Traces of the Spirit

Traces of the Spirit

The Religious Dimensions of Popular Music

Robin Sylvan

NEW YORK UNIVERSITY PRESS
New York and London

NEW YORK UNIVERSITY PRESS
New York and London

Library of Congress Cataloging-in-Publication Data
Sylvan, Robin.
Traces of the spirit : the religious dimensions of popular music /
Robin Sylvan.
p. cm.
Includes bibliographical references (p.   ) and index.
ISBN 0-8147-9808-X (cloth) — ISBN 0-8147-9809-8 (pbk.)
1. Popular music—Religious aspects. 2. Popular culture—Religious
aspects.   I. Title.
ML3470 .S97 2002
781.64'112—dc21   2002000536

New York University Press books are printed on acid-free paper,
and their binding materials are chosen for strength and durability.

Manufactured in the United States of America
10 9 8 7 6 5 4 3 2 1

Contents

Acknowledgments   *vii*

Introduction: Traces of the Spirit: The Hidden
Religious Dimensions of Popular Music   1

I   Theoretical, Structural, and Historical Background   15

1   The Connection between Music and Religion   19

2   West African Possession Religion and American
Popular Music   45

II   Popular Music Subcultures as Religion: A Comparative
Analysis Based on Ethnographic Research   77

3   *Eyes of the World*: The Grateful Dead and
the Deadheads   83

4   The Dance Music Continuum: House, Rave, and
Electronic Dance Music   117

5   Stairway to Heaven, Highway to Hell: Heavy Metal
and Metalheads   152

6   *The Message*: Rap Music and Hip-Hop Culture   182

Conclusion: There's More to the Picture than
Meets the Eye   214

Appendix   *223*
Notes   *231*
Bibliography   *271*
Index   *281*
About the Author   *291*

Acknowledgments

I would like to thank Charles Long for taking me under his wing early in my graduate career and making it possible for me to do exactly the kind of work I had envisioned. He provided a larger theoretical context for this work and his brilliant problematizing always pushed me to new levels of insight and perspective. I am proud to be part of an intellectual lineage of religious studies scholarship that I can trace back through him to his teacher, Joachim Wach, and through him to his teacher, Rudolf Otto. I am grateful that he saw my Ph.D. process through to completion even after he left Santa Barbara to return to North Carolina.

I would also like to thank Catherine Albanese for her strong on-the-ground involvement with this book. Her close reading of my drafts, her surgical use of the red pen, and especially her insistence on my doing fieldwork have contributed immeasurably to enhancing the quality of this project. My appreciation as well to Dwight Reynolds for his accessibility and musician's perspective, and to Douglas Daniels for his expertise on African American music.

I want to thank my parents, Irwin and Sally Sylvan, for their enormous and unwavering support, both psychological and financial. Simply put, my academic career would not have been possible without them and I hope I have done them proud. Thanks also to my brother, David Sylvan, whose sage advice on the arcane machinations of graduate school helped me at numerous stages along the way. Gratitude to my friend and mentor, Kenyth Freeman, for his ongoing support and for being my only reliable link between the academic world and the other worlds I inhabit.

I am very thankful for my close friends and fellow scholars Darryl Caterine, Dave McMahan, and Katie Komenda. We've been in the trenches together and helped each other at many points along the way. I treasure the spirit of cooperation and mutual support we created and the lasting connections we've forged. To all my nonacademic friends in different communities up and down the West Coast—in Ojai, in Santa Barbara, in the

Bay Area, and in Bellingham—my thanks as well. I know that the rigors of academia took their toll on me as a human being, and I appreciate everyone's patience and support, particularly when I was not the easiest person to be with.

Much gratitude to the great people who helped me with my fieldwork, both in West Africa and in the Bay Area, especially Samba Doumbouya in Dakar, John Collins in Accra, Patti Clemens in Oakland, and James Romero in San Francisco. Thanks to all the interviewees for their time and energy; I learned something from each session and was impressed with everyone's depth and integrity. I hope that I have done justice to the spirit of the sessions, the people, the music, and the respective scenes. Best wishes to all in their musical and spiritual endeavors.

Finally, I am thankful for the gifts of music and spirit that have touched me in my life in so many profound ways and I am grateful for the opportunity to give something back. If this book makes some small contribution to a greater awareness and deeper understanding of the spiritual and religious dimensions of music and/or inspires anyone in work of their own, then all the effort will have been worth it.

Introduction

Traces of the Spirit: The Hidden Religious Dimensions of Popular Music

I had an experience of the most complete identity with the Creator.
... and experienced—it's hard to describe, but there was an underlying sensation of a giant wheel and sort of a picture of a mandala.
But it wasn't a visible picture; it was kind of an underlying feeling
and it was also a visceral sensation at the top of my head, opening
up, and of just complete identity with all life and creation and unity
with people.

I felt the presence of the Creator of all, and identity with, in other
words, immanence of the presence. And looking through my eyes.

It turned me back on to life, because I had really kind of given
up [on] the possibility of life being fulfilling and joyful and exciting, you know, being completely alive. It's like I felt so completely
alive in a really unadulterated way that I remembered what I felt
like, what I was here for, I remembered "oh, okay." We're here to be
like this.

It approaches more closely the sacred than anything else I've ever
experienced.[1]   —Bill Lyman

I really did feel like at times I was subtracted from the individual
and became part of the whole. Maybe blending into the field which
binds all of the molecules of the universe, ... the energy that binds
the entire world together. ... [I] experienced things from a higher
plane of existence.

There were definitely times where I felt like I was existing ... as
everything all at once.

I would blend into the cosmic mind. ... I felt like I was a part of
that. ...

I consider it to be a very spiritual experience. In fact, I can say
that prior to doing that, my sense of spirituality was pretty weak,
pretty undeveloped, pretty dormant in me. ... But I definitely felt a
very strong sense of spirituality and mostly the spirituality was kind

1

of a personal transformation into just understanding that oneness, that concept of the one.

At that point in my life, things really transformed in me. I really started feeling like I had a more noble purpose in life.[2]

—Jeff Taylor

It was like a whole new world that I walked into. And it was a world I wanted to stay in for the rest of my life. . . . It was just amazing. . . .

The feeling was an arrangement of excitement, self-love. Being myself means I love myself. . . . My social life, my family. I found a love. I found a positive attention. I found a release. . . .

That's where I built my definite structure on "this is what it's all about" and it was a great night. I'll remember it for the rest of my life. . . .

My life did shift, I would say, to the positive, at least. Because if I had kept going the way I was, I would either go and kill people or I would kill myself or both. . . . It made me a stronger person. It made the depression go away. . . . I would have to say it's a positive religion, what I believe in. . . . I live a pretty positive life.[3]

—Lance Ozanix

It's the ancients. It's definitely the ancients. . . . [It] just called my soul. It would make my soul jump out of my body, literally. . . . It's just a link. Something touches you one day, just sparks your whole consciousness. . . .

I look around at everything, and everything I absorb is God and I can express that, literally. . . . It's like praying. It's like being with God, literally, like being with God.

It just gives you a purpose. It shows you why you're here. . . . [It's] a spirituality. And it's everything that I can think of. . . . It just links and connects to all that. It knows that I know God every day.

It's in my day-to-day every day. . . . It's not different from my life. It's what I do. It's just what's in my life. Every day I'm hearing it. I'm always shaking like that.[4]

—Jorge Guerrero

These four quotations read like classic descriptions of religious experiences of a profound, life-changing nature. If one did not know the specific circumstances which gave rise to these experiences, one might assume that they took place within the framework of traditional

religious or esoteric mystical practices. However, they did not occur within such contexts. They are, in fact, descriptions of experiences which took place at popular music events under the powerful influence of highly amplified rhythmic music in combination with repetitive movement, unusual lighting, and other consciousness-altering factors. The first description comes from a concert by the now-defunct San Francisco Bay Area rock band the Grateful Dead. The second is from an all-night electronic dance music party known as a rave. The third is from a concert of the heavy metal subgenre of rock music. And the fourth is drawn from the speaker's involvement with rap music and the larger hip-hop culture of which it is a part.

Observers of culture and scholars of religion have said many things about the slow decline of religion and the death of God in Western civilization. Yet for the millions of people who have experienced something similar to the accounts above, religion and God are not dead, but very much alive and well and dancing to the beat of popular music; the religious impulse has simply migrated to another sector of the culture, a sector in which religious sensibilities have flourished and made an enormous impact on a large portion of the population. Right under our noses, a significant religious phenomenon is taking place, one which constitutes an important development in the Western religious and cultural landscape. Yet, because conventional wisdom has taught us to regard popular musics as trivial forms of secular entertainment, these religious dimensions remain hidden from view, marginalized and misunderstood. In this book, using a variety of theoretical and methodological tools, especially those from the field of religious studies, the religious dimensions of popular music will be brought forward, front and center, for full examination and analysis, and acknowledged as the important phenomena they represent.

Experiences similar to those described above, whether mainstream or underground, live band or DJ mix, lower or upper class, white, African American, or Latino, are commonplace occurrences which play themselves out nearly every night in clubs and bars, arenas and stadiums, warehouses and fields throughout the United States and around the planet. Since the 1950s, when rhythm and blues crossed over to become rock and roll, moving from a predominantly African American context to a mainstream white youth audience, beat-driven popular music has provided the sound track for the lives of millions of people and, in the process, spawned a multibillion dollar industry. For teenagers and young adults especially, the musical subculture to which they belong provides as all-encompassing an orientation to the world as any traditional religion.[5] They buy the recordings and listen to them constantly, memorizing music and lyrics in great detail. They follow the subculture through whatever media channels are available to them: magazine, newspaper, radio, television, and the Internet. They dress in the particular style of their subculture, move with its particular body language and mannerisms, speak its particular lingo. They spend their time with friends who are equally devoted to the same music, listening to it and discussing it, forming their own musical community. And of course, whenever they can, they participate in the most highly valued ritual expression of their community, the live concert or dance hall, where they experience a sense of ecstatic communion.

Thus the musical subculture provides almost everything for its adherents that a traditional religion would. In the heat of the music, it provides a powerful religious experience which is both the foundation and the goal of the whole enterprise, an encounter with the numinous that is at the core of all religions. It provides a form of ritual activity and communal ceremony that regularly and reliably produces such experiences through concrete practices, something that all religions do. It provides a philosophy and worldview that makes sense of these experiences and translates them into a code for living one's day-to-day life, something that all religions do. Finally, it provides a cultural identity, a social structure, and a sense of belonging to a community, something that all religions do.[6] On many important levels, then, the music functions in the same way as a religion, and the musical subculture functions in the same way as a religious community, albeit in an unconscious and postmodern way.

I use the word "unconscious" here because many people in these subcultures (and in general) do not think of these phenomena as religious (although, as I will show, some do); rather, the music is often seen as a form of entertainment with aesthetic, social, and economic dimensions. The musical subculture functions as a religion in these people's lives, but they do not consciously recognize it as such; thus, it is unconscious. I use the word "postmodern" here because this is not religion in the sense of a traditional form grounded in a stable cultural context, expressing some essential defining quality; rather, this religion is an eclectic pastiche of diverse musical, religious, and cultural components thrown together and grafted onto an oligopolistic corporate entertainment industry that exploits the stylistic trends of marginal subcultures for the marketing of its commodified products.[7] Clearly, this is not religion in the form that one would normally expect to find it, but it is, I contend, religion neverthe-less. One of the important tasks of this study will be to explain how a gen-uine religious impulse went underground and became entangled in the hodge-podge hybrid now called popular music.

To begin with, there needs to be a broader framework for what is meant by "religion," a framework that goes beyond the narrow reified in-stitutions which that word normally describes. This broader framework was, in fact, developed decades ago by some of the pioneering scholars in the field of the history of religions. In this approach, the emphasis is on the numinous as the central ordering structure for human beings.[8] The human encounter with the numinous, the religious experience, forms the basis for subsequent developments that lead to social expression and the organized exterior forms that we call "religion." Implicit in this perspec-tive is the notion that religion, in a broader and more fundamental sense, is the underlying substratum for all cultural activity and serves as the foundation for culture in general. As historian of religions Charles H. Long writes: "Religion is thus understood to be pervasive not only in reli-gious institutions, but in all the dimensions of cultural life."[9] Phenome-nologist of religion Gerardus Van der Leeuw puts it even more succinctly when he states that "ultimately, all culture is religious."[10]

What happens, however, when the encounter with the numinous, the religious experience, can no longer find adequate expression in the tradi-tional religious institutions provided by the culture? This question is cru-cial to the current investigation for both contemporary and historical reasons. First of all, this appears to be the situation encountered by many of today's young people—the traditional religious institutions do not meet their spiritual needs. Secondly, this was also the situation encoun-tered by African slaves brought to the Americas, but for very different reasons—they were literally forbidden, often on penalty of death, to practice their traditional religion. The African diaspora is important be-cause there is a strong current of the West African religious sensibility in popular music, as I will show shortly. In both these cases, and in general, when the religious impulse cannot find adequate expression in tradi-tional religious institutions, it will then seek expression in other sectors of cultural activity. Historian of American religions Catherine L. Al-banese has called this phenomenon "cultural religion."[11] And while there are many sectors of cultural activity in which "cultural religion" can be located, the particular sector of cultural activity in which the religious impulses of these particular groups has found expression is music.

This is no accident. Music is one of the most powerful tools for conveying religious meaning known to humankind. Music and religion are intimately linked in almost every culture and in almost every historical period.[12] In chapter 1, I will examine this nearly universal connection between music and religion in greater detail and suggest some very powerful reasons why music is a particularly good medium for the expression of the religious impulse. Foremost among these is the fact that music is capable of functioning simultaneously at many different levels (physiological, psychological, sociocultural, semiological, virtual, ritual, and spiritual) and integrating them into a coherent whole. So for a complex multidimensional phenomenon like religion, which also functions simultaneously at multiple levels, the fact that music is capable of conveying all these levels of complexity in a compelling and integrated package makes it a vehicle par excellence to carry the religious impulse. Moreover, the musical experience that integrates all these levels represents a unique phenomenological and ontological mode of being-in-the-world in which the dualities of subject-object, body-mind, and spiritual-material are transcended. It is only natural, therefore, that music would become a sphere of expression for the religious impulse beyond traditional religious institutions.

This intimate and universal connection between music and religion provides us a general, theoretical answer to the question of why the religious impulse seeks expression in the cultural sector of music. And there is a more specific *historical* answer which has to do with the particularities of how West African diasporic religion adapted to the radically different circumstances of the New World, transformed itself in a variety of ways in order to survive, and, in the process, created uniquely African American religious traditions. In its original context, a large focus of West African religious activity was the ceremonial practice of possession dances. These were sacred gatherings where drum ensembles and singers supplied beat-driven polyrhythmic music and initiates danced themselves into ecstatic trance states in which the gods would take possession of their bodies and be physically present among the community for the purposes of counseling, healing, divination, and so forth.[13] When West Africans were brought to the Americas by force in the devastating horror of the slave trade, they were forbidden to practice this complex of musicoreligious ceremonies. So their religious impulse went underground and found expression in other ways. One of the ways they did this was to graft a Catholic veneer on top of what were essentially West African deities and possession practices. This can be seen in Bahian Candomble, Haitian Vodun, and Cuban Santeria. In these religions, the West African musicoreligious possession complex has survived largely intact, although clearly transformed. Another approach was that taken by the black church in the Protestant United States. This involved a much more thoroughly traditional Christian liturgical form but with elements of West African religious sensibility finding expression in musical practices and possession-like ecstatic trance states.[14]

Finally, and most importantly for my investigation, this impulse also found expression in "secular" entertainment musics in the United States. African American musics such as blues and jazz carried within them many of the musicoreligious practices and experiential states of West African possession religions, although these were now transmuted into a form hidden within a different cultural sector.[15] These musics then formed the basis for what was to become rock and roll when it crossed over to a mainstream white audience, carrying within it this hidden West African–African American religious sensibility. As rock and roll evolved into a major cultural force and spawned a variety of different musical youth subcultures, several generations of Americans of all classes and ethnicities came of age under the influence of this hidden religious sensibility, which became part and parcel of the fabric of our common cultural heritage. In chapter 2, drawing on scholarly sources, as well as my own fieldwork in West Africa and personal experience, I will examine these historical developments and the structural evolution of these crucial transformations in greater detail.

It is important to remember that the entry of rock and roll into the American cultural mainstream did not come easily or without fierce opposition. Ed Sullivan, for example, resisted the idea of putting Elvis Presley on his influential television show for a long time, until Presley was too popular to ignore. Even when Sullivan finally relented, the camera showed Presley only from the waist up, editing out his rhythmic pelvic dance movement. The idea that "black" music could become a popular music was anathema to the bearers of mainstream cultural standards. This fact was not lost on young people who wanted to break out of the constrictions of 1950s mainstream culture. Ever since it crossed over to a white audience, rock and roll has been a music of youthful rebellion, a vehicle to express the awakening consciousness of the newly emerging post–World War II youth culture.[16] As it evolved into an ever-burgeoning variety of diverse musical youth subcultures (that is, acid rock, heavy metal, disco, funk, punk, house, alternative, rap), rock and roll developed distinctive stylistic articulations of this rebellious youth energy into coherent cultural expressions. This history of rock and roll's complex evolution will also be explored in chapter 2.

These two chapters, the first theoretical and the second historical, together comprise the first section of the book, in that they provide the larger framework for its more specific focus, namely, the four musical subcultures mentioned at the outset. In Part Two, I examine these four musical subcultures in depth, devoting a chapter to each one in turn. The first part of each chapter introduces the particular subculture and its historical, cultural, and musical background. Chapter 3 looks at the archetypal 1960s psychedelic rock band which emerged out of the San Francisco Haight-Ashbury hippie counterculture, the Grateful Dead, and focuses special attention on the Deadheads, the devoted community that has constellated around the Dead's music and live concerts since the 1960s. Chapter 4 examines the techno dance music subculture in its more important articulations, from its origins as house music in the Chicago and New York club scenes, to the large all-night psychedelic raves in the late 1980s in England, to some of its many contemporary variants. In chapter 5, I examine the heavy metal music subculture and its religious dimensions, which, although tending toward the darker side of the spectrum (that is, Satanism, violence, and a death orientation), are clearly considerable, and play a major role in the lives of its adherents. Finally, chapter 6 looks at the rap music hip-hop subculture in its various articulations, and explores its continuities with, and differences from, African and African American musicoreligious themes and practices.

This connection between beat-driven popular music and youth subcultures is not simply coincidental. Adolescence is one of the most important transitional periods in an individual's life and is usually marked by some sort of rite of passage acknowledging and guiding the transformation from child into adult.[17] These rituals emphasize the liminal, "betwixt-and-between" quality of this time of life by separating the initiates from the rest of society, stripping them of their normal social identities, and placing them in their own temporary form of alternative community that Victor Turner has called "communitas."[18] The hormone-driven rebellious quest for intense experience characteristic of this age group is often channeled into various types of initiatic trials, such as body mutilation, fasting, dancing until exhaustion, use of psychotropic plants, and going on vision quests. These aspects of liminality, communitas, and initiatic trials can be clearly seen in most contemporary musical youth subcultures.[19] The enormous difference between these youth subcultures and traditional cultures, however, is that the latter provide a framework within which the young people can complete their initiation and be reintegrated back into society in their new social status as adults. There is no such conceptual framework and ritual mechanism for the reintegration of youth-transformed-into-adults in our culture. So there continues to be an enormous divide between young and old, each side viewing the other with suspicion and derision. And beat-driven popular music continues to be one of the principal means of expressing the oppositional energies of the youthful side of this dichotomy.

For this and other reasons, rock and roll and popular youth culture have only very recently begun to be taken seriously by the scholarly world. In the last several decades, the notion of popular culture as a legitimate arena for serious expression has increasingly gained acceptance among a new generation of religious studies scholars, theologians, sociologists, literary critics, cultural studies scholars, and ethnomusicologists, and that is all to the good. Yet even among this pioneering group, the idea that popular culture in general, and popular music in particular, contains profound *spiritual* and *religious* dimensions is still a new and relatively unexplored area within mainstream academia.[20] In contrast, for those of us who came of age in post–World War II youth culture, outside the constrictive paradigms of academia, such an idea strikes a chord of resonance and seems natural and obvious.

If one takes seriously the idea that beat-driven popular music and its attendant youth subcultures can be understood as religious phenomena, then the next logical task for the scholar of religion is to begin to investigate the nature of the religious phenomenon in question. In other words, what kind of religion is it? How does one characterize its experiences, practices, rituals, symbols, myths, beliefs, values, and social organization? While each musical youth subculture is different, I believe they all have certain features and qualities in common. To begin with, they all have strong elements of the West African and African American musicoreligious complex discussed above; they are danced, embodied religions employing beat-driven music in communal, ritual contexts to produce ecstatic, quasi-possession states.

However, given the myriad historical and structural transformations this musicoreligious complex had to go through to emerge in these forms, it would be too simplistic to argue for an exclusively West African and African American interpretation. There are also strong European influences in these "religions," such as the frenzied abandon of the destructive Dionysian impulse, the folkish paganism of the Celts and other indigenous tribes, the pantheistic mysticism of the Romantics, and the occultism of Western magical traditions.[21] Shamanism, the ancient, nearly universal, ecstatic, tribal protoreligion, serves as an illuminating model for comparison as well.[22] Fetishism, that peculiar religious innovation that emerged from the European encounter with Africa and the New World, is also a crucial component in these "religions" which operate within the economic context of a corporate industry selling commodified products.[23] And I have already noted the structural and psychological parallels between adolescent rites of passage in traditional cultures and the ritualized communal activities of the live concert.[24]

In each of the chapters of Part Two of the book, I focus on the religious dimensions of the four musical youth subcultures I have chosen, and undertake a comparative analysis of their essential qualities—the religious experience, the ritual process, and the philosophy and worldview. The material for these chapters comes out of the year and a half I spent living in the San Francisco Bay Area, conducting research and immersing myself in these four musical subcultures. I should note that the location for fieldwork means that the results of my study most accurately reflect these subcultures as they have developed in the specific context of that region, particularly with regard to the strong influence of alternative spirituality that has been a distinctive feature of the Bay Area for many decades. Nevertheless, I think the results of my research also provide a firm foundation for a larger discussion of the religious dimensions of these four musical subcultures, and popular music and popular culture in general. In the chapters of Part Two, I have tried to let the members of the subcultures speak for themselves as much as possible, using extensive quotations from interviews that I conducted.

In the second part of each chapter, I explore the religious experience, looking at the particularities and nuances of the altered states of consciousness, the feeling tone of such states, the sense of self, relationality to the larger world, somatic experience, and the use of drugs. Reliable progressions or sequences of these experiential states are noted, as well as aspects like conversion and spillover to day-to-day life. In addition, the specific spiritual and religious metaphors used by the interviewees to describe their experiences are also explored. The traditional possession metaphor is that of the rider and the horse, in which the possessing deity is the controlling rider and the dancer/initiate is the horse. While it is clear that such classic possession does not occur within these musical subcultures, it is equally clear from the compelling testimonials that participants have powerful experiences which put them in the general vicinity. This comparison raises intriguing issues about the religious experience—unitive versus dualistic, personal versus impersonal, conscious versus unconscious, in-body versus out-of-body—which I discuss.

In the third part of each chapter, I apply the same kind of approach to the ritual dimensions of these subcultures for analysis, using four sets of categories drawn from the subfields of ritual and performance studies, my own observations in the field, and those of the participants.[25] The first of these categories is the temporal aspect, which includes the frequency of musical event and the regular sequence of activities which take place within that event. Such sequences obviously have a very strong musical component, and specific musical structures, such as the musical motto, which I also explore. The second category is the spatial aspect, which includes the type of venue, the placement of objects, people, and space within that venue, and the directional interrelationships between them. This spatial aspect is closely connected to the third category, the organization of the body, including characteristic movements and gestures, dress and fashion, and somatic experiential states. Fourth, there is the aspect of social bonding which is central to most rituals and certainly central to the musical events of these subcultures. I examine what kinds of interactions and connections take place at these events, particularly in the heat of the musical experience, and how they create bonds which form the basis for a coherent subcultural community. In addition, I also look at the metaphors of traditional rituals used by participants to describe their activities, as well as some of the classic Turnerian ritual categories mentioned earlier (initiation, liminality, antistructure, and communitas).

In the fourth part of each chapter, I explore the worldviews and philosophies implicit in the "religions" of these musical subcultures, as well as their codes for how to live one's life. In this regard, because music is capable of integrating multiple levels of experience and meaning, the template for each subculture's worldview can be found within the structure and feeling of the music itself. I examine these musical templates, their philosophical analogs, and the perspective each subculture has on an individual's life, the sociopolitical world, and the larger universe. An obvious theme here is their critique of and oppositional stance to mainstream culture, and an accompanying sense of being an "alternative," which again has strong qualities of liminality, antistructure, and communitas.[26]

Another major theme is the centrality of the body as the site of experience and the locus of integration of meaning, this in contrast to the inherited Cartesian mind-body dualism of mainstream culture.[27] In this body-oriented worldview, play, pleasure, sexuality, and intense feeling are highly valued. The symbol of the crossroads, prominent in West African religion and in the blues, is an important metaphor expressing the intersection of the physical and spiritual worlds.[28] The goal is not escape from the physical world into some imagined purely spiritual realm, but an experience of the spiritual *in* this physical body and world, an integration, rather than an opposition, of the two. However, it is quite clear that these musical youth subcultures do not, by any stretch of the imagination, express the same worldview and set of values. One need only take a cursory glance at the Deadheads' trust in the divine nature of the improvisational process, the dance-floor mysticism of rave, heavy metal's fascination with darkness and death, or rap's concern with the African American historical legacy to see enormous differences.

As one can see from this preliminary discussion, the religious dimensions of beat-driven popular music and its attendant youth subcultures are abundant and complex. As one situates these phenomena within the cultural and religious landscape of our contemporary world, their significance looms large. This is true not only in terms of the sheer number of adherents and the intensity of their devotion, but it is also true because the popular music industry is the stylistic trendsetter of our time, sending its images and sounds across the world into all sectors of all cultures. If one reflects for a moment on the huge impact of a group like the Beatles on the planetary culture, the enormous power of popular music becomes readily apparent. Scholars and cultural critics have had endless debates about the ramifications of this power—is its potential for social change and political mobilization being effectively tapped? or is it being co-opted by the corporate industry? I think these are the wrong questions to be asking in order to get at the true nature of popular music's power and the implications that flow from it, implications I will explore in the conclusion.

The real power of popular music is spiritual and religious, and it has already irrevocably changed the lives of millions of people across several generations not only in terms of the texture of day-to-day living, but also in the way they see the world and the social forms which have sprung from those epistemologies. As a religious and cultural phenomenon, popular music has already precipitated the end of centuries of dominance of the mind-body split. And it signals the emergence of a significant alternative religious choice that bypasses the narrow opposition between traditional religious institutions and secular humanism. These are important changes with large implications that should not be underestimated. Moreover, the dynamic and innovative creativity with which these subcultures continually find new forms of expression indicates that one can expect them to be a source of religious vitality and evolution for generations into the future. We appear to be entering a time when these hidden religious dimensions are no longer hidden but brought consciously into full view, acknowledged and celebrated for their spiritual power.[29] After so many significant and unexpected transformations to become the spiritual force popular music is, who knows what significant and unexpected transformations lie ahead? One can only watch and listen with anticipation and wonder, feeling an excitement similar to that experienced in the heat of the music, catching a small glimpse of traces of the spirit.

PART ONE

Theoretical, Structural, and Historical Background

In 1995, I journeyed to the West African countries of Senegal, Mali, and Ghana to explore their music and religion firsthand. As my plane flew for what seemed like endless hours over the blue waters of the Atlantic Ocean and then over the vast yellow expanses of the Sahara Desert, I was struck by the immense geographical distance between North America and Africa. During the subsequent months I spent living and traveling in West Africa, I came to realize that the cultural distance between these two continents is perhaps even greater, or so it felt to me at the time. Appearances, however, can be deceptive and things are not always what they seem to be at first glance. Despite these distances, North America and Africa are inextricably connected in a variety of significant ways and share many important commonalities.

In the same way, at first glance, music and religion too appear to be distinct phenomena separated by large classificatory distances. In particular, the distance between popular music and sacred religious traditions seems to be especially large. Yet, to continue the parallel, closer examination reveals that music and religion are also inextricably connected in a variety of significant ways and share many important commonalities. Moreover, the connection between music and religion and that between North America and Africa are also linked to *each other*. In other words, North America and Africa are strongly linked *through* the connection between music and religion. These linkages and connections between seemingly divergent phenomena raise crucial theoretical, structural, and historical issues regarding the nature of music, religion, culture, Africa, and America. It is these issues that I will explore in the first section of this study.

One of the ways I was able to bridge the cultural gap during my time in West Africa was by virtue of having brought a guitar with me. The simple visual symbol of the guitar allowed people to see me as a musician, which opened many doors for me into their rich musical world. As I attended and participated in numerous musical events, I began to see that, for Africans, music is not simply an aesthetic performative genre that can be separated from the rest of life and other cultural expressions, including religion. Music permeated all aspects of life, connecting them into an integrated whole. Music also provided a powerful, almost visceral link to the spiritual world not only in formal religious ceremonies, but at simple informal musical gatherings as well. As African American musicologist Samuel A. Floyd, Jr., writes:

> The musical artistry of Africans supported their ritual in a profoundly mystical universe, a universe in which African peoples sought union with the invisible—God, lesser gods, spirits, and the living-dead. . . . Understanding this universe is important if one wishes to understand African music either for its own sake or as the antecedent of African American music. Elements of African ritual, myth, and legend reside in, are supported by, and parallel those of African Dance, Drum, and Song.[1]

Thus, in Africa music and religion are not separate at all but are intimately interconnected aspects of a larger spiritual universe that provides the culture with its fundamental orientation.

Similarly, as I noted above, North America and Africa are not separate either but are intimately connected parts of a larger African and Afro-diasporic culture that is shaped by this fundamental orientation. One of the most compelling examples of this intimate connection is that of African Americans who, despite the devastation of the trans-Atlantic slave trade and over three hundred years of oppression in North America, nevertheless managed to maintain continuity with this larger culture and orientation in radically changed forms. Not surprisingly, one of the primary means through which they did so was music. Ethnomusicologist Portia Maultsby discusses the dynamics of this continuity:

> West African musical concepts form the foundation for the various musical genres Black Americans have created. During each phase of its development, Black music has exemplified the collective attitudes, values, philosophies, and experiences of the Black community. The social organizations as determined by environmental factors encouraged the retention, reinterpretation, and revival of various African concepts. In adapting to environmental changes over three hundred years, Blacks have con-

tinued to rely on familiar traditions and practices for self-preservation. Musical forms have been recycled through age-old concepts. The musical tradition the slaves established continues to persist in the twentieth century, reinterpreted as the social times demand. Whatever social changes arise in the future, African concepts will continue to form the basis of Black musical expression. . . . Hence, the Black musical tradition will continue to evolve and mirror new values, attitudes, philosophies, and lifestyles, but it will never lose its West African essence.[2]

And because a crucial aspect of this essence is the connection to the larger spiritual universe, African American music also contains powerful religious dimensions that permeate all aspects of life. However, as African music was imported from its indigenous context to the Western context of North America, not only did its musical forms change, but its religious dimensions took on new meanings in response to the vastly different context. The new musical forms African Americans created and their new religious meanings for African American culture in the United States constitute a change of enormous proportions.

An equally momentous change took place when these new musical forms moved beyond the confines of African American culture to become the foundation of most white American popular music. Philosopher Cornel West calls this "the Afro-Americanization of popular music." He writes: "The salient feature of popular music . . . is the appropriation and imitation of Afro-American musical forms and styles. The Afro-American spiritual-blues impulse . . . serves as a major source for popular music in the West."[3] Not surprisingly, as African American music was imported from its African American context to the new context of American popular music, its forms changed again and its religious dimensions again took on new meanings. This series of importations, recontextualizations, and transformations has resulted in a complex hybrid of musicoreligious phenomena that is significantly different from its African and African American origins.

At first glance, three of the four popular music subcultures of this study appear to be almost completely unrelated to their African and African American forebearers. Yet, once again, closer examination reveals that these phenomena are also inextricably connected in a variety of significant ways and share many important commonalities. As cultural historian Michael Ventura notes, there are still powerful traces of the "West African essence" to be found in American popular music:

[Rock and roll] does preserve qualities of that African metaphysic intact so strongly that it unconsciously generates the same dances, acts as a major antidote to the mind-body split, and uses a derivative of . . . techniques of possession as a source, for performers and audiences alike, of tremendous personal energy.[4]

In this first section, using theoretical, structural, and historical approaches, I will explore these connections between music and religion, and North America and Africa, in greater detail.

1

The Connection between Music and Religion

At first glance, it may seem odd to suggest that popular music has significant religious dimensions. Music, after all, is regarded in popular Western culture as a form of entertainment operating primarily at an aesthetic level, a form having only superficial sociocultural implications. However, when one looks at the larger sweep of history in a broad spectrum of cultures around the world, it becomes clear that there is an almost universal connection between music and religion. For example, in shamanism, the most ancient of religious traditions, shamans use songs accompanied by trance-inducing drumming to carry them on ecstatic journeys to celestial realms where they interact with the spirits for the well-being of the community. The drum is often seen as the horse which the shaman rides while on this journey. In Australian aboriginal religion, which goes back fifty thousand years, the spiritual power of the creation myths are sung into *churingas,* sacred receptacles for the totemic ancestors, in a rhythmic chant accompanied by the percussive beating of sticks. The sound of the bull-roarer, a wood board swung by a string, thought to be identical to that of the totemic ancestor, is considered so sacred that no sound recording of it has ever been allowed. Drumming and chanting are similarly central and sacred to virtually every Native American group's religious practices, from the songs of the Kachina dances of the Hopi in northern Arizona, to the powerful drummed chants of the Sun Dance of the Oglala Sioux and other Plains Indians, to the pan-Indian peyote meeting of the Native American Church, a form of prayer in which the chief activity consists of cycles of sacred songs accompanied by rattle and water drum.

I have already discussed the importance of polyrhythmic drum ensembles in the possession religions of West Africa and the African Diaspora. Indeed, the use of drumming and dancing as central components of sacred ceremonies is found throughout the entire African continent. In Hindu traditions in India, music and sound are understood as being synonymous with God (Nada-Brahman), the stuff of which the universe is made. Thus, music is seen as a path through which one can attain union with God, whether it occurs in the context of classical ragas, devotional chants, or Brahmanical rituals. In all forms of Buddhism, chant is also a central practice, particularly the use of mantras, sacred seed syllables thought to contain potent spiritual power.

Chanting is similarly important in Islam, particularly the chanting of verses from the holy Qur'an in the daily prayers, a practice so sacred that it is not technically considered to be music. In Islam's mystical Sufi sects, music and dance are used by the dervishes to attain profound ecstatic states of union with God. Music has been central in Judaism throughout its history, from the blast of the Shofar (ram's horn trumpet) on the most holy day of Yom Kippur to the use of the lyre by the prophets and King David, to the cantor's chanting of Hebrew prayers and blessings in contemporary services. And finally, there is the use of hymns in Christian liturgy in a myriad of forms, from the solemn tones of Gregorian chant to the orchestral brilliance of Bach cantatas to the African American stylings of gospel choirs.

These are but a few examples from a list that could go on and on and that, in itself, could constitute the focus of a lengthy study. For my purposes here, however, I simply wish to make the point that music and religion are closely linked in virtually every religious tradition. Conversely, music and religion are closely linked in many *musical* traditions as well. Ethnomusicologist David McAllester has written eloquently on the universal power of the musical experience, a power fraught with spiritual implications:

> I would say that one of the most important of the universals, or near-universals, in music is that music transforms experience. Music is always out of the ordinary and by its presence creates an atmosphere of the special. Experience is transformed from the humdrum, the everyday, into something else. Music may heighten excitement or it may soothe tensions, but in either case it takes one away into another state of being. There are many of these musical states of being. . . . In all the ways it is used it seems to heighten experience. You might even say it is an actualization of the mystical experience for everybody. We are not all practicing mystics and most of us do not experience God easily. But when we

hear music, something like that is happening to us. We are lifted out of ourselves.[1]

Thus, music and religion are closely linked from *either* side of the equation—there are important musical dimensions to religion, and there are important religious dimensions to music.

In this chapter, I will examine why this is so and sketch out in detail some of the intricacies and complexities of this connection. My basic working premise, stated briefly in the introduction, is that music functions simultaneously at many different levels—physiological, psychological, sociocultural, semiological, virtual, ritual, and spiritual—and integrates all these levels synergistically into a coherent whole greater than the sum of its parts, a unified field that can be directly accessed and powerfully experienced. Because of this, it is the vehicle par excellence for a complex multidimensional phenomenon like religion, which also functions at all these different levels and seeks integrated expression. I will begin the exploration, therefore, with a brief survey of each of these levels, keeping in mind that they combine and overlap.

The Physiological Level

It seems appropriate to start at the most fundamental level, namely, that of music as physical vibration and the way it affects the physiology of the human body. Music is produced by voice or instruments as the result of some type of physical activity, be it the forcing of air through a chamber or a set of vocal chords, or the striking of a drumhead or a set of strings. This physical activity creates sound in the form of vibrational wave patterns that travel through the air and are received primarily through the hearing apparatus of the ear. However, for anyone who has ever attended an amplified rock concert, a dance club with a powerful sound system, or any other loud musical event, it is clear that the sound is received by the entire body and not just the ears. For example, the impact of a booming bass and drum in the lower register can often be felt in the area of the stomach and solar plexus.

That music operates at a physical level seems fairly obvious. What is of interest for this discussion is that the physical impact of music is capable of creating a shift in the physiological functioning of the human body. In the early 1960s Andrew Neher did some of the only experimental work in the laboratory in this regard. While investigating the impact that sonic driving (rhythmic drumming) had on human subjects, Neher found that at certain frequencies and speeds electrical activity in the brain was affected, unusual perceptions were produced, and muscular twitching occurred.[2] More recently, some scholars have examined the effects of rhythmic driving on the human neurobiology in greater detail, mapping out patterned discharges in the sympathetic and parasympathetic nervous systems, resulting in "synchronization of cortical rhythms."[3] The idea here is that musical rhythms have the effect of "tuning" the rhythms of the human body and its various subsystems, including circadian rhythms, heartbeat, breathing rate, and muscular activity. They "synchronize with the rhythms of muscular activity centered in the brain and nervous system. . . . The external rhythm becomes the synchronizer to set the internal clocks of these fast rhythms."[4] Thus music, particularly strongly rhythmic music, provides a mechanism for the synchronization of the body and its various subsystems.

There are other aspects of music that affect human physiology besides that of rhythmic driving. Ethnomusicologist Gilbert Rouget has noted the efficacy of a combination of acceleration of tempo (accelerando) and increase in volume and instrumental density (crescendo) as a nearly universal cross-cultural technique in bringing about trance and possession states.[5] And musicologist James Mursell, in discussing classical music, has written that it "has a marked effect on pulse, respiration and external blood pressure. . . . [It] delays the onset of muscular fatigue . . . [and] has a marked effect upon the psychogalvanic reflex." He goes on to speculate that the power of "tone as such," or tonal stimulation, is responsible for the physiological responses.[6] In addition, there is also the widespread cross-cultural practice of dance and movement as an adjunct to the use of music in religious ceremonies. In this regard, I have already mentioned the West African possession dance, the Hopi Kachina dance, the Oglala Sioux Sun Dance, and the Sufi whirling dervishes, among others. Composer and musicologist Olly Wilson, discussing African and African American religious music, suggests that in these traditions music and movement constitute integral components in a unified whole:

> In traditional sub-Saharan musical cultures body movement must be seen as an integral part of the music-making process. Although it is true that physical motion, especially as dance, frequently accompanies music in many cultures, in most instances that physical activity is extrinsic to

the act of making music. . . . In sub-Saharan cultures, conceptually, the two activities are viewed as interrelated components of the same process. The Western conceptual assumption of a division between consciously organized sound (music) and movement associated with that sound (dance) usually does not exist here. That is why in many traditional music-making situations the dancers and the musicians frequently are one and the same.[7]

Regardless of whether body movement is extrinsic or intrinsic to the act of making music, however, the importance of this physical aspect of music is undeniable.

In addition to simple movement and dance, there are some extreme variants which illustrate the overwhelming power of music on the human body in the context of religious ceremony, in particular the sometimes violent shaking and convulsing found in traditions of spirit possession. Anthropologists Walter and Frances Mischel have given a classic account of the extreme physical changes which occur in a woman during possession in the religious ceremonies of the Shango cult in Trinidad, where strongly rhythmic music plays an integral role:

> When the "spirit begins to manifest on" or "catch" Tanti, a dramatic physical transformation takes place. If in a standing position, she staggers, appears to lose her balance, begins to sway, and may fall either to the ground or into the arms of bystanders. Her entire body begins to vibrate, while her arms are either rigid at her sides or stretched out above her. Her feet are planted widely apart and she may lurch back and forth from toe to heel. The vibrations increase in intensity, and somewhat resemble the convulsions of a seizure state. At the same time, she emits deep grunts and groans. Her jaw begins to protrude, her lips pout and turn down sharply at the corners, her eyes dilate and stare fixedly ahead.[8]

The Mischels go on to describe how Tanti begins to take on the physical demeanor of Ogun, the deity who is possessing her, from body posture to stylized movements on down to being dressed in appropriate clothing. Clearly, a physiological transformation of enormous proportions takes place.[9]

The physiological impact of music can be observed and measured objectively from the outside. But it is important to emphasize that this impact is also strongly felt subjectively, from the inside, as a bodily experience. The body is, in fact, the locus of integration of the many dimensions of musical experience, which shade from the more physically oriented phenomena noted above to the psychological states examined next to the more mystical experiences of spiritual worlds. Musicologist Susan McClary has written about the centrality of the body in understanding the power of music:

> Music is foremost among cultural "technologies of the body," it is a site where we learn how to experience socially mediated patterns of kinetic energy, being in time, emotions, desire, pleasure and much more. . . . Music thus provides a terrain where competing notions of the body (and also the self, ideals of social interaction, feelings and so on) vie for attention and influence. An emergent group often announces its arrival first and most intensely in the ways its music constitutes the body.[10]

Thus, the body is not only an agglomeration of various physiological systems but it is also the locus of integration for feelings, emotions, desire, pleasure, and the self; in short, it is the site of important psychological dimensions as well. I will return to this notion of the centrality of the body in the musical experience in greater detail later, but for now, this provocative quotation from McClary provides a transition from the physiological dimensions of music to its psychological ones.

The Psychological Level

The power of music to evoke strong emotional responses is well known not only in Western musical forms, but in all musics around the world. As Rouget notes: "Of all the arts, music is undoubtedly the one that has the greatest capacity to move us, and the emotion it arouses can reach overwhelming proportions."[11] Certainly, most people have had the experience of being touched deeply by a piece of music—moved to tears of sadness or joy, stirred to passions of anger or love, carried to heights of inspiration or the depths of despair. Music seems to have an unparalleled power to reach into our psyche and pull out intense feeling states to experience. Why is this? What are the mechanisms taking place at the psychological level that allow music to evoke these strong emotions?

The answer is not a simple one; there are a number of elements in this process that make it quite complex, elements involving other dimensions of music that I will examine shortly. For now, however, it will be useful to look to traditional psychological models for an explanation. In the Western rationalist tradition of the Enlightenment, the Cartesian maxim "I think, therefore I am" forms the foundation for the way our culture views and/or structures the psyche. The "I," or the ego, or the self, is identified with rational thought, and most of our energy and attention is invested in that modality. Consequently, other human modalities such as feeling, the irrational, and the body are often relegated to the unconscious, where they continue to exist but receive little conscious attention. An individual tends to think of him- or herself as a solid, single entity, rather than as a complex agglomeration of equally complex subsystems or selves. This single entity is usually identified with the rational thinking self. This Western way of viewing the psyche thus leaves one with a hegemonic structure in which a small part of the totality, the rational thinking self, tends to subjugate the other subsystems.

However, the rational thinking self may not even be the most crucial aspect of what constitutes our humanness. Many of humanity's greatest creative works and cultural achievements are expressions of the irrational, the intuitive, the emotional, the physical, and the unconscious. But because these modalities have been subjugated by the ego-dominated hegemony of the psyche, there needs to be some means by which they can be reinvoked and reintegrated. Music is a powerful means of accomplishing this. What happens when one listens to music that evokes a strong emotional response is that the ego is temporarily relieved of its dominant position, and other parts of the self, such as emotions and feelings, can come to the surface to be experienced. In other words, there is a temporary restructuring of the psyche.

A powerful example of this temporary restructuring can be found in the phenomenon of possession. In certain West African and African American religious traditions, the central goal of the ritual activity is to bring about a state of possession in one or more of the participants, in which the presiding deity takes control of the person's body and becomes physically present in the human world. The primary means by which this is accomplished, after the preliminary prayers and offerings, is through percussion-heavy music, singing, and dancing. Particular songs, or sets of songs, as well as particular rhythms, are associated with particular deities and it is during his or her songs or rhythms that the deity possesses someone. The possessing deity is identified by his or her characteristic movements and behavior.

After the onset of possession, the deity is often dressed in special clothing, performs special duties, and interacts with people according to his or her unique personality structure.

The metaphor employed by these cultures is that of the rider and the horse—the deity is the rider and the person's body is the horse. Almost uniformly, the people who are possessed report that they experience a kind of blackout during possession and they have no recollection of any of their activities while possessed. So one can say that the normal rider (or ego structure, in the model we are discussing) of the possessed person is replaced by the rider (or ego structure) of the deity. This replacement of riders is complete and detailed, down to mannerisms, movements, speech patterns, and behavior. Thus it seems clear that the normal operational structure of the possessed person's psyche has been altered in a profound way.

I should state at this point that possession is an extreme example of the psychological effects of music, and I have used this example to illustrate the effects in the strongest possible terms. But it is equally true that music induces psychological effects in a whole range of lesser ways. In order to set up a framework for discussing this, it will be helpful to introduce and develop the notion of altered states of consciousness, a term that came into use in the 1960s in response to the widespread use of psychedelic drugs, spiritual and meditational practices, and numerous types of therapies. Altered states of consciousness have been defined by Dr. Arnold Ludwig as:

> Those mental states, induced by various physiological, psychological, or pharmacological maneuvers or agents, which can be recognized subjectively by the individual himself (or by an objective observer of the individual) as representing a sufficient deviation, in terms of subjective experience or psychological functioning, from certain general norms as determined by the subjective experience and psychological functioning of that individual during alert, waking consciousness.[12]

Put more simply, an altered state of consciousness is a state of consciousness which differs significantly from the normal consciousness of day-to-day experience.

Among the "maneuvers or agents" that Ludwig referred to, music is considered by some to be one of the most efficacious. Certainly, this is what McAllester was saying earlier in discussing the power of music to transform experience and create different musical states of being.[13] Fellow ethnomusicologist John Blacking concurs:

> Although heightened experience or altered states of consciousness are not qualities peculiar to music, music has advantages over many other ways of heightening human experience, because of the special relationships between people and the kind of coordination of the body that are often required for performance.[14]

Moreover, both Blacking and McAllester have made the connection between musically produced altered states of consciousness and religious experience.[15] Again, it is interesting to note the importance of the body as the locus of integration of these ecstatic, mystical quasi-religious experiences.

> I have described the sorts of movement and sound that can emerge from the body in a state of ecstasy or altered consciousness. I am suggesting that dance and music are cultural developments of proto-dance and proto-music, and that one important purpose of these arts is to restore, if only temporarily, the open state of cosmic consciousness that is the source of their existence. The process of communication is like that of a telephone or tape-recorder, in which sounds are converted into a magnetic code, which can then be translated back into the original sounds.[16]

Blacking's speculations propose an interesting model for understanding the connection between music and religion at the level of psychology, consciousness, and personality structure.

The Sociocultural Level

Thus far, for the sake of simplicity and focus, I have been discussing the impact of music on the individual. Yet it is clear from looking at our examples that the use of music almost always takes place in a social or group context. In this regard, the notion of an isolated individual who experiences music in a solitary manner is practically unheard of. For most peoples around the world, in fact, there is no concept of music as separate from the social context of day-to-day life in which it is embedded. Even in the West, predominant musical genres like classical or rock and roll are inseparable from certain social forms that reflect particular sets of beliefs and values common to their respective social groups. In many cases, involvement with the music is an essential criterion for entry into these social groups, and one may even develop a strong social identity based on musical affiliation. Thus, music is usually a highly social phenomenon.

Even if it were possible for an individual to be isolated from his or her social group and have a musical experience (through composing, playing, or listening), it would still reflect his or her larger social context. In this sense, the term cultural may be more accurate than social, because I am really talking about culturally shaped ways of perceiving and organizing (musical) reality. And this points to a fundamental question underlying any study of this kind, namely, what is music? Music is obviously different from simple noise or sound. Yet one culture may have a very different sense of what constitutes music from another, which is why the cultural aspect is so important. Blacking makes this point succinctly:

> Music is a product of the behavior of human groups, whether formal or informal: it is *humanly organized sound*. And, although different societies tend to have different ideas about what they regard as music, all definitions are based on some consensus of opinion about the principles on which the sounds of music should be organized. No such consensus can exist until there is some common ground of experience, and unless different people are able to hear and recognize patterns in the sound that reach their ears. . . . Music is a cultural tradition that can be shared and transmitted.[17]

> Musical systems . . . are made up of socially accepted patterns of sound that have been invented and developed by interacting individuals in the contexts of different social and cultural systems.[18]

The key phrase here, which I have italicized, is that music is "humanly organized sound." The structure of that organization is one expression or reflection of the culture in which the music exists. Therefore, even if I listen to music in the solitude of my home, I am still participating in the organized conceptual structure of my culture.

This recognition of the cultural variability of music is one of the key contributions that ethnomusicology has made to the study of music. In other words, music does not take place in some sort of cultural vacuum; it is not a universal language in a simple mechanistic sense, as many traditional musicologists have tried to claim. There are differences in musical systems and people's relationships to them, which reflect larger differences in the cultures in question. These musical and cultural differences are also reflected in religious practice and sensibility. The beat-driven musics associated with possession religions are very different from, say, the Gregorian chants of Christian monastic religion. Each reflects a very different culture, a very different religious practice and sensibility, and a very different musical form. Moreover, those melodies, harmonies, or rhythms that might evoke a powerful response from someone in one culture may have absolutely no effect on someone from another culture; generally, the physiological and psychological effects do not occur except within the learned meaning system of a particular sociocultural context.

The Semiological Level

These meaning systems are constructed through a complex process of symbolization, or signification, in which structured musical patterns come to be associated with particular resonant meanings. The field of scholarship that studies the mechanics of symbolization or signification is called semiology, and I will be utilizing some of its conceptual tools to look at the semiological dimensions of music. Most of the basic terms in this field were developed to analyze language and then expanded to apply to other systems of signification. For my purposes, which are admittedly elementary, it will be useful to begin with language as a first example to illustrate these terms. The word "book" will serve as a basic *sign*. In semiological terms, a *sign* is made up of two constituent parts, the *signifier* and the *signified*. The *signifier* is the word "book," which takes the form of printed ink spelled with the letters b-o-o-k, or the form of the sound "book," which is produced by small mouth noises. The *signified* is the actual physical object made of paper to which the *signifier* refers. In language systems, there is usually a pretty stable one-to-one correspondence between the *signifier* and the *signified,* with some obvious exceptions.

In music, however, it is a very different situation.[19] One can say that particular musical phrases are *signs* and that they are also *signifiers*. But it is difficult to identify exactly what is being *signified*. For example, I may listen to a particular phrase in a piece of music and, for me, it could signify a feeling of joy. Someone else could listen to it and take it to signify a particular person or place. It may even be the case that the composer had something else in mind while writing the piece or, further, that the performer had something else in mind while performing it. In other words, in music there is not the same type of stable, clear, one-to-one relationship between the *signifier* and the *signified* as in language. In fact, in most cases (and I will be examining the notable exceptions shortly) the connection between *signifier* and *signified* is very tenuous indeed, and the *signified* seems to be somewhat free-floating and chameleonic. This makes for a situation in which a multiplicity of meanings can be invoked by a single piece of music.

Another factor contributing to the free-floating nature of the *signified* in music is that musical phrases (*signifiers*) have an interesting dual capacity to refer both extrinsically and intrinsically.[20] Extrinsic referring means that the *signifier* is referring to something external to the piece of music, whether it be, to use our previous examples, a feeling of joy or a particular person or place. Musical semiologist Jean-Jacques Nattiez says that one "can establish a division into three large fields" of extrinsic referring: "the spatio-temporal, the kinetic, and the affective."[21] In other words, music can refer outside itself to specific things, to people or places, to times or events, to movements or processes, or to various states of feeling.

Intrinsic referring, on the other hand, means that the *signifier* is referring to something within the piece of music. For example, a particular musical phrase with a descending line is repeated within the course of a piece. But at the finale the phrase is repeated with an ascending line, creating a powerful effect by deviating from the expectation that was created by the previous descending repetitions. In this case, the ascending line is referring intrinsically, deriving its meaning and power by referring to something within the piece of music. Music's capacity for intrinsic referring is one of the keys to understanding its power to create virtual realities. And as I will show later, this power to create virtual realities makes music an especially potent vehicle for conveying the sacred or the spiritual. So when one says that music has the dual capacity for both extrinsic and intrinsic referring, it means that music is capable of simultaneously opening out into the external world and plunging inward into internal worlds, much the same as religion has the capacity to touch both the visible and the invisible realms.

In addition, there is also the matter of secondary associations or significations. The classic example in Western popular culture would be that of a couple falling in love while a particular song is playing. Thereafter, the song comes to be associated not only with that particular event but with the whole complex of subsequent feelings, meanings, and history of that couple's romantic relationship. So one can say that while the song continues to have its own primary set of significations, both extrinsic and intrinsic, it also comes to have a secondary set of significations for the couple in question. This example is what one might call an accidental or random case; the song just happens to be playing while certain important events or feelings occur or, conversely, certain events or feelings happen to occur while an important piece of music is being played.

But in cultures that recognize this power of secondary musical signification, such associations may be consciously created and utilized, and may indeed be elevated to a position of primary importance. This is particularly true when we look at music that is used within a ceremonial or ritual religious context. Through formal repetition in a proscribed ritual sequence of sacred activities, the music comes to be associated with those activities and with the effects or associations which those activities produce. Such is the case with almost all religious ceremonies, whether we are talking about the sound of the water-drum in the Native American Church peyote meeting, the drum ensembles in West African and African American possession religions, the gospel choir in American churches, the call to prayer in Islam, the devotional chanting in Hindu Krishna sects, or any other countless examples.

Rouget has supplied a particularly good example for illustrating both the primary and secondary semiological power of music. He has developed a sophisticated and nuanced explanation of the mechanics of musical trance induction through the concept of the "musical motto." This motto is a musical phrase or theme which is identified with a particular deity or spirit, and is played when the participants wish to invoke that deity or spirit to come and take possession of one of the initiates in the ceremony. Rouget finds evidence of this type of use of musical mottoes in Bali, Vietnam, Tibet, Madagascar, Mozambique, Ethiopia, Niger, Senegal, among the Dogon, the Yoruba, the Fon, in Brazil in Candomble, in Haiti in Vodun, and, interestingly, in Europe in Tarantism. He writes that the musical motto

> plays a central role in possession. It can be defined as a sign whose "signified" is the god to which it refers and whose "signifier" has three facets: linguistic, musical, and choreographic. The signifying power of this sign is peculiarly extensive, since it involves spirit and body, intelligence and sensibility, the faculties of ideation and movement, all at the same time.

This is evidently what makes it, for the adept, the most powerful means available for identifying himself with the divinity possessing him.[22]

In this statement, we begin to get a sense of how music is a preferred medium for conveying religious meaning by virtue of its ability to operate simultaneously at several different levels.

Before concluding this section, I should also briefly mention that language itself has this same signifying power, and language often appears in music in the form of lyrics or texts. Language here also has a dual nature—it is simultaneously both a semiological system and a form of musical expression, a vocalization that functions in the same way as a musical instrument. There is another sense in which language used in a musical context has a dual nature, namely, the poetic aspect of song or chant lyrics. Poetry constitutes a different use of language from functional day-to-day language, the language of intellectual discourse, or even the language of storytelling narrative, in that poetry's purpose is primarily to evoke rather than to describe literally. Using semiological terms, one can say that in poetry the *signified* is less rigidly tied to the *signifier* than in simple descriptive language while, at the same time, the *signifier* itself is freed from a purely descriptive role into a more aesthetic, evocative function. And paradoxically this situation allows poetry to evoke the *signified* with greater power. Hence one can see the second dual nature of language in a musical context: it is more literally descriptive than music itself and yet it is also poetically evocative; it weakens the link between the *signifier* and the *signified* and yet it strengthens the evocative power of this link.

There are numerous musicoreligious practices that clearly demonstrate this evocative power of language. In Hindu traditions, for example, the practice of mantra chanting consists of repeatedly vocalizing the name of a deity in order to invoke his or her presence or power:

> A mantra containing the name of a god—for instance namah Sivaya—is indeed regarded as embodying the energy of the god which is activated by pronouncing the formula. The knowledge of, and meditation on, a mantra enables the adept to exert influence upon the god, to exercise power over the potencies manifesting in it, to establish connections between the divinity and himself, or to realize his identity with that divinity.[23]

It might be more accurate to use the word "*in*vocative" rather than "evocative" in describing the magical power of vocalized language to *in-*

voke the presence of the deity. Mantra is just another example of how the semiological properties of music clearly play an important role in the connection between music and religion.

The Virtual Level

The phenomenologist of religion Gerardus van der Leeuw has written that "music is a world in itself."[24] In this section, I will explore this seemingly simple statement in greater detail, attempting to understand why this is so and the mechanics of how it works. In order to do so, I introduce some terms and concepts borrowed from cybernetics and computer science. In the mid-1980s, science fiction author William Gibson developed the notion of cyberspace, a virtual dimension that transcends the limits of two-dimensional screens and allows one to experience a complete visual and visceral consensus reality system.[25] Since then, subsequent developments in computer technology have given us the term and concept of *virtual reality*.[26] Virtual reality refers to the world one enters into through the computer screen, a virtual world not bound by the rules of the physical universe, a world that opens out into the realm of the imagination. These innovative notions have captured the imagination of a new generation of computer enthusiasts and cultural trend-setters.

Long before the invention of computers, however, human beings were experiencing a powerful form of virtual reality through the medium of music. As Van der Leeuw puts it: "Music is a world in itself, with its own space and its own time, in which not only spatial, but also temporal existence is subsumed."[27] In other words, music creates a virtual reality by setting up its own version of space and time. It will be useful to focus first on the temporal, since that is the virtual dimension of music that is more immediately apparent and that yields more easily to analysis. To begin with the obvious, one can say that music is a temporal form because it requires the passage of time in order to unfold in its totality. It is not the same as a painting, for example, which is frozen, as it were, in a single eternal moment in which it can be seen in its entirety.

There are several types of temporal activity within music, which can be given distinct visual representations. In music, the sound, although transient and part of a larger whole, can only be heard in the present moment. In this respect, it is the "eternal now," which can be represented visually with the symbol of the point. At the same time, however, one must also apprehend music as a line, as a sequential unfolding of notes which form the larger whole of the piece. One can only make sense of the tone sounding in the present moment by referring to previous and subsequent tones. In this sense, one is experiencing not only the present moment but also the past and the future, within the context of the entire musical event of which all three temporal aspects are a part. Finally, there are the recurrent aspects of music, such as the statement and restatement of a melodic theme, or the repetitive beat of the rhythm, which are similar to the cyclical time of nature and can be represented by a circle, or even a spiral (since some repetition includes embellishment or change).

All these are ways of viewing time objectively, from the outside. One of the distinctive features of virtual reality, however, is that one can enter into it and it can create a subjective experience not bound by the realities of the external world. This is also true of music. Blacking has said that "the essential quality of music is its power to create another world of virtual time."[28] How does this happen? The rhythm and tempo of a piece of music set up a temporal framework that creates a sense of time unique to that piece. The tempo can increase or decrease, thereby changing the feeling tone or texture of the music. I showed earlier, for example, how the acceleration of tempo can bring about the onset of possession trance in West African and African American ceremonies. Moreover, the rhythm can shift and thereby create a corresponding shift in musical texture. I also showed that there are different rhythmic patterns for the different possessing deities in these religious traditions, so that a shift in rhythm would literally mean calling in an altogether different god, with altogether different energies and characteristics. In addition—and this is particularly true of African musics—it is possible to have more than one rhythm occurring at the same time in the same piece of music. These simultaneously occurring multiple rhythms, or polyrhythms, are capable of creating simultaneously occurring multiple temporal realities within a single piece of music. One can now begin to see how these temporal structures move beyond simple mechanical time into the creation of complex virtual temporal realities, each with its own texture, feeling tone, characteristics, and presiding deity.

These temporal structures of rhythm and tempo only set up the broad framework of the piece. They are, metaphorically speaking, the form or the container, while we can consider the melody and harmony to be the actual contents.[29] To continue the metaphor, then, one can say that the rhythm and tempo of a piece of music provide the temporal grid for that music's virtual reality, while the melody and harmony serve as the analog of the virtual spatial grid. When a piece of music introduces a particular theme and then goes on to vary it, articulate it, and develop it, there emerges a complex set of virtual, spatial, and temporal relationships. The different qualities (or virtual aspects) of a piece of music interact with each other and create a whole new set of qualities through their interrelationships. Thus music can provide much subtlety and nuance in its virtual dimensions. It is also important to remember that these different qualities, aspects, and feeling tones that are generated by rhythm, harmony, and melody also have sets of semiological meanings attached to them, thereby further filling in the texture and detail of the virtual realities the music is creating.

The Ritual Level

I now have the pieces in place to explore how music actually functions within a religious ritual context. I have already shown how music is a powerful medium for the transformation of experience. When it is put in a ritual context, however, this power is channeled toward specific religious ends in conjunction with another set of interlocking ritual components. The result of this conjunction is to amplify music's already considerable power, making it an even more effective tool for triggering particular religious experiences. In certain traditions, such as the West African and African American possession cults, for example, a particular piece of music heard outside a ritual context may have no effect whatsoever on the listener, while when heard within the ritual context it has a profound effect. In this section, I am going to examine why this is so. Why do music and ritual seem to work so well together, and what are the dynamics of the way that interaction actually works?

In the introduction, I briefly discussed some of the seminal concepts in ritual studies: the universality of rites of passage for transitions from one phase of life to the next; the three stages of separation, liminality, and reintegration; and notions of structure, antistructure, and communitas. I would now like to introduce some more recent theoretical innovations in ritual studies developed by historian of religions Jonathan Z. Smith. To begin with, Smith argues that nothing is inherently sacred but that things, places, persons or times are *made* sacred by ritual activity. He proposes that we look at ritual as a way of focusing or directing attention in a highly marked way. It is this quality of ritually focused attention that, in his view, makes something sacred. If we link this type of attention with the concept of altered states of consciousness, we can propose further that ritual activity is a means of attaining particular altered states of consciousness that permit one to invoke the sacred. Given that music is a powerful tool both for effecting altered states of consciousness and for invoking the sacred, it should come as no surprise that it is a major component in ritual activity around the world.

Smith's next theoretical insight takes a common assumption in ritual studies and stands it on its head—that participants in rituals believe in sympathetic magic, the idea that an action performed in a ritual context will magically bring about the same effect in the real world. Smith, for his part, suggests the opposite interpretation—that participants are keenly aware that their ritual activity does *not* correspond to actual events in the real world:

> We must presume that he is aware of this discrepancy, that he works with it, that he has some means of overcoming this contradiction between word and deed. This work, I believe, is one of the major functions of ritual. I would suggest that, among other things, *ritual represents the creation of a controlled environment* where the variables (i.e., the accidents) of ordinary life may be displaced *precisely* because they are felt to be overwhelmingly present and powerful. *Ritual is a means of performing the way things ought to be in conscious tension to the way things are in such a way that this ritualized perfection is recollected in the ordinary, uncontrolled course of things.*[30]

Ritual, then, takes place in a controlled environment where everything is in its proper place and all activity unfolds in the correct and perfect way. In essence, this is a description of a type of virtual reality. Aware that things do not go perfectly in everyday reality, people create a virtual reality in ritual activity in order to have at least one place where everything is exactly right. It is natural, therefore, that music, with its unique capacity to create virtual worlds, particularly worlds of virtual time, would be a prominent tool used in ritual contexts for the creation of a virtual reality. Both ritual and music are systems that create virtual realities, and they are somewhat complementary systems at that: ritual excels at the creation of virtual space, while music excels at the creation of virtual time. This is not to say that ritual does not also create virtual time—it does. And this is also not to say that music does not create virtual space—it does. But ritual creates its virtual space within an actual real-world physical place. Smith puts a great deal of emphasis on the importance of place in ritual—the notion that things are made sacred by being put in their proper place and that place serves as a focusing lens for directing attention in a ritual manner. And I have already discussed music's remarkable capacity to manufacture virtual time. So I am suggesting that ritual and music work together synergistically to create a compelling virtual reality with spatial *and* temporal dimensions.

There is also a strong semiological aspect to ritual activity, not only because symbols per se play such a central role, but because structural components such as spatial arrangement, sequence of events, gesture and movement, vocal and speech structure, dress, altars, implements and objects, and roles all have important symbolic significance within a ritual context that provides a coherent meaning system.[31] And these semiological systems can be quite complex, each symbol having multiple, and even contradictory, meanings.[32] In this regard, one can see once again that music is a particularly powerful and appropriate ritual component in light of its already considerable semiological dimensions. The image here takes on an almost fractal character—music, a semiological system comprised of smaller components, itself functions as a smaller component within the larger semiological system of ritual.

However, lest these virtual and semiological aspects of music and ritual become too abstract and disembodied, let me emphasize that they also have a powerful bodily component. Victor Turner felt that an important dimension of the power of ritual symbols is their ability to affect people on a visceral, sensory level.[33] Another contemporary scholar in ritual studies, Ronald Grimes, has also done work along these lines, devoting a great deal of attention to bodily experience and feeling states as data in his research.[34] Grimes understands that something profound can transpire in the context of a ritual, and that this something is, in fact, one of the central purposes of that ritual: "When 'It works,' [it] generates a sense of wonder and awe among the participants. This 'It' is elusive, powerful, fragile, and highly valued. And one needs to be in a highly tuned state of body-mind to encounter it."[35] Given that this powerful experience of "It" is so critical for a successful ritual, it is not surprising that music is an important component in ritual, especially in light of what we have already seen about music's capacity to affect one's bodily experience and feeling state.

At this point, it will be useful to examine a particular ritual to see some of the specific and practical functions that music performs in a real-life ceremonial setting. I have chosen Ann Dhu Shapiro and Ines Talamantez's article on the Mescalero Apache girl's puberty ceremony, a rite of passage from adolescence to adulthood. Shapiro and Talamantez make note of several interesting functions that music performs in the course of this four-day ceremony. First is its role in highlighting certain activities so as to make them stand out: "The effect of such close coordination between song structure and action is to focus attention on the specific action and to enhance it."[36] Second, they note "the strong aural experience created by the songs, bound up with equally strong physical and visual experiences."[37] Next they point out that the repetitive structure of the songs "gives them an aesthetic design that matches other portions of the ceremony, from the tipi shapes against the sky to the geometrical designs painted on the Gaahe."[38]

Finally, Shapiro and Talamantez observe the function of music in shaping and defining the structure of the ceremony and the way this serves to create a ritual world of virtual time:

> The songs of the ceremony are structured and grouped in such a way as to unify the diverse portions of the ritual and to create the impression in the participants that *no* time has elapsed from beginning to end—and that, in fact, this ceremony joins others in its own re-creation of the realm of mythological time.[39]

The notion of no time elapsing and of the re-creation of mythological time brings us very close to the thought of Mircea Eliade in his classic work *The Myth of the Eternal Return*. Eliade saw one of the main functions of ritual is to return the participants to the primordial time of creation, *in illo tempore*.[40] Talamantez and Shapiro have given a concrete example of how music is an effective tool used within a specific ritual context to achieve this end.

Through both concrete example and theoretical model, then, one can begin to see how the multidimensional nature of music, its ability to function simultaneously at several different levels, makes it particularly well-suited to religious activity in a ritual context. Because music works at multiple levels—the physiological, the psychological, the sociocultural, the semiological, and the temporal/virtual—it is the ritual component or technique par excellence.

The Spiritual Level

Having examined the many levels on which music operates, I can now turn my attention to the main topic of this chapter, namely, the spiritual and religious dimensions of music. And this brings us face to face with the central mystery of the spiritual realm. Whether one calls it the sacred, the holy, the numinous, the absolute, the place of the archetypes, the world of the spirits, the realm of the gods, or God, it is a dimension of reality that is of paramount importance to human beings. But it does not yield easily to rational analysis; over the millennia, many thinkers have, on the one hand, tried to explain it away with clever arguments and, on the other, suspended critical analysis in favor of mushy platitudes. My task, in contrast, will be to face the mystery head on and, while respecting its compelling power, marshall resources, both intellectual *and* intuitive, to try to illuminate it. To begin with, one needs to take seriously the notion that there is such a thing as the spiritual realm and to develop a set of scholarly concepts and terms to discuss it intelligently.

Here, I must return to one of the concepts mentioned in the introduction, an idea developed by Rudolf Otto—one of the first scholars of religion in the modern sense—the idea of the numinous. Otto developed this idea and term in order to make some useful distinctions in discussing the complexities of the spiritual realm. First, there is the distinction between the phenomenal, things as they appear in the external observable world of form, and the numinal or numinous, things as they are in their essence.[41] Second, there is the distinction between our idea of the holy or sacred as good or morally justified, and our intense *experience* of it, the "unique original feeling-response," which Otto also called the numinous.[42] So there are two aspects to the numinous, that which stimulates the feeling-response, the spiritual realm, which Otto called the "wholly other"; and the feeling-response itself, our human mode of apprehending the numinous, which Otto called the "mysterium tremendum and fascinans." Otto argued that the human encounter with the numinous forms the basis for religious experience, which in turn forms the basis for religion per se.

Otto clearly enjoyed music and wrote about the musical experience:

> It releases a blissful rejoicing in us, and we are conscious of a glimmering, billowy agitation occupying our minds, without being able to express or explain in concepts what it really is that moves us so deeply. . . .

Music, in short, arouses in us an experience and vibrations of mood that are quite specific in kind. . . . The resultant complex mood is, as it were, a fabric, in which the general human feelings and emotional states constitute the warp, and the non-rational music-feelings the woof. . . . The real content of music is not drawn from the ordinary human emotions at all, and . . . is in no way merely a second language, alongside the usual one, by which these emotions find expression. Musical feeling is rather (like numinous feeling) something "wholly other."[43]

Essentially, then, Otto is saying that musical feeling is *analogous* to numinous feeling but is not *identical* with it. He warns: "We must beware of confounding in any way the non-rational of music and the non-rational of the numinous itself."[44] In speaking of the analogy between music and the numinous, however, Otto goes on to say that "the former may become a means of expression of the latter," that music may become a means of expressing the numinous.[45]

Four decades later, Gerardus Van der Leeuw took up the same discussion and elaborated on it. Using the same terminology as Otto, he wrote of music that it "seems to be an expression of the holy," and that "we find ourselves in the presence of the wholly other."[46] He also wrote that "music speaks the truth, that deeper truth which comes from another world. Music is a direct revelation of the secret of the world."[47] Notice that he does not say that music *is* the secret of the world, but a revelation of it. In my earlier section on virtual reality, I introduced Van der Leeuw's comment on music's ability to create its own virtual world. Van der Leeuw's key contribution in this regard is the notion that this virtual musical world serves the function of pointing to the spiritual dimension:

It [music] can very easily be an expression of a reality which is by no means amusical, but more than musical. Music is neither the reproduction of the "world" nor of nature nor of the spirit. But in spite of this it can be the revelation of that of which the "world" is only an incomplete revelation. . . . In heaven there is music, but heaven is more than just music.[48]

The heavenly song cannot be heard on earth; it is that *canor* of which the mystics speak, the song which sounds first above, then within, the human being. Earthly music can only remind us distantly of this song. The most beautiful music is only an echo of the eternal Gloria.[49]

So the virtual world that music creates can be an analog of the heavenly world. When one hears music and it stirs the spiritual impulse within, one is reminded of the spiritual realm; one is given, as it were, a small taste of what that realm is like.

This view of music advanced by Otto and Van der Leeuw is a sophisticated and nuanced explanation of the spiritual power of music. However, for all its insights, it still works within the framework of the Western intellectual tradition of the Enlightenment, a framework that continues to posit a separation between the everyday world, the world of music, and the world of spirit. A more radical view would acknowledge the possibility that pathways and linkages can be established between these worlds, and that two-way travel along these pathways can occur. In order to find this type of radical view, however, one must look toward those non-Western cultures that have more fully developed it.

Not surprisingly, West Africa is one region where such a view is eloquently articulated, in this case, by African musicologist W. Komla Amoaku of the Ewe of Ghana:

> This view, accepted by all the Ewe, holds that the invisible world of spirit, the world of man, and the visible world of nature form an indivisible unit; that the visible world of nature is the reflection of the true, invisible world of spirit. . . . Music among the Ewe is viewed as an expression . . . which involves the visible as well as the invisible worlds. . . . The Ewe have demonstrated consistently in the ritualization of practically every aspect of traditional music that, indeed, no musical activity is devoid of the Ewe worldview. I have never participated in a traditional musical activity in which there was no allusion to the gods or spirits, some gesture intended to link the visible with the invisible world.[50]

Amoaku goes on to make this link between intersecting worlds and music even more explicit:

> For me, it [music] is the involuntary alteration that occurs in my psyche, the spiritual upliftment, my transcendental imaginations of a spirit world, my oneness with the gods and spirits of departed relatives, and that temporary transformation of my body into spirit. Whenever I participate in this music, whether physically or silently, I look for the properties that make the activity spiritually satisfying and fulfilling—properties that link me with the invisible world and constantly remind me of a world beyond.[51]

I will explore this typically African view of the intersection of worlds and the spiritual power of music in more detail in the next chapter.

I should point out that West Africa is by no means the only region that demonstrates a recognition of the profound importance of music as a link with the spiritual world. In India, for example, there is the beautifully articulated and developed idea of sound as God, or Nada-Brahma. Master sitarist Ravi Shankar writes:

> Our tradition teaches us that sound is God—Nada Brahma. That is, musical sound and the musical experience are steps to the realization of the self. We view music as a kind of spiritual discipline that raises one's inner being to divine peacefulness and bliss. We are taught that one of the fundamental goals a Hindu works toward in his lifetime is a knowledge of the true meaning of the universe—its unchanging, eternal essence—and this is realized by a complete knowledge of one's self and one's own nature. The highest aim of our music is to reveal the essence of the universe it reflects. . . . Thus, through music, one can reach God.[52]

This view of music as a spiritual path is part of a larger sonic cosmology in which music is seen as the stuff out which the universe is made. If the universe is composed of sound, it follows that the skillful use of sound in music can bring one back to the source of creation. There have been extensive treatises written throughout Indian history that elaborate this cosmology in great detail, of which the *Sangita Ratnakara* of Sarngadeva is generally considered to be the greatest. In his introduction to this revered work, Raja says: "The musical notes are the physical manifestations of the Highest Reality termed Nada-Brahman. Music is not a mere accompaniment in religious worship; it is religious worship itself."[53]

One can see in these Hindu and Ewe cosmologies the explicit articulation of the tremendous spiritual and religious power of music. These traditions have consciously cultivated this spiritual power in sophisticated and elaborate systems in order to utilize it for specific religious ends. However, it should be clear from all the material discussed in this chapter that this power is present in the music, *whether it is consciously recognized or not*. Music *does* affect people in all the ways I have described: at the physiological level, it affects the body and its subsystems; at the psychological level, it affects the structure of the psyche and the state of consciousness; at the sociocultural level, it affects and reflects the social order and the cultural paradigms; at the semiological level, it provides symbolic structures which create affective meaning systems; at the virtual level, it creates compelling temporal and spatial worlds into which one is drawn; at the ritual level, it fits into a larger set of ritual activities, with their own functions and purposes; and, finally, at the spiritual or religious level, it establishes a link to the spiritual world and the contours and dynamics of that world. Moreover, music affects people in all these ways *simultaneously,* integrating all the levels into a powerful and harmonious whole that is greater than the sum of its parts.

I would like to emphasize that this integration takes place in an *experiential* state, and that this state is a unique phenomenological and ontological mode of being-in-the-world in which the subject-object, body-mind, and spiritual-material dualities are transcended in a unified field. In this state, the body is the central locus through which experiential integration occurs. Ethnomusicologist Steven M. Friedson developed these pioneering ideas in his work with the Tumbuka healers of Malawi in their possession dances, and it is worth quoting him at length.

What do we make of worlds possessed by spirits, spirits moved by music? How do we interpret a world that is neither given nor experienced in Cartesian duality? This oppositional structure breaks down in the face of such porous corporealities as dancing prophets. There the body has an ontological status different from its status in Western conceptions of the individual, with their connotations of a bounded, delimited, and inviolate space. When Tumbuka healers dance, they reach beyond and place themselves through subject-object distinctions, into a fundamental relationship with *the things themselves.*

Tumbuka healers, in an ontological sense, dance an authentic existence, an openness to Being, which must be understood first and foremost in its existential status as a mode of being-in-the-world. . . . The term "mode" is to be taken not only in its general ontological meaning as a way of Being, but also in a more strictly musical sense as a tonal/rhythmic structuration. In trance dancing there is no separation between the two: lived experience *is* a musical mode of being-in-the-world. . . .

Within the acoustical *and motional* properties of singing, clapping, drumming, and dancing, people experience profound modes of being-in-the-world. This is not the sharing of an interior state of consciousness but a gathering together of intersubjective experience through the objective process of making music together. . . . If making music together is truly intersubjective, then it is a transcendent process and in this sense its presence is objective. The invisible spirits are refracted through the bodily process of the trance dancer, and *vimbuza* [spirits] and Tumbuka, as equally viable presences, partake of the same experiential realm of sound and motion.[54]

Partaking of this musical realm, participants step into a unified field where the spiritual dimension is directly experienced in a powerful phenomenological mode that is integrated with all the other dimensions.

In most cultures around the world, throughout the history of humankind, this spiritual power of music has been acknowledged, cultivated, and celebrated. It is an important part of our common heritage, one of the great expressions of the human endeavor. We recognize it when we hear it and experience it; we feel the power, even when our culture has no conceptual category for it, even when we are listening to a seemingly trivial popular song. "We are not all practicing mystics and most of us do not experience God easily. But when we hear music, something like that is happening to us."[55]

2

West African Possession Religion and American Popular Music

Now that I have explored the nearly universal connection between music and religion, and the reasons for it, I will turn my attention back to the *specific* music and religion in this study, namely, contemporary American popular music and its connection to West African possession religion. As I noted earlier, there is a long and complex history to how these two phenomena came to be intertwined, a history which I will recount in this chapter. There are many twists and turns along the way, from the indigenous forms of possession religion in West Africa, to the devastating dislocations of the trans-Atlantic slave trade and the brilliantly transformed expressions in the Americas. There is the entry into entertainment musics in North America, the development of great African American musical traditions like the blues, and rhythm and blues' crossover to white youth audiences as rock and roll. Finally, there is the rise of rock as a major cultural force and a multibillion dollar corporate industry, to the emergence of distinct musical youth subcultures. I will cover each of these in turn, starting in West Africa.

Possession Religion in Indigenous West Africa

I have made numerous references to West African possession cults and their musicoreligious practices in previous chapters, but now I will look at these religions more systematically and in greater detail. In using the term "West African," I am referring primarily to the Ibo, Yoruba, Fon, Ewe, Ga, and Ashanti peoples located within the modern nation-states of Nigeria, Benin, Togo, and Ghana. Among these cultures, the Fon and the Yoruba figure most prominently, not only because they were the dominant cultures at the time of the slave trade, but also because they were the most influential among those peoples brought to the Americas and their influence on African American religions is very strong.[1] A brief survey will help to illustrate key structural elements of this complex of practices.[2]

To begin with, each culture has its own pantheon of deities (called *loa* among the Fon and *orishas* among the Yoruba), many of which are linked to natural phenomena. Among the Yoruba, for example, Shango is the *orisha* of thunder, Ogun the *orisha* of iron, and Yemaya the *orisha* of the ocean. Each deity has particular powers and qualities associated with him or her, as well as personality traits, movement styles, and clothing. So one prays to particular deities for the blessing of their particular power; that is, if one has problems in love, one prays to Erzulie, *loa* of love. Each of these deities has its own cult dedicated exclusively to him or her, with its own shrines, altars, priests and priestesses, initiates, songs and dances, weekly consulting days, and annual festival days.

Traditionally, to be an initiate, one has to be called by the deity, which usually means that one is spontaneously possessed in the course of observing a ceremony.[3] The priest or priestess is able to identify the possessing deity by a variety of indications, such as the song playing at the onset of possession or the type of movement and behavior evinced during possession. Once called, one goes through an initiation involving all the classic stages of rites of passage: separation from normal life, seclusion with fellow initiates in a liminal state, trials and training in which one is taught how to handle the possession as well as the ins and outs of group activities, and reintegration into society in the new role as a member of the group. These initiation and training periods can be quite rigorous and demanding, sometimes taking as long as seven years.[4]

The weekly consulting days are the central focal point of the ongoing group activities. It is here that community members come with their particular prayers and concerns to ask the help of the deity. These concerns can range from health problems to job prospects to affairs of the heart. It is here also that the possession dances occur on a regular basis. These are "in-house" dances, as it were, primarily for the members of the group and interested members of the community. It will be useful at this point to give a thumbnail sketch of a typical possession dance—its spatial and human organization, and the sequence of activities—in order to get a feel for what it is like in its indigenous context.

Most shrines have at least one inner room where the altar is located along with other ritual objects. The composition of the altars can vary, but they usually have some sort of representation of the primary deity, whether a statue or drawing or painting, and a place to pour libations. The dances typically take place outside, in a courtyard setting, with the large central area left open for the dancers. The members of the group congregate on one side, with special areas for the priests and priestesses, the drummers, and the rest of the initiates. Community members and observers form a ring around the rest of the perimeter. Dances often begin with the pouring of libations, usually some alcoholic beverage, as a means of honoring the deities and the ancestors and of consecrating the ceremony. At some point along the way, a chicken (or goat) is sacrificed by slitting its throat, and the blood is also spilled on the ground or altar as an offering. The sequential order of the libations and sacrifice varies from group to group. After this initial consecration, the songs and drumming and dancing begin in earnest.

The drum ensemble traditionally consists of three drums and two percussionists, usually bell and shaker, although this can vary. The drummers are highly skilled and trained musicians, and their role in the ceremony is of paramount importance.[5] There is a repertoire of sacred songs, each with its own rhythm, the order of which is keyed by the priest or priestess. These songs usually last anywhere from five to ten minutes, followed by a brief pause and then the next song. The priest or priestess is the lead vocalist, with the initiates providing vocal accompaniment. The initiates often supplement the rhythm with some percussion instrument, like sticks or shakers. When the songs begin, the dancing does too. Typically, at the outset one dancer comes out for each song and dances alone, although this too can vary. As the ceremony progresses and picks up energy, however, other dancers begin to join in and the dance space can become quite crowded. The dances are highly stylized and, for the most part, restrained, consisting of simple repetitive stepping motions, often in a line or a circle. Of course, this changes with the onset of possession, after which the dancing can be very dramatic and animated.

In some religious groups, possession comes in the middle of the dance. The dancer might be dancing in a restrained manner when, suddenly, his or her body is thrown back violently, as if struck by electricity or some powerful physical force. This may happen several times and is usually followed by a rhythmic shaking and trembling all over the body. Often the eyes roll back in the head, and the body assumes a completely different stance. When these signals indicate the onset of possession, an assistant goes to the possessed initiate, physically restrains her, and then takes her to the altar room.[6] Here, the assistants change her clothing and jewelry, replacing it with the appropriate garb of the possessing deity. This includes giving the possessed person ritual objects, such as a broom, an axe, or a staff, each of which symbolize particular attributes of the deity. The possessed person is then led back outside to the courtyard, and the dancing resumes. At this point, however, the dancing is of a completely different nature. The dance does not necessarily become wild and abandoned—it is often still highly stylized and restrained—but it reflects a completely different vocabulary of movements and body postures, expressing a completely different personality structure, that of the deity. The dance may, in fact, become frenetic, but that depends on whether the personality of the possessing deity is frenetic.

Another common way in which a group member becomes possessed is while she is sitting. This is not so dramatic and animated, but it is no less obvious. In this case, the initiate simply begins shaking in a rhythmic manner, accompanied by shifts in physical demeanor. Here again, an assistant goes to the possessed person, restrains her, and changes her clothing in her seat. After this, the possessed person gets up and dances, again with a completely different persona, and the process continues as described above. For example, in the Ga village of Konkonuru in Ghana, I spent many hours with the local priestess Otutuwa Abenaa at her shrine and home prior to the Sunday afternoon possession dance, enough time to become familiar with her speech patterns and body language. Later, during the dance, the possession came on her while she was seated, indicated by a series of shakes and shudders, followed by a half-faint in which she fell backward in her stool. Already moving to some internal rhythm, she got up to dance with her scarf removed, barebreasted, holding a broom which was the ritual implement of Kwasitutu, the possessing spirit. When her dance brought her near me, I could see that her face was visibly different, as was her whole demeanor. She showed no signs of recognizing me.

Sometimes, an initiate may be seen to be close to the onset of possession, and the lead drummer skillfully accentuates certain parts of the rhythm so as to induce possession. The lead drummer also figures prominently in the dance which takes place after the onset of possession and the change of clothes, using his drumming technique to interact with the dancer and, often, to raise the level of energy. The possessed dancer also interacts with the audience, slapping hands with them, sitting on them, talking to them, or even attacking them. In the case I witnessed, while possessed, Abenaa went around the periphery of the ceremony to greet everyone in the audience. At this same dance, an unassuming older priestess who was possessed by a spirit began attacking a spectator, driving him from his seat. When he returned, she tried to beat him with her cane.

At a certain point, the possessed dancer may be led by an assistant into the altar room and receives community members for consultations. These consultations often address some problem the person is experiencing—marital difficulties, financial woes, or illness. The possessing deity analyzes the cause of the problem and prescribes a remedy, usually in the form of ceremonial offerings to the gods. In the West African worldview, the worlds of nature, humans, and the gods constitute one continuous interrelated whole which only functions normally when they are all in correct and harmonious relationship. Problems arise when these relationships are neglected and fall into disharmony. Conversely, problems are resolved when the correct relationships are restored, and this is done through ceremonial offerings. For example, in a Tigare cult dance I attended in the village of Kisame, a possessed priestess holding a broom grabbed my local companion and took him into the consulting room. She recounted the story of how his mother had gone to a Tigare dance for help because she had not been able to conceive a child. There, his mother was dedicated to the possessing spirit, given the name of her yet-to-be-conceived son, and instructed never to use a broom at night. My friend was stunned, because it was impossible that the priestess could have known this information through normal channels. The priestess told him that the difficulties he was experiencing in his life could be rectified by making a sacrifice to the possessing spirit.

It is important to emphasize that, in these consultations, one is actually meeting face-to-face with the *deity,* in a human body, in the physical world. Such a meeting is the *goal* of the possession ceremony—to allow the deities to become physically present among the community in the human world, in the world of nature, in order to receive the benefit of their wisdom and spiritual powers. As African art historian Robert Farris Thompson writes: "To become possessed by the spirit of a Yoruba deity . . . is a formal goal of the religion, is to 'make the god,' to capture numinous flowing force within one's body."[7] Thompson goes on to state that the deity's powers, in addition to the more practical focus of the consultations, can also be "manifest in prophecy and predictive grace; hence, persons possessed by the spirit of a Yoruba deity are believed to speak of things yet to come."[8] Healing is another important manifestation of the magical powers of the possessing deity, and the occurrence of miraculous cures within the context of a possession dance is commonplace.

In addition to the weekly dances and consultations, there are also annual festivals for each of the major deities. These are large celebratory occasions which last all day or several days, where the whole community gathers, and outsiders (including priests and priestesses from other cults and villages) travel from great distances to join in. These gatherings feature costumed processions through the village and culminate in large public possession dances. In these dances, it is common for many different deities to take possession of the dancers and for many deities to be dancing at the same time, so much so that sometimes the courtyard becomes crowded with possessed dancers. Spurred on by the energy of the large crowds, the dances often become very animated and wild. I attended the Kpledzo festival in the Ga beach village of Nungua in Ghana, along with a crowd of three to four hundred people. As the dancing reached its apex in the late afternoon, there were over a dozen priestesses dancing at the same time, the crowd was shouting and gesticulating, and the energy level built to a fever pitch. The atmosphere at such gatherings is very different from the practical focus of the weekly dances; it is more festive and carnival-like, a celebration of the deities and their presence in the community.

In both these contexts, the music of the drum ensemble is key, both in stimulating the onset of possession and in directing its subsequent unfolding. This is one of the great examples of the efficacy of music as a ritual tool to establish a link to the spiritual world. It will be useful, therefore, to look more closely at the mechanics of how this actually works. In order to do so, I need to survey some of the distinguishing characteristics of African music, which is organized along different principles from Western music. To begin with the obvious, the emphasis is on *rhythmic* development and complexity, while the Western musical emphasis is on harmonic and melodic development and complexity.

One of the central distinctive features of African rhythmic structure is that more than one rhythm occurs at the same time—at least two, and often three or more. These rhythms lock into each other in specifically structured ways, interweaving into a richly textured rhythmic fabric. These interlocking rhythms, known as polyrhythms, form the basis for virtually all African and African-derived musics. The most common example is a four-beat rhythm laid over a three-beat rhythm; they each repeat their pattern within the same interval, yet may only share one beat in common. The two rhythms pull against each other, creating a dynamic tension which is resolved by the common beat. This interactive poly-rhythmic dynamic provides greater propulsion than a single rhythm. Many terms are used to describe this propulsive interlocking polyrhyth-mic drive—scholars employ terms like "concrescence" and "plexus," and musicians use terms like "beat" and "groove." "Getting in the groove" and staying there is the whole point of the musical endeavor.

Sometimes the common beat is not actually played, although everyone is aware of it, and it is up to the dancers and audience to complete the polyrhythm by supplying it either in their own minds or through their movements. This awareness of the common beat is called the "metro-nome sense," and it is crucial to the success of any polyrhythmic en-deavor.[9] As ethnomusicologist and drummer John Chernoff writes:

> Though the rhythms are played apart, the music is unified by the way the separate rhythms fit together into a cross-rhythmic fabric. Only through the combined rhythms does the music emerge, and the only way to hear the music properly [is] to find the beat, and to develop and exercise "metronome sense."[10]

In contemporary popular music, the most common way of supplying the beat is by tapping one's foot in time to the music. In African music, the most common way of supplying the beat is to get up and dance, an activ-ity which, in possession religion as well as in most other African musical events, is one of the central features of the proceedings. This connection between music and dance is a singular aspect of African music.

The fact that the dancers and audience need to complete the poly-rhythm illustrates another organizing principle of African music—its es-sentially participatory nature. In contrast to Western music's rigid distinc-tions between performer and audience, African music is a highly participa-tory medium in which the musicians, dancers, and audience are all crucial players in the cocreation of musical events. Active participation in the mu-sical event is not simply a welcome addition—it is a *necessary* component. One example which illustrates this principle and which also serves as an im-portant feature of African music in and of itself is the phenomenon of call and response. Here, a single voice calls out a phrase, and a group of voices call back a response to that musical phrase, either identical or slightly dif-ferent. This back-and-forth interaction may continue for some time, per-haps even for the length of the piece. This type of interaction is not limited to vocals; call and response can take place among drummers or any other instrument for that matter. Both types of call and response occur within the music of possession dances: the lead singer does a call and response with the other singers, and the lead drummer does a call and response with the other drummers. Obviously, no such interaction could take place without a high degree of collective participation.

Another classic example of call and response is found in work songs, in which the rhythm of the work activity, such as hoeing or scything, is called by a leader and answered by the rest of the work force.[11] This example demonstrates another important principle of African music, namely, its functional nature. In other words, music is not a purely aesthetic activity pursued for its own sake, standing separate from the rest of life, as in the West. On the contrary, African music is always linked to functional nonmusical or extramusical activities, such as possession religion, work, or state affairs. It is not simply that music is an *accompaniment* to these activities, but that music is integrated into virtually all aspects of African culture and its ongoing functions. It will be crucial to keep this in mind later in this chapter when I examine how West African possession religion transferred its sensibilities and practices to secular entertainment musics in North America.

Another crucial aspect of call and response is the embellishment and transformation of musical ideas. This often occurs through the process of improvisation, another important feature of African music. In possession dances, for example, the lead drummer improvises while the other drummers maintain the rhythmic groove, often to raise the energy of the proceedings or to bring about the onset of possession in a dancer. These improvisations play off the established rhythms, shifting them so as to supply new accents or cross-rhythmic patterns. Sometimes two drummers will have a musical conversation, as it were, exchanging and transforming musical phrases through their interaction. When vocalists improvise, as they often do, they utilize a variety of characteristic African vocal techniques: falsettos, gutturals, melismas, nonverbal interpolations, shouts, and moans. These improvised techniques serve to inject surges of emotional intensity into the music. So while there are set rhythms and vocal lines, improvisation supplies the particular character of a specific musical event. In the case of possession dance music which I am examining, there are set songs with set rhythms and set dances for particular deities, but it is often the improvised drumming and singing, playing off the set rhythms and vocals, which brings on possession. The dancing after the onset of possession may also contain a high degree of improvisation, indicating the particular inclinations of the possessing deity.

To sum up so far: each group has its own deity (with its own personality, powers, movements, clothing, and objects), shrine, priests and initiates, weekly dances, annual festivals, and songs with set rhythms and dances. Possession, the formal goal of the ceremonials, in which the deity becomes physically present in the community, is brought on by specific musicoreligious practices in a specific spatial arrangement within a specific sequence of ritual activities. These practices indicate a musically based religion that is *danced*, in which the skillful use of polyrhythms and other African musical techniques create a conduit through which the human and the spiritual worlds can be linked. It is this complex of practices, experiential states, and relationships between the human and spiritual worlds that constitutes what I have referred to as the West African religious impulse and sensibility. I will now examine how this complex underwent a series of transformations as many of its practitioners were forcibly removed from their indigenous context.

The Trans-Atlantic Slave Trade and Subsequent Transformations in the African Diaspora

While the religious systems described above were by no means static or unchanging, continually evolving through cross-cultural contact as well as environmental and political-economic pressures, the fundamental forms and practices remained relatively stable. However, all that changed in dramatic fashion with the arrival of white Europeans and the subsequent horrors of the trans-Atlantic slave trade. While it is beyond the scope of this study to go into this enormous subject in detail, a general survey of the big picture and relevant facts will nevertheless be useful. Although the slave trade began as early as the sixteenth century, it did not reach its critical mass until two centuries later. Scholars identify the period of 1701 through 1810 as the peak. Current estimates put the total number of Africans brought to the Americas during the entire slave trade at approximately 12 to 15 million people.[12]

This is a staggering number, considering the technology for transport at the time—wooden ships crowded to inhuman capacity in unsanitary conditions on a voyage that took two to three months. Many people did not survive the passage, with death rates sometimes as high as 50 percent.

Those who did survive were faced with even more oppressive circumstances as slaves working in brutal conditions on plantations in the New World. Of these 12 million people, taken from an area stretching from modern-day Senegal to modern-day Angola, approximately 50 percent were brought from the area of West Africa I have been focusing on in this study.[13] Interestingly, less than 5 percent of the overall slave traffic was brought into the United States. The Caribbean islands (42 percent) and South America (49 percent, 38 percent of that to Brazil) were the primary destinations.[14] I mention this fact not only because it goes against popular perception of the United States as a major player in the slave trade, but also because it serves to highlight the enormous demographic differences between slavery in the United States and in the Caribbean and South America. These differences are important because they influence the different routes taken by slaves for the adaptation and survival of African religious practices.

With such a huge influx of slaves in the Caribbean and South America, Africans constituted around 90 percent of the population in the areas to which they were imported. These areas were primarily extremely large plantations, often in rugged and previously unsettled locations. Because large numbers of Africans were congregated together in one place, in the hundreds and sometimes in the thousands, it was relatively easy (though still difficult, to be sure) to preserve some form of traditional African religious practice. With many ethnic and linguistic groups thrown randomly together, the practices of the Fon and Yoruba cultures tended to dominate not only because of their larger numbers, but also because of the prestige and dominance they enjoyed in Africa. But due to the devastating dislocations of the slave trade, large chunks of the traditions were lost or transformed. A highly trained priest or priestess was not necessarily available; the same was true of a fully initiated group membership, including drummers and dancers.

George Simpson has suggested that "in the Catholic countries, permission to organize religious fraternities along ethnic lines encouraged the preservation of African religious traditions."[15] Moreover, the ritual forms of Catholicism and its pantheon of saints rendered it somewhat compatible with African religions and made it possible for a considerable body of traditional practices to continue under a Catholic veneer. In Haitian Vodun, Cuban Santeria, and Bahian Brazilian Candomble, the musicoreligious practices of Fon and Yoruba possession cults were preserved nearly intact. It is simply that the liturgical elements had a Catholic flavor (with prayers to Jesus and the Trinity), and the *loa* and *orishas* had been subsumed under the personae of the Catholic saints. For example, now Shango was worshiped as Saint Barbara or Ogun as Saint Peter. But the ritual forms, the music and dancing, the phenomenon of possession itself—all these remained largely the same. Now, however, each group was not dedicated exclusively to *one loa* or *orisha*, but to *all loa* or *orishas*. And some new loa and orishas, such as Native American deities, were added to the pantheon to reflect the realities of the radically different circumstances in the New World.[16] There were also other adaptive variations of African religious practices which arose in the Caribbean and South America—ancestor cults like Kumina in Jamaica and Big Drum in Grenada, Protestant revivalist cults like the Shouters in Trinidad and the Shakers in St. Vincent, or eclectic possession hybrids like Macoumba and Umbanda in Brazil—all of which also had strong African elements.

In general, then, it is clear that significantly more of the musicoreligious possession practices of West Africa were preserved relatively intact in these areas than in North America. I have already touched on some of the probable reasons. In the United States, far fewer total slaves were imported and they constituted a much smaller percentage of the total population. Moreover, the plantations were much smaller than those in the Caribbean and South America, and were often run by families who were more involved in the private lives of their slaves.[17] Both these factors made it difficult for large groups of Africans to congregate together and establish a strong sense of African cultural identity. Also, "by 1860, 99% of the slaves in the U.S. were native-born, and most of them were second to fifth generation Americans. These persons had not had any personal contact with Africa" and therefore had no firsthand knowledge of African traditions.[18] In addition, the United States was (and is) primarily a Protestant country, and Protestant forms of Christianity were not nearly as compatible with the West African possession religions as was Catholicism. Last, but certainly not least, is the fact that traditional African religious practices were largely forbidden, as were traditional musical practices, such as playing the drum.[19] This was due to white slave owners' fears that such religious and musical practice would foster a stronger sense of group identity and solidarity and could lead to insurrection.

Taken as a whole, traditional expression of West African religious forms was largely suppressed in the United States for the reasons cited above and had to go underground and transform itself in significantly more radical ways than in the Caribbean and South America. As I mentioned earlier, the two major avenues for this transformed expression were Protestant churches and secular entertainment musics. In both cases, traditional expression occurred primarily in music and dance styles which were clearly African in flavor but which had no explicitly African thematic content.

For example, one of the main forms of worship for African American slaves in the southern United States was the ring shout, which would occur regularly on the plantations, either openly in the church or secretly out in the fields. Ostensibly, the participants were singing a Christian spiritual, but the form showed clear elements of West African possession practices. Here is an account of a ring shout in South Carolina in 1862:

> A true "shout" takes place on Sundays or on "praise" nights through the week, and either in the praise-house or in some cabin in which a regular religious meeting has been held. . . . Very likely more than half the population of the plantation is gathered together . . . all stand up in the middle of the floor, and when the "sperichil" is struck up, begin first walking and by-and-by shuffling around, one after the other, in a ring. The foot is hardly taken from the floor, and the progression is mainly due to a jerking, hitching motion, which agitates the entire shouter, and soon brings out streams of perspiration. Sometimes they dance silently, sometimes as they shuffle they sing the chorus of the spiritual, and sometimes the song itself is also sung by the dancers. But most frequently a band, composed of some of the best singers and tired shouters, stand at the side of the room to "base" the others, singing the body of the song and clapping their hands together on their knees. Song and dance alike are extremely energetic, and often, when a shout lasts into the middle of the night, the monotonous thud, thud of the feet prevents sleep within half a mile of the praise-house.[20]

The first African American churches in the United States were Baptist, beginning in 1789 in South Carolina and Georgia. The first churches for freed slaves were Methodist, beginning in 1817 in Philadelphia.[21] Generally speaking, the liturgies, worship activities, and Christian themes were basically the same as any traditional Methodist or Baptist churches.[22] However, the singing of hymns took on many features of traditional African musicoreligious practices—strongly rhythmic and polyrhythmic orientation (with clapping taking the place of drumming), call-and-response singing, improvised vocalizations with clearly African stylistic techniques (falsettos, gutturals, melismas, nonverbal interpolations, shouts, and moans), and vigorous rhythmic dancing as a means of participating in the music. The singing and clapping and dancing would often build to ecstatic states of trance and possession extremely similar to those attained in the traditional West African cults. People would begin shaking uncontrollably, moving in radically different ways than normal (usually more frenetically), and even speaking with different voices in different languages. Here is an account of an African American service in South Carolina in 1920, fifty-five years after the end of slavery:

> Several men moved their feet alternately, in strange syncopation. A rhythm was born, almost without reference to the words of the preacher. It seemed to take shape almost visibly, and grow. I was gripped with the feeling of a mass-intelligence, a self-conscious entity, gradually informing the crowd and taking possession of every mind there, including my own.... A distinct melodic outline became more and more prominent shaping itself around the central theme of the words, "Git right, sodger!" ... Scraps of other words and tunes were flung into the medley of sound by individual singers from time to time, but the general trend was carried on by a deep undercurrent, which appeared to be stronger than the mind of any individual present, for it bore the mass of improvised harmony and rhythms into the most effective climax of incremental repetition that I have ever heard. I felt as if some conscious plan or purpose were carrying us along, call it mob-mind, communal composition, or what you will.[23]

Stylistically and functionally, these phenomena can be seen as classic examples of West African possession religion.[24] However, the ritual and conceptual framework had become completely Christian. Instead of identifying the possessing spirit as a *loa* or *orisha*, the Holy Spirit was said to have come upon the shaking person. Instead of speaking with the voice of the deity, the person was said to be speaking in tongues. Rather than the work of the devil, which was how traditional West African religion had been characterized, this was the work of the Lord and confirmed one as a good Christian.

There are various thematic aspects of Christianity which made it particularly well-suited for African Americans in the United States. One was that Jesus had targeted his ministry to the poor, powerless, and down-trodden, promising that if they were good Christians that status would ultimately be reversed, either in this world or the next. Certainly, this message spoke directly to the oppressive circumstances African

Americans found themselves in, and provided them a sense of hope. Another important theme was the Old Testament story of the Jewish people's exile from the land of Israel, their suffering, and eventual return. Clearly, this story paralleled the African diaspora and provided hope for a return to Mother Africa. For these and other reasons, the combination of overt Christian liturgy and covert West African musicoreligious practices proved to be a powerful one. In the postemancipation era, as African Americans became free to create their own unique forms, the black churches developed rich and distinctive religious traditions which brilliantly reflected and transformed the particularities of their historical situation. As the early Methodist and Baptist churches were followed by the Holiness and Pentecostal congregations, a strong tradition of black churches was established in the United States and continues to the present. Moreover, during the "great awakenings," large revival camp meetings that swept across the country several times, these Christianized, West African–influenced, African American musicoreligious practices crossed over to white Americans, and became firmly established in a wide variety of congregations which also continue to this day and exert a strong influence on American culture.[25]

Entry into North American Entertainment Musics

While these West African–influenced African American musicoreligious practices were being incorporated in vastly transformed form into American religious traditions, they were also following a parallel process with American musical traditions. I now turn my attention to the second major avenue for the transformed expression of the West African religious impulse in the United States, namely, secular entertainment music. Despite the ban on playing drums and other African instruments, African American slaves nevertheless continued to play music in the forms available to them. Among themselves, African idioms continued in the form of work songs, field calls, and "shouts." Among the whites, musical forms were primarily of European derivation, both classical and folk idioms. Musically skilled slaves were employed by their masters to perform at dances and concerts and became very proficient at playing stringed instruments like the violin, banjo, and guitar. It even became possible to constitute bandlike ensembles which performed regularly and achieved a certain degree of popularity among whites.

Over time, the phenomenon that had occurred with Christian liturgies recurred with European secular musics—the formal exterior structures gradually became permeated by West African styles and sensibilities, particularly in the postemancipation era as the population of the free community grew and the music was no longer bound by the restrictions of the white masters. The range and diversity of these new musical expressions, so different from their African origins, is a testimonial to the creative ability of African Americans to adapt to their dramatically altered social, political, economic, and musical context. Instead of preserving their traditional music as a repository of static forms, they moved forward with brilliant innovation, creating original African American idioms that reflected their new circumstances. The music these bands played shifted from purely European folk idioms to the first true hybrid African American music, syncopated dance music (a term coined by African American musicologist Portia Maultsby), consisting of highly rhythmic fiddle and banjo accompanied by hand claps and body pats.[26] This music was incorporated into touring variety shows in a form known as blackface or Ethiopian minstrelsy, the modern descendant of which is blackface comedy. Although these shows reinforced negative stereotypes, they allowed dance and musical figures like Master Juba (William Henry Lane) to became quite popular in the 1840s.

Another African American musical idiom that became highly popular around this time was the brass band, best exemplified by Frank Johnson (1792–1844) and his highly acclaimed band. Both these musics contained strong elements of the West African musicoreligious practices discussed above: rhythmic and polyrhythmic orientation (with clapping taking the place of drumming), call and response singing and playing, improvised instrumentals and vocalizations with clearly African stylistic techniques, and vigorous rhythmic dancing as a means of participating in the music. Maultsby has called these the "common aesthetic features" that "link the secular and religious traditions."[27] These musics laid the foundation for the subsequent development of the two musical styles most commonly associated with African Americans: blues and jazz.

New Orleans provides a particularly clear example of how the West African religious sensibility began to feed into secular entertainment musics. As the major port city with access to the Caribbean, and because of its French cultural ties to Haiti and other islands of the French Antilles, New Orleans was the site of a very strong Vodun influence in its African American community. And as I mentioned earlier, Vodun retained very strong elements of West African musicoreligious practices largely intact, specifically those of the Fon. Although formally outlawed, clandestine Vodun ceremonials were a common occurrence in and around the city. What is unique about New Orleans, however, is that it was one of the only places "in the United States where slaves were allowed to gather among themselves for their 'entertainments,' as they were called, and, most importantly, to play drums."[28] And the major place in New Orleans where these lawful gatherings of West African drumming and dancing occurred every Sunday was Congo Square.

These were huge animated gatherings, with not only large numbers of African American participants but also large numbers of white spectators. Here is a firsthand account by a white observer:

> Upon entering the square the visitor finds the multitude packed in groups of close, narrow circles, of a central area of only a few feet; and there in the center of each circle sits the musician, astride a barrel, strongheaded, which he beats with two sticks, to a strange measure incessantly, like mad, for hours altogether, while the perspiration literally rolls in streams and wets the ground; and there, too, labor the dancers male and female, under an inspiration of possession, which takes from their limbs all sense of weariness, and gives to them a rapidity and a duration of motion that will hardly be found elsewhere outside of mere machinery. The head rests upon the breast, or is thrown back upon the shoulders, the eyes closed, or glaring, while the arms, amid cries, and shouts, and sharp ejaculations, float upon the air, or keep time, with the hands patting upon the thighs, to a music which is seemingly eternal.[29]

This scene has all the flavor of a traditional West African possession ceremony, but with a major difference—there is a white audience observing it for entertainment purposes.

Cultural historian Michael Ventura has written eloquently on the far-reaching implications of this crucial shift in context, a shift that impacted all the dimensions of music—physiological, psychological, sociocultural, semiological, virtual, ritual, and religious:

> For the first time in the New World, African music and dancing was presented both for Africans and whites as an end in itself, a form on its own. Here was the metaphysics of Africa set loose from the forms of Africa. For this form of *performance* wasn't African. In the ceremonies of

Voodoo there is no audience. Some may dance and some may watch, but those roles may change several times in a ceremony, and all are participants. In Congo Square, African music was put into a Western form of presentation. . . . It is likely that this was the first time blacks became aware of the music *as music* instead of strictly a part of ceremony. Which means that in Congo Square, African metaphysics first became subsumed in the music. A secret within the music instead of the object of the music. A possibility embodied by the music, instead of the music existing strictly as this metaphysic's *technique.* On the one hand, something marvelous was lost. On the other, only by separating the music from the religion could either the musics or the metaphysics within it leave their origins and deeply influence a wider sphere.[30]

And New Orleans, a rather singular city regarded by many as the birthplace of jazz, was clearly one place where the music did begin to deeply influence a wider sphere. The types of gatherings which took place in Congo Square, as well as the widespread clandestine practice of Vodun, formed the underlying context and ethos in which the early pioneers of jazz and blues were to make their musical innovations. The West African spiritual sensibility, separated from its moorings in a specifically religious context, was now free to feed into the growing efflorescence of uniquely African American secular entertainment musics, with New Orleans as one of its primary centers.

Blues

At the same time that the groundwork was being laid for the development of jazz, the other great African American secular musical tradition, the blues, emerged in the late 1800s. Many people consider blues to be the greatest achievement of American culture—not only African American culture, but *all* American culture. Blues is certainly the African American music par excellence: it distills the difficulties and contradictions of the slave and postslave experience into a musical form with coherent themes of suffering and redemption; it transforms the West African spiritual expression from large religious drum and dance ensembles to one man playing the guitar and then back into newly configured musical ensembles in a completely different context; it integrates European and West African musical principles into a distinctive and original idiom; it provides the musical foundation on which virtually all subsequent popular musics are built; and last, but not least, it creates its own musical subculture which has its own "priests," "congregations," and forms of "worship." In this regard, blues is an excellent example of how music functions simultaneously on many different levels in an integrated fashion.

Blues began in rural areas throughout the South in the difficult transitional dynamics of the postemancipation period. It came to be known as "country" or "rural" blues and was typified by such archetypal figures as Robert Johnson (1911–38) and Bukka White (1909–77) from the Mississippi Delta, and Blind Lemon Jefferson (1893–1929) and Lightnin' Hopkins (1912–82) from Texas—just one man and his acoustic guitar.[31] By the World War I era, however, as more and more African Americans migrated from rural areas to the cities for greater opportunity, there was a corresponding shift in the blues to a form known as "city" blues. City blues was played by ensembles of musicians and, because of the need to play the changes together, musical structures which had previously been fluid began to be formalized.[32] Piano replaced the acoustic guitar as the main instrument, and women singers like Ma Rainey (1886–1939) and Bessie Smith (1894–1937) predominated in the 1920s. With the subsequent invention of the electric guitar and drum kit, seminal bluesmen like Sonny Boy Williamson (1910–65), Muddy Waters (1915–83), Howlin Wolf (1910–76), and Jimmy Reed (1925–76) began to develop the classic sound of the electric guitar-based blues band in the 1940s, often accompanied by harmonica. Later, the harmonica was often replaced by saxophones, and a style known as "urban" blues emerged in cities like Kansas City (typified by Joe Turner [1911–85] and Jimmy Rushing [1903–72]) and Memphis (typified by B.B. King [b. 1925], Albert King [1923–92], Freddy King [1934–76], Bobby Blue Bland [b. 1930], and Junior Parker [1932–71]).

Ethnomusicologist John Storm Roberts has identified several of the key characteristic African musical features in the blues: the importance of improvisation, call and response structures, rhythmic and polyrhythmic orientation (transposed to the guitar or piano), African vocal and instrumental phrasings (the guitar, for example, exhibiting similarities to West African stringed instruments like the *chalam* or *kora*), audience participation, and the close connection between music and dance.[33] Ethnomusicologist Charles Keil, in his classic work *Urban Blues,* has done more than perhaps any other scholar to make clear the *religious* dimensions of the blues:

In spite of the fact that blues singing is ostensibly a secular, even profane, form of expression, the role is intimately related to sacred roles in the Negro community. . . . As professions, blues singing and preaching seem to be closely linked in both the rural or small-town setting and in the urban ghettos. We have already noted some of the stylistic common denominators that underlie the performance of both roles, and it is clear that the experiences which prepare one for adequately fulfilling either role overlap extensively.[34]

I should like to discuss the concept of soul and its many dimensions, because in this notion of an "unspeakable essence" we have the foundation of the ideology which both guides and is embodied in any contemporary blues ritual. The word "ritual" seems more appropriate than "performance" when the audience is committed rather than appreciative. And from this, it follows, perhaps, that blues singing is more of a belief role than a creative role—more priestly than artistic.[35]

Keil goes on to analyze the performance context of blues artists like Bobby Blue Bland and B. B. King within the conceptual framework of religious ritual, with the bluesman as the priest, the audience as the congregation, and the music and dancing as the primary tools through which prayer and communion are achieved. In the heat of the music and dancing, one can experience the "unspeakable essence" in one's body. Here is a clear continuity with West African possession religion.

It is also important to briefly discuss some of the "theological" implications of the blues. Traditionally, the spirituals and the blues have been seen as the two parts of a basic dichotomy of African American musics and their attendant spiritual sensibilities.[36] The spiritual, as a general term, represents the continuation of the great African American musicoreligious singing traditions within the black Christian churches. These traditions began as psalm and hymn singing, evolved into spirituals per se with the Fisk Jubilee Singers in the 1870s, and continued to evolve as gospel music with figures like Thomas Dorsey, Lucie Campbell, Sallie Martin, and Mahalia Jackson in the 1920s on up to the present day.[37] As I noted earlier, although these musicoreligious practices showed a clear continuity with West African possession religion, their liturgical form and thematic content were definitely Christian: they sought to escape the hardships of suffering in this world by placing their faith in deliverance in the next. This position continues the Western Christian split between body and spirit, the human world and the spiritual world, opting to emphasize the latter at the expense of the former.[38]

In contrast, the blues refuses to make such a split, focusing on the suffering experienced as slaves and former slaves in the African diaspora, and seeking a measure of whatever this-worldly redemption can be achieved through embodied sexuality and solidarity within the African American community. In this sense, the blues are the legitimate heir to the metaphysics and theology of West African possession religion; the goal is still the intersection of body and spirit, the world of humans *and* gods, and it is no accident that the crossroads, the place of that intersection, figures so prominently in blues mythology. As theologian James Cone so eloquently writes:

> The blues are a lived experience, an encounter with the contradictions of American society, but a refusal to be conquered by it. They are despair only in the sense that there is no attempt to cover up reality. The blues recognize that black people have been hurt and scarred by the brutalities of white society. But there is also hope in what Richard Wright calls the "endemic capacity to live." This hope provided the strength to survive, and also an openness to the intensity of life's pains without being destroyed by them. . . . That black people could sing the blues, describing their joys and sorrows, meant that they were able to affirm an authentic hope in the essential worth of black humanity. . . . Unlike the spirituals, the hope of the blues is not located in the concept of heaven. . . .
>
> They [blues people] are looking for a home that is earthly *and* eschatological. Home would always be more than a plot of land, more than a lover, family, and friends—though it would include these. Home would be the unrestricted affirmation of self and the will to protect self from those who would destroy self. It would be self-reliance and self-respect. In short, home could only be freedom, and the will to create a new world for the people I love.[39]

The metaphysics and theology of the blues, just like its musical form, represent a truly African *American* articulation of the West African spiritual sensibility. The blues takes stock of the new realities of life among whites in America and adapts to them while preserving the core values and experiences of its West African roots. And just as all subsequent popular musical forms are built on the foundation of the blues, so too are their attendant metaphysics and theologies, as I will show in later chapters, particularly with respect to rap and hip-hop.

The Crossover from Rhythm and Blues to Rock and Roll

So far in this chapter, I have been tracing the labyrinthine path of the West African musicoreligious complex as it went through a series of transformations on its journey into American culture. Up until this point, its expression remained largely within the boundaries of communities of primarily African origin.[40] But as the blues continued to evolve and innovate, taking the form of rhythm and blues in the late 1940s and early 1950s, artists like Fats Domino, Chuck Berry, Little Richard, and Bo Diddley began to attract white teenage audiences and started crossing over into white culture. The first white audiences to listen to rhythm and blues were poor, young, rural, southern working-class people, like the young Jerry Lee Lewis, Elvis Presley, and Carl Perkins. They slipped into the African American juke joints in the highly segregated South to listen to the music which captivated them, crossing rigidly defined cultural and social boundaries in the process. However large the cultural and racial barriers were at that time, and they were considerable, these young white, rural, southern working-class poor nevertheless felt some affinity with their African American counterparts, an affinity that was transmitted through the music.[41] As Michael Ventura writes: "The moment this black music attracted these white musicians was one of the most important moments in modern history."[42]

The increasing popularity of rhythm and blues and its potential to cross over to white audiences were not lost on key people in the recording industry. They knew, however, that the rigid racial divisions of the time made it difficult or impossible for an African American artist to cross over to a wider white audience. So Sam Phillips, founder of the legendary Sun Studios in Memphis, decided to seek a white artist to market rhythm and blues to the white audience, and he found the perfect one in Elvis Presley. This was certainly not the first time that white musicians had deliberately copied and appropriated an African American musical style in order to market it to a white audience; the whole history of African American music is filled with such appropriations virtually every step of the way.[43] It was, however, the first time that a white musician appropriating an African American style had crossed over in such a hugely successful manner. Presley's white versions of rhythm and blues music struck a responsive chord in white American culture and catapulted him to incredible popularity.

Within a short time span, Elvis-mania was in full swing. By 1956, Elvis had a number of hit singles riding the top of the charts, was causing widespread hysteria in his sold-out public performances, and shook the nation with his electrifying appearance on the Ed Sullivan show.[44] Mainstream white America had never before been exposed to the propulsive rhythmic intensity of both the music and the dance exhibited by Presley and his band. His trademark dance with gyrating hips, so similar to traditional African dance with its characteristic pelvic thrust, was edited out of Sullivan's television broadcast, as Presley was shown only from the waist up. Even so, the dance still had an enormous impact. Texas singer and songwriter Butch Hancock recalls: "Yeah, that was the dance that everybody forgot. It was the dance that was so strong that it took an entire civilization to forget it. And ten seconds on the Ed Sullivan Show to remember. . . . All their effort to make us forget the dances—and they can be blown away in an instant."[45] Finally, and suddenly, the West African–African American religious sensibility and the practices of beat-driven music and dance had penetrated a mainstream white audience. "Elvis was the first product of African metaphysics in America which the official culture could not ignore."[46]

The style of music, essentially still rhythm and blues, but with some traces of country and western, was now called rock and roll, and Elvis's breakthrough success opened the floodgates for one of the greatest waves of musical and cultural activity ever to sweep across the country.[47] Jerry Lee Lewis, Carl Perkins, Buddy Holly, and a whole host of white musicians began to score hit singles and attain massive popularity with their own rock and roll appropriations of rhythm and blues. African American artists like Little Richard, Chuck Berry, and Fats Domino also reaped the benefits of the rock and roll explosion with increased airplay on white radio stations and hits of their own, although most African American musicians did not share in the economic boom and were angry about their music being appropriated. Respectable white people were now listening to African-derived music and dancing African-derived dances. Moreover, they began to adopt new styles of dress, speech, and social activities. With the advent of rock and roll, not only had African American music crossed over to white America but, in the process, it had also launched a whole new form of cultural expression.

There were several historical and social factors which made this type of crossover possible. First of all, the post–World War II era was a time of great economic prosperity in the United States. Consequently, there was a great deal more disposable income available to be spent on music in its various forms than at any previous time. Second, for the first time in the history of the nation, a distinct youth culture had emerged, one made possible by the combination of increased affluence and leisure time. Young people now had the money and time to become a potent consumer force, thereby creating their own markets. And the development of these markets was increasingly defined by another important factor in the mix, the ascendance of mass media technologies. Certainly, records and radio had been around for decades, but now they were targeted specifically at youth audiences.

However, television was the new medium that forever changed the nature of mass communications, projecting images of the new youth culture across the entire country. Dick Clark's *American Bandstand*, a staple of American youth rock and roll culture in the 1950s and 1960s, is the classic example of the connection between television, youth, and rock and roll. Another factor was the extension of higher education from an elite minority to the great middle class. This meant that the liminal time of youth was stretched out over a longer period, that it grew to include a larger percentage of the population, and that it was more closely linked with the relatively free thought of the universities.[48] This also meant that young people were beginning to question the values of their culture and, in some cases, to openly oppose them. This type of youthful opposition can be seen in popular 1950s cinematic figures like the leather-clad biker Marlon Brando in *The Wild One* or James Dean in *Rebel without a Cause*.

The oppositional stance of white youth culture is one of the main reasons why teenagers began to turn to the rhythm and blues music of the African American community in the first place. It was a means of rebelling against the stifling conformity of mainstream 1950s culture, typified by bland, safe, clean-cut figures like crooner Pat Boone or television icons Ozzie and Harriet Nelson. African American culture represented an alternative worldview grounded in a different value system—poor and dispossessed rather than middle class; sexual and embodied rather than repressed; exotic, angry, and even dangerous rather than bland and safe; "hip" rather than "square." These qualities, however, were projections of unfulfilled parts of the white teenage psyche rather than accurate reflections of the complex realities of African American life. Nevertheless, embracing these values and styles was an effective oppositional tool, drawing the outrage of parents and authority figures alike. This process of youth turning to African American culture as a means of rebelling was nothing new; the beats and hipsters had already trodden this ground with their appropriation of jazz.[49] But, again, what *was* new was the vast scale on which this took place. Unlike the beats and hipsters, who remained a small minority, rock and roll had spread to become *the* major musical and cultural expression of teenage youth.[50]

Thus, from the beginning, rock and roll was an appropriation of the African American blues tradition which carried within it hidden traces of the West African spiritual sensibility and its musico-religious practices. However, an important transformation had occurred in the process: the music and styles had been removed from their original context and placed in a new context where the forms took on changed meanings. In crossing over to white teenage audiences, these hidden West African traces became embedded in the new context of the emerging white oppositional youth culture. From the mid-1950s on, generations of white American youth grew up with an experience of the West African spiritual sensibility, albeit in a radically transformed context, as an important part of their lives. As Ventura writes:

> The Voodoo rite of possession by the god became the standard of American performance in rock'n'roll. Elvis Presley, Little Richard, Jerry Lee Lewis . . . —they let themselves be possessed not by any god they could name but by the spirit they felt in the music. Their behavior in this possession was something Western society had never before tolerated. And the way a possessed devotee in a Voodoo ceremony often will transmit his state of possession to someone else by merely touching their hand, they transmitted their possession through their voice and their dance to their audience, even through their records. We feel a charge of energy from within us, but it is felt as something infectious that we seek and catch and live.[51]

> Which is not to say that rock'n'roll is Voodoo. Of course it's not. But it does preserve qualities of that African metaphysic intact so strongly that it unconsciously generates the same dances, acts as a major antidote to the mind-body split, and uses a derivative of Voodoo's techniques of possession as a source, for performers and audiences alike, of tremendous personal energy.[52]

The Rise of Rock as a Major Cultural Force

There are numerous well-written histories of rock and roll detailing the many stars and styles which rose to popularity over the subsequent decades (the 1960s, 1970s, and 1980s).[53] This section will not be such a comprehensive history. Instead, it surveys some of the more important developments which pertain to the subject at hand—the religious dimensions of popular music and its modes of expression. After Elvis Presley and the first wave of rock and roll in the 1950s, the next major group to have a comparable impact was the Beatles, and their enormous success paved the way for a host of other British bands like the Rolling Stones and the Kinks in the 1960s. In many ways, the Beatles are the prototypical rock band. To begin with, their rise to stardom—from a local band in Liverpool, to the top of the charts in England, to their historic "conquest" of the United States, to the spread of Beatlemania around the planet, to their continuing evolution as brilliant songwriters and musicians, to their ascendance as the voice of a whole generation, and even to their acrimonious breakup—formed the model for the success of rock bands. Any subsequent band's success would henceforth be measured by the standards set by the Beatles.

But perhaps even more importantly, the unparalleled scale of their success gave them unprecedented influence in shaping popular consciousness. By the late 1960s, the Beatles had attained such a degree of popularity that they were a household name in England and the United States and many countries around the world, and everything they did and said had an enormous impact. There is no greater example than John Lennon's remark that the Beatles were more popular than Jesus. This seemingly offhand comment in one among hundreds of interviews set off a firestorm of controversy. Subsequent backlash from offended Christian parties led to events like record burnings and boycotts and eventually to a vague public apology by Lennon. There are two aspects of this episode that are relevant to this discussion. First, it demonstrates the degree to which even the smallest comments and gestures by the Beatles were scrutinized and given major cultural significance by fans and detractors alike. Second, Lennon was probably correct in noting that the Beatles were more popular than Jesus, at least among young people in the United States and England, a comparison which underlined the religious fervor with which their fans followed the group. Later in their career, the Beatles would begin to consciously make use of their position as global icons to inject a message of peace and love into the cultural discourse. Whether or not one agreed with the content of their message, the magnitude of their influence was unquestioned.

The specific case of the Beatles serves to highlight what was happening in a general way—rock and roll (now simply called "rock"), the rebellious upstart, had evolved into a major cultural force in the United States and around the world. In the late 1960s, with the advent of the antiwar movement and the psychedelic hippie counterculture, rock music became an important voice in the political and cultural changes sweeping across the country. Nowhere was this seen more strongly than in the huge three-day rock festival which took place at Max Yasgur's farm in Woodstock, New York, from 15 to 17 August 1969. The first gathering of its kind, Woodstock featured a virtual who's who of the most prominent rock artists of the time and, exceeding the expectations of its organizers and promoters, drew over half a million participants—a staggering number—to a muddy field in the middle of rural upstate New York. Not even rain and mud and crowded conditions could dim the spirits of the audience, who danced ecstatically to the music for hours and days on end in an incredible display of spontaneous community. And, if half a million people actually showed up, how many untold millions more must have been influenced by the events, music, and styles? The saga of the "Woodstock generation" represents perhaps the maximum penetration of the countercultural values and styles of rock music into the mainstream in the course of its history. The eminent scholar of American religions William McLoughlin has argued that there is a continuity between gatherings like Woodstock and the religious revival camp meetings of the "great awakenings" in the eighteenth and nineteenth century and, indeed, that the subsequent proliferation of rock festivals and concerts after Woodstock can be seen as part of a larger religious and cultural transformation he calls the "fourth great awakening."[54]

Parallel to the rise of rock as a major cultural force and mirroring its influence in the economic sector was the emergence of a corporate rock music industry. The enormous profit potential of rock music demonstrated by the huge record sales of the Beatles and large festivals like Woodstock did not go unnoticed by the major record companies. They mobilized their resources to sign new bands and market them to take advantage of the widespread popularity of the rock phenomenon. During the decade of the late 1960s and early 1970s, with the rise of the long-playing (LP) record as the major form of recorded music and national concert tours of huge arenas as the new form of live music, the popular music industry became one of the most lucrative sectors of the economy. As large corporations suddenly had windfall profit margins and significant investments in capital and labor to protect, economic considerations began to crowd out artistic and cultural ones, and the inexorable logic of the bottom line took precedence over musical innovation. To a large degree, rock music lost its rebellious stance and countercultural values, except insofar as these were marketable qualities which sold well. The industry consolidated into an oligopoly of seven megacorporations with billions of dollars in sales. Any new musical or stylistic innovations were quickly appropriated by the industry, marketed until their profit potential had been exhausted, and discarded in favor of the next fad. The West African–African American musicoreligious complex, which had crossed over to white America and become a major cultural force, had taken another turn and was now enmeshed in the complex economic dynamics of an oligopolistic corporate system.

During this whole time, African American music continued almost unaffected by the rock phenomenon. African American artists were bitter that their music had been stolen and that white people were reaping the profits. But, even though the monetary stakes were higher, this kind of appropriation was certainly nothing new. There continued to be great music and new styles produced within the African American community: the classic soul music of the 1960s with artists like James Brown, Aretha Franklin, and the Temptations; the beat-heavy funk bands of the early 1970s like Parliament-Funkadelic or Kool and the Gang; the disco craze of the mid-1970s with artists like Donna Summer; and the newly emergent phenomenon of rap in the late 1970s and early 1980s, pioneered in its formative years by the likes of DJ Kool Herc, Afrika Bambaataa, and Grandmaster Flash.[55] Although there was a certain amount of crossover and appropriation, black music remained largely distinct and separate, carrying on as one of the most long-standing and important repositories of the West African spiritual impulse in the African American community.

The Emergence of Distinct Musical Youth Subcultures

I must note one final development in the long and winding path of the West African spiritual impulse in America. That is the emergence of distinct musical youth subcultures. So far, in this discussion of rhythm and

blues, rock and roll, and rock music I have been speaking in broad gener-
alities about the people involved in these phenomena, focusing primarily
on the performers, and only occasionally making reference to class, race,
age, and geography. However, the history of these musics has always been
about specific styles arising in specific conditions in specific communities. I have already shown how blues arose in the difficult postslavery conditions among African Americans in the rural South and took on new
forms as it moved into the northern cities. Another example is how rock
and roll arose as poor rural southern whites copied rhythm and blues and
tapped into a newly affluent white teenage audience looking to rebel
against their parent culture. As beat-driven popular music became a mass
phenomenon controlled by a huge corporate behemoth, however, new
circumstances developed which changed the dynamics of the specificities
of these musics and their communities.

Beginning with Elvis Presley and reaching its maximum expression
with the Beatles, beat-driven popular music reached unprecedentedly
large audiences comprised of numerous constituencies rather than one
specific group.[56] Certainly, as I noted earlier, these constituencies were
primarily young people, but they were diverse in terms of class, ethnicity,
and geography. Moreover, these constituencies began to develop new cultural affinities based not only on the music but on a shared enthusiasm
for their musical heroes and an adoption of behaviors shared by their
group. For example, devotees copied the distinctive haircuts of Presley
and the Beatles, their clothing, their movement style, and their "rebellious" social behavior. They put posters of their icons up on the walls of
their rooms and may even have had some sort of altar with objects associated with them. A good portion of their time was spent with other fans,
listening to the music, discussing subjects related to the group, and engaging in social activities like dances where the music of their group was
played, or even going to live shows, if they were fortunate enough. In
short, they were spontaneously forming their own subculture devoted to
their particular singer or band.

These subcultures had powerful but unconscious religious dimensions, not only because of the hidden traces of West African spirituality
implicit in the music, but also because they were deifying their musical
heroes and engaging in what might be described as a form of worship.
This type of "worship" represents a further transformation of West
African religious sensibilities and practices, but one now based on a fundamental confusion at the cosmological level. Instead of viewing the pos-

sessed individual or performer as the "horse" and the possessing deity as the "rider," this type of "worship" makes no such distinction and conflates the two. Thus, the performer exhibiting traits traditionally associated with possession by the deity, is worshipped as the *deity him- or herself,* and elevated to a godlike status.

After the unparalleled success of the Beatles, no other band to the present would subsequently attain the same degree of mass popularity and the ability to cut across the boundaries of class, ethnicity, and geography in quite the same way. However, the impulse to form subcultures based on a band or a genre of music continued on. Musical youth subcultures began to devolve from mass audiences to smaller, more specific "niches" which arose out of, and spoke to, particular constituencies.[57] As these musical youth subcultures developed strong followings among themselves, they often drew the attention of the large record companies, who then appropriated the emergent style and marketed it to a mass audience.[58]

The classic example of this type of process is found in the history of British punk. Punk began in London in the mid-1970s as a response to the increasingly corporate nature of rock music and the growing emphasis on artistic pretensions and slick, overblown production in the music and shows of popular English bands like Yes or Pink Floyd. In contrast, punkers adopted an attitude of "do it yourself," forming their own bands with little or no musical training, playing loud, simple, aggressive, angry, pounding rock music at local clubs for their own punk compatriots. To a large degree, punk rock grew out of the disaffected white working class whose economic opportunities were bleak and getting worse in the early 1970s England of conservative prime minister Margaret Thatcher. There was a sense of profound pessimism about the future, bordering on nihilism, which generated an intense rage against the status quo and an impulse to anarchy. This rage and anarchic stance were reflected not only in the harsh sonic attack of the music but in the overall style of the subculture. Punk fashions of bleached or colored spiky hair, torn clothing, skin-piercing safety pin jewelry, and metal and leather bondage gear were outrageous for the time and offended the prevailing sensibilities of the day.

Social behavior among the punks was equally outrageous, manifesting itself not only in defiant gestures and obscene epithets toward authority figures and mainstream culture, but also among the punks themselves at their own concerts. It was punk that developed the mosh pit at the front of the stage where the ritual of slamdancing took place. Here, audience members banged against each other in a kind of Dionysian frenzy. The prototypical

London punk band, the Sex Pistols, would often adopt a confrontational tone with their audience: cursing at them and being cursed at, spitting at them and being spat at, throwing objects at them and having objects thrown back at themselves, and sometimes getting into fistfights with the audience, either onstage or down in the mosh pit. Incendiary songs like *Anarchy in the U.K.* or *God Save the Queen,* written by leader Johnny Rotten (John Lydon), became punk anthems. The outrageous antics and self-destructive behavior (including heroin addiction) of bassist Sid Vicious (John Ritchie), which ultimately led to his death, became a model for punks everywhere. Even their stage names reflected this penchant for outrage.

The punk subculture, although anathema to mainstream behavior and values, grew so popular and influential that the record companies could no longer ignore its profit potential. Many authentic punk bands, like the Sex Pistols and the Clash, were signed to major labels (Virgin and CBS) and marketed to mass audiences. They were followed by many copycat bands, groups who were not originally punk but who jumped on the bandwagon when it became popular. A good example of these bands was the Police, whose tamer, more radio-friendly version of punk went on to attain far greater mass success than the real thing, not only in England but in the United States as well. Concerts moved from underground clubs to stadiums and arenas, attended by mainstream audiences. Watered-down punk was played on mainstream radio and appeared on television in softened guises. Punk fashions now began to be marketed by trendy boutiques and bought by a middle- and upper-middle-class clientele. Within a few short years, punk had gone from being a genuinely subversive underground subculture to being a nonthreatening set of styles and fashions marketed by mainstream institutions to a mainstream audience. What was left of the original subculture declined and died a slow death, while the punk "fad" went the way of so many other marketed fads—on the junkheap, to be replaced by the next new thing.[59] Punk had been successfully appropriated by the popular music industry, marketed to a mass audience, and when its profit potential had been exhausted, discarded.

This dynamic was to be subsequently repeated many times with a variety of musical youth subcultures, including, among others, the appropriation of the styles of reggae, glam, disco, heavy metal, new wave, new romantic, and, more recently, house, rap, techno, acid jazz, punk-funk, alternative, and grunge music. Because the industry itself was not capable of generating the vitality and creative innovations evinced by these subcultures, it sent its representatives out to scout for the next new phenomenon. A curious symbiotic relationship developed between musical youth subcultures and the popular music industry. It took an authentic subculture, developing in its own alternative context, to generate the music and styles which were vibrant and cutting edge. These subcultures became the emergent form through which traces of West African and African American spirituality found a communitarian expression for their musicoreligious practices. However, once a subculture had developed a substantial following and a coherent style that was trendy and appealing, it was inevitably exploited by the popular music industry in the pattern of appropriation I have been discussing. And the time it took for this whole process to occur grew shorter and shorter. The rapidity with which the Seattle grunge "scene" in the early 1990s went from an underground subculture to mainstream success to a plethora of copycat bands and twenty-something poseurs to passé and out-of-date is a clear example of the increased speed of appropriation.

Nevertheless, new subcultures continue to invent themselves with equally astonishing speed and to flourish in a variety of locations and contexts throughout the United States, England, and the world. Many young people, caught in the difficult transitional time between adolescence and adulthood, seem to crave the intense initiatic experience, the sense of solidarity and community, the expression of oppositional values which these subcultures provide. Some feel intuitively drawn to the underground stream of West African spiritual power implicit in the music, as well as the ritual forms of the live concert which still contain elements of traditional possession practices. While the mainstream religious institutions become more and more irrelevant to the lives of many young people, they find some fundamental need for spiritual expression fulfilled by these musical subcultures. So, even though the West African religious complex has gone through a myriad of major transformations on its journey into American culture and is now tied into a white youth audience and a corporate economic structure, its transformed expressions still thrive and have the capacity to profoundly affect people's lives in powerful ways.

> Anyone who has felt it knows it is a precious energy, and knows it has shaped them, changed them, given them moments they could not have had otherwise, moments of heightened clarity or frightening intensity or both; moments of love and bursts of release. And, perhaps most importantly, we could experience this in a medium that met the twentieth century on its own terms.[60]

PART TWO

Popular Music Subcultures as Religion

A Comparative Analysis Based on Ethnographic Research

In 1996, I moved to the San Francisco Bay Area to conduct research and do fieldwork in the four popular music subcultures of this study—the Grateful Dead and the Deadheads, rave and electronic dance music, heavy metal and metalheads, and rap and hip-hop. There were a variety of factors that went into my selecting the Bay Area as a site for this research, but the most important of these was simply the fact that all four of these subcultures had thriving, vibrant scenes that were reasonably accessible. During the year and a half that I conducted this research, I attended dozens of musical events, from intimate underground settings to enormous commercial arenas, spanning the spectrum of the diverse popular musics discussed in this study.

I also had the opportunity to spend time with people from these subcultures outside these musical events, which helped me to get a feel for the texture of their daily lives. This constitutes what I call the participant-observer component of my fieldwork, which enabled me not only to have direct personal experiences of the subject matter, but also to make detailed firsthand observations. In addition, I interviewed twenty-five individuals who were strongly involved in these subcultures so that they could speak for themselves in their own voices on the subject, and I have included extensive direct quotations from these interviews in the chapters of this section.[1] While I do not claim that these musical events and individuals constitute a representative sample of their respective subcultures, nevertheless it is clear to me that this fieldwork did allow me to deepen my understanding of these subcultures, their forms, experiences, and meanings.

Once the research and fieldwork had been completed, my next task was to analyze the material to bring out the dynamics, nuances, and contradictions of these subcultures as religious phenomena. This was no easy project; as I noted in the introduction, these musical subcultures do not constitute religion in the form that one would normally expect to find it. First of all, they are not formal churches and congregations with clearly delineated theologies, liturgies, and organizational structures, but ephemeral phenomena spontaneously arising within a popular culture context often viewed as superficial and disposable entertainment. In addition, their religious dimensions are tangled up with other important features not normally associated with traditional institutional religion, such as mass media transmission, sophisticated digital technology, and oligopolistic corporate economics, to name just a few. Finally, the religious dimensions are often not consciously recognized as such by the actual members of the subcultures themselves. Thus, the religious dimensions are not laid out in an obvious straightforward manner and, consequently, do not fit neatly within a standard religious analysis. Nevertheless, as we enter life in the twenty-first century, with all its speed and complexity, the religious landscape is rapidly evolving in unexpected ways, and we need to develop analytic tools that enable us to make sense of its newly emerging forms.

In this regard, there is a growing body of scholars who recognize that, as traditional institutional religion has become increasingly irrelevant to many people, the sector of popular culture has become the new arena for their religious expression. Theologian Andrew Greeley has argued that "popular culture is a 'locus theologicus,' a theological place—the locale in which one may encounter God. Popular culture provides an opportunity to experience God."[2] This shift from institutional to cultural religion is summed up in the title of Jon Wiley Nelson's book, *Your God Is Alive and Well and Appearing in Popular Culture.*[3] With respect to popular music in particular, theomusicologist Jon Michael Spencer has written insightfully of this shift, and it is worth quoting him at length:

> People in America are as religious today as they ever have been, but religion is far more diffused throughout culture. . . . In addition to traditional institutionalized religious belief and practice, religion has . . . been relocated from the church to the streets, nightclubs, concert coliseums, and music festivals. . . . Religion's relocation to the nightclubs includes the weekly oscillation of secularists to the rite and ritual of the Friday

and Saturday night function. Its relocation to concert coliseums and music festivals includes weekly, annual, or seasonal excursions to sacred gathering centers where groups of people find themselves in more comfortable spaces. The purpose of these events is to maintain cultic bonds and to achieve heightened forms of community that reaffirm mythologies and theologies and generate the kind of cosmological orientation and spiritual empowerment needed to sustain the members of these groups until subsequent gatherings.

Obviously, research into revelations of and reflection on the spiritually sacred, the ethically didactic, and the mythologically ultimate cannot be restricted to the church and church music. The depths of secularity must be plumbed for disclosures of sacramentality, spirituality, and even scripturality if ever we are to understand the nature of humanity. . . . To catch the masses in their natural living and in their casual thinking, we must peer through the transparency of popular music into the religious imagination of the populace.[4]

Historian of religions Charles Long has identified two key elements that I think are extremely helpful for understanding this new type of religiosity which is imbedded in popular culture, the first of which is "the mode of transmission."[5] Popular music illustrates this point perfectly. Its mode of transmission is intimately bound up with beat-heavy music, electronic instrumentation and amplification, digital recording, mass production technology, corporate marketing, radio and television airplay, live performance, and home stereo technology, as well as with the individual's unique way of receiving and processing the music. Each of these aspects has its own particular set of parameters and dynamics which, taken in sum, account for many of the complexities of popular music as religion. I should note that each has a strong material component as well.

The second element is the "cognition afforded by the modes of transmission" which, because of powerful contemporary mass media technology, has been greatly intensified.

Considerations of this sort raise issues regarding the locus and meaning of religion in contemporary industrialized societies. Because of the intensity of transmission, the content of what is transmitted tends to be ephemeral; thus, the notion of religion as establishing powerful, pervasive, and long-lasting moods and motivations is shifted away from content and substance to *modes of experience.* Popular religion is thus no longer defined in terms of sustaining traditions, but in the *qualitative meaning of the nature of experience.*[6]

In the case of popular music, then, the key to unpacking its religious significance lies in understanding the intense experiential states which it engenders. In an intriguing article written at the height of the psychedelic counterculture of the late 1960s and early 1970s, sociologist William C. Shepherd noted the many similarities between religious and musical experience, and explored the idea that they were analogous in some fundamental way. He found that the analogy broke down in traditional Western theistic religions because the truth claims they made about God had no analog in music. The psychedelic counterculture, however, made no such truth claims about the religiosity they found in the powerful experiential states of rock music and drugs. Therefore, wrote Shepherd:

> While the analogy between religion and music is invalid with reference to the standard forms of religiosity in our culture, it seems to me valid with reference to a newer form of religiosity emerging among the young. . . . I would argue that we are witnessing the birth of a new religious life style in which religious experience *is* precisely analogous to the aesthetic experience of music. For the incompatible elements so basic to other sorts of Western religiosity, dogmas or truth claims about supersensual entities, are truly missing here. If the analogy between religion and music fails as regards traditional theistic religions, even of the very liberal variety, it succeeds as regards the emerging religiosity among a good proportion of our young.[7]

And the primary emphasis of this emerging religiosity, he argued, along lines closely parallel to Long, is on the *experience,* which is both musical *and* religious at the same time.

Thus, the first and most important aspect of my analysis of the religious dimensions of these musical subcultures focuses squarely on the powerful experiential states their members attain through the music, states that are clearly analogous to a variety of classic religious experiences. I see this focus on the primacy of religious experience as continuing and updating a long-standing tradition of religious studies scholarship that emphasizes the encounter with the numinous as the central ordering structure for human beings. This primary religious experience then becomes the basis for subsequent developments that lead to social expression and the organized exterior forms that we call "religion." In this section, I will look closely at two of these developments in particular: First, the ritual forms that bring participants together in religious communion; and second, the worldviews, philosophies, and codes for living that provide them an orientation to the world and a meaning system through which to construct their ongoing reality.

I was struck by the ritual forms both because they uncannily reproduce so many components of classic religious rituals and because they provide the same kind of regularly recurring sacralizing function in members' lives that traditional rituals do for their respective members. The worldviews, philosophies, and codes for living caught my attention because they demonstrate the ways in which the religious dimensions of these subcultures have been integrated into members' daily lives and have changed them for the better. Obviously, religious experience, ritual practice, and orientation do not necessarily constitute religion per se in and of themselves and I am not arguing that they do. But I *am* arguing that these features do provide compelling evidence of a phenomenon which has powerful religious dimensions, and which serves as the functional equivalent of religion for the people involved.[8]

Religious experience is one of the most difficult subjects for scholars of religion to analyze because it is of a uniquely subjective personal nature that cannot be objectively observed or empirically measured. What one can do, however, is to examine seriously the accounts of individuals who have had such experiences and to use techniques of comparative analysis to tease out consistent threads of similarity and difference. This is the approach that William James took in his classic study *The Varieties of Religious Experience,* an approach that could be characterized as a kind of radical empiricism.[9] While clearly useful for marshaling objective evidence of a subjective phenomenon and identifying structural patterns, such an approach, however, still leaves one on the outside looking in, separated by a glass wall from the interior texture of the experience.

As a corrective, therefore, certain strategies have been developed within the discipline of religious studies which seek to overcome this separation. Joachim Wach's strategy is found in the hermeneutic enterprise, the attempt of the scholar to interpret the data using not only the intellect, but his or her total person, which also includes emotion, will, and experience. He writes: "A love letter will appear meaningless and silly to anybody not in love. . . . By the same token a religious utterance will bewilder, frustrate, or repel anyone whose religious sensitivities have not been developed."[10] In similar vein, Gerardus Van der Leeuw's phenomenological approach balanced objective techniques of epoche (bracketing and temporary suspension of presuppositions) and analytical categorization of phenomena with the scholar's empathetic interpolation of his or her own experiences. He called for "a systematic introspection; not only the description of what is visible from the outside, but above all the experience born of what can only become reality after it has been admitted into the life of the observer himself."[11]

In terms of the life of this observer, I can say that popular music has exerted a tremendous influence on me since my adolescence, an influence that has continued into my adulthood. I regularly acquire and listen to vast amounts of recorded music and regularly go to numerous concerts and dance clubs, all purely for my own personal edification, independent of academic concerns. I am also a musician who has played and performed in a variety of contexts, and this has been an important part of my life. Therefore, I have a natural empathy for the subject I am studying as well as a set of powerful experiences I can draw from in making my interpretations. The material that follows arises out of my own lifetime of experience with music, my year and a half of fieldwork in the Bay Area, and methodological aspects of James's radical empiricism, Wach's hermeneutics, and Van der Leeuw's phenomenological techniques of epoche, analytical categorization, and empathetic interpolation.

3

Eyes of the World
The Grateful Dead and the Deadheads

Perhaps the best example of a popular music subculture with obvious religious dimensions is the band the Grateful Dead and its followers known as the Deadheads. The Grateful Dead got their start in San Francisco in 1965, beginning as an acoustic bluegrass jug band called Mother McCree's Uptown Jug Champions, which included core members Jerry Garcia, Bob Weir, and Pigpen (also known as Ron McKernan). Soon thereafter, the band decided to switch to electric instruments and a more rhythm-and-blues-oriented sound, changed their name to the Warlocks, and incorporated other core members Bill Kreutzman and Phil Lesh. After discovering that another band already had the name the Warlocks, the group changed its name to the Grateful Dead, an appellation based on a motif from a cycle of folktales that Garcia had seen in a dictionary.

The Dead, as they are affectionately known by aficionados, began recording and performing around the Bay Area in a configuration that was to continue with few changes for the next thirty years: Garcia on lead guitar and vocals, Weir on rhythm guitar and vocals, Pigpen on keyboards, harmonica, and vocals, Lesh on bass and vocals, and Kreutzman on drums. Pigpen died in 1973 of alcohol-related liver disease and was replaced by an unlucky succession of keyboard players, several of whom also died. Drummer and percussionist Mickey Hart joined the band in 1967 and became a core member. Robert Hunter, the lyricist who was Garcia's songwriting partner, was not a member of the band but was nevertheless a key figure throughout its history.

From the very beginning, the Dead were strongly identified with the psychedelic hippie counterculture of the 1960s and 1970s. They participated in, and were the house band for, several of the famous "Acid Tests" put on, as Shenk and Silberman write, by novelist Ken Kesey and the Merry Pranksters in the Bay Area and Los Angeles in '65 and '66, featuring improvised music, strobes and black lights, films and projections, tape loops, hidden microphones, and LSD—which was still legal—dissolved into Kool-Aid. . . . Combining free-form jamming, garage science-fiction weirdness, participation by everyone, and psychedelics, "the Acid Test," as Garcia reflected, "was the prototype for our whole basic trip."[1]

The Dead's home base was San Francisco's Haight-Ashbury district, the epicenter of the counterculture. The Haight, as the neighborhood was known, became host to legions of long-haired, colorfully clothed hippies who congregated in Victorian apartments and on the streets, consumed marijuana and LSD, attended rock concerts at venues such as the Avalon Ballroom and the Fillmore West, and participated in events such as the Human Be-In in Golden Gate Park in January 1967. The peak time for the movement was later that year, the so-called "Summer of Love," in which seventy-five thousand people inundated the small neighborhood. Theirs was an ethos of idealism and expectation of social change that explored the values of peace and love, communality, creative expression, and Eastern forms of spirituality such as yoga and Buddhism. Participants used psychedelics and other mind-altering agents, and experimented with unorthodox forms of sexuality and sensuality. The Grateful Dead were right in the middle of it all, living together in an apartment at 710 Haight Street, participating in the various events, and playing many concerts, free and otherwise, both outdoors and indoors.[2]

Their music, though rooted in traditional styles of bluegrass and rhythm and blues, began to shift with the influence of psychedelics and the exploratory ethos of the countercultural context. This was particularly evident in their live performances, in which tightly structured three-minute songs would be stretched out to ten and twenty minutes or more, filled with highly experimental instrumental jams (improvisations) that took the music far afield from its original form. These jams became the Dead's trademark, mirroring the unpredictable intensity of the LSD experience that most of the audience was going through. A symbiotic relationship between band and audience began to emerge, in which the Grateful Dead became the guides for a collective psychedelic journey. As the lead guitarist responsible for much of the musical direction in these exploratory jams, Jerry Garcia assumed a kind of semiguru status that earned him the name "Captain Trips."[3] The Dead attempted to translate these live psychedelic musical journeys into studio recordings, with mixed results.[4] Their second and third albums, *Anthem of the Sun* (1968) and *Aoxomoxoa* (1969), featured a variety of experimental production techniques, studio effects and electronics, unusual compositional forms, and extensive multitracking in an attempt to recreate the psychedelic experience on record. However, the concert experience was more faithfully captured on live albums like the classic *Live/Dead* (1969).

Along with other San Francisco psychedelic bands such as Jefferson Airplane, Quicksilver Messenger Service, Big Brother and the Holding Company, and Moby Grape, the Dead were pioneers in developing a sound that came to be known as "acid rock."[5] Initially, this sound was primarily a regional phenomenon, but it soon crossed over to a larger audience. The Dead participated in two of the rock concert festivals most responsible for this crossover. The first, the Monterey Pop Festival, held from 15 to 17 June 1967, brought the San Francisco sound to national prominence. The second, the Woodstock Music and Arts Festival in 1969, to which I have already referred, marked the high-water mark of the counterculture's penetration into mainstream America. It demonstrated the ability of the counterculture to create what seemed to many a workable alternative community on an unprecedented scale based on the values of peace and love with music as the cornerstone. After Woodstock, hopes were high for a cultural transformation of even larger proportions.

Such a transformation, however, was not to be. A third major rock festival at which the Dead were scheduled to play was to irrevocably shift the trajectory of the 1960s counterculture, effectively signaling its decline and fall. Organized as a free concert by the Rolling Stones at Altamont Speedway in the San Francisco Bay Area in December 1969 to conclude their tour of the United States, this festival included several bands from the San Francisco scene and was attended by over three hundred thousand people. Peace and love were definitely *not* the prevailing themes, however, as Hell's Angels motorcycle gang members, hired as security, beat up members of Jefferson Airplane during their time onstage. The Dead, shaken by this ugly turn of events, decided not to play and helicoptered out. Not long thereafter, during the Rolling Stones' performance, the Hell's Angels stabbed a young man to death directly in front of the stage. Three other people were killed in the chaos, and numerous others were hospitalized or arrested. As Bill Thompson, manager of Jefferson Airplane, put it, "Altamont was the end of the sixties. It was December 1969, and that was the end. Of the whole feeling."[6]

Other grim events were to follow quickly, including the drug-related deaths of rock stars Jimi Hendrix, Janis Joplin, Al Wilson, and Jim Morrison, and the National Guard's shooting of four student demonstrators at Kent State University in Ohio. In the meantime, the Haight was inundated by a crush of curious onlookers and crass commercialization, diluting its idealistic community feel and forcing the Dead to move their base of operations north across the Golden Gate Bridge to Marin County. Following the subsequent breakup of the Jefferson Airplane and Quicksilver Messenger Service, the Dead remained the primary survivors of the San Francisco psychedelic counterculture. As Dead chronicler Sandy Troy writes:

> It fell upon the Grateful Dead to carry on the psychedelic tradition of the 60s. More by default than design, the Grateful Dead were thrust into the position of being representatives of the 60s to a generation of high school kids and college students who wanted to be part of the Woodstock nation. . . . To a large segment of American youth, the Grateful Dead came to symbolize what the counterculture was all about.[7]

So a curious dynamic occurred: after the counterculture ran the course of its rise and fall from prominence, the Grateful Dead became one of its last strongholds, a refuge where countercultural values and psychedelic experience could continue to flourish, even in increasingly conservative times. This dynamic was to continue and even strengthen over the years; the countercultural significance of the Dead seemed to increase in direct proportion to the decline of the counterculture in mainstream America.

The Dead retreated somewhat from their acid rock orientation, at least in their next two studio albums, *Workingman's Dead* (1970) and *American Beauty* (1970), which had a more straightforward folk-rock sound. However, their live shows continued to evolve in the direction of psychedelic-influenced jamming, as they ceaselessly toured, both nationally and internationally, attracting a larger and larger audience along the way. These tours produced music for two of their best-loved live albums, *Grateful Dead* (also known as *Skull and Roses*, 1971) and *Europe '72* (1972).[8] As these tours brought the Dead greater financial success, they sought ways to bypass mainstream corporate America and to create their own more "in-house" corporate structure. They formed their own record label and subsidiary, Grateful Dead Records and Round Records, and started their own travel agency, Fly by Night Travel.[9] They also developed their own state-of-the-art sound system for concerts, a twenty-five-ton production called "The Wall of Sound," which required a large crew to transport it, set it up, and break it down.[10]

Eventually, however, the weight of this huge enterprise began to take its toll, as the economics became unmanageable. The band actually "retired" briefly in 1974 and 1975, taking time off from touring and restructuring their financial and corporate organization. After this short hiatus, the Dead came back with renewed energy. They recorded top-notch studio albums like *Blues for Allah* (1975) and *Terrapin Station* (1976). They released *The Grateful Dead Movie,* a cinematic document of the live Grateful Dead concert experience. And they toured incessantly, playing many large shows across the country and around the world, including famous 1978 concerts at the Great Pyramid in Egypt.

It was during the 1970s that the Grateful Dead's followers emerged as a distinct subculture known as the Deadheads. Initially, the Deadheads began in 1971 as a mailing list for devoted Grateful Dead fans who wanted to be kept informed about tour schedules and album releases and to get insider access to concert tickets. Within three years, this list had grown to about forty thousand people with its own regular newsletter.[11] But the ramifications of being a Deadhead went far beyond being on the mailing list. Being a Deadhead meant that the Grateful Dead became a central focus in your life in one way or another. The classic example was the people who followed the Grateful Dead to all the shows on their tours, fans known as "Tourheads." "Heads on tour drive from venue to venue—often all night—living in tourbuses, inexpensive motels, or nearby dorm rooms or student co-ops for each run," recounted Shenk and Silberman.[12] Such an enterprise could be very challenging, both logistically and financially, requiring great dedication and creativity. Yet for Deadheads the rewards clearly were worth the effort. "Take a train, take a bus, hitchhike, just to get there. It was incredible, the effort put into following that band. . . . It is the best way to travel. You get to be a tourist in every city that you visit. . . . That was the magic of tour . . . the most unbelievable energy."[13]

For those aficionados who could not go on tour with the Grateful Dead, there were other ways to be a Deadhead. One was to acquire not only all the Dead's official albums, but to record live shows on tape and to acquire tapes of live shows that other Deadheads had recorded. Unlike most other popular bands, which discourage taping at their shows, the Grateful Dead had a designated area set aside specifically for taping, called the tapers' section, right behind the soundboard. Some tapers had accumulated hundreds and even thousands of hours of recordings of Dead shows. There was, and continues to be, an extensive network of Deadheads who traded tapes for no profit, meeting at shows, through Deadhead fanzines (fan magazines), or over the Internet. Tapers compile lists of their tapes, along with information like location, date, quality of recording, quality of music, and order of songs, creating detailed documentation for quick reference.

The tourheads and tapers are examples of an intense, almost obsessive devotion to the Grateful Dead. Such fanatical devotees constituted an important segment of Deadheads.[14] Not all Deadheads, however, took their devotion to such lengths, nor was this required in order to consider oneself a Deadhead. As sociologist Robert Sardiello writes: " An appreciation of the music is . . . the most elementary ingredient of Dead Head identity."[15] In addition to this simple musical appreciation, there was definitely also a sense of family and community and an implicit philosophy and set of values or spirituality which characterized the Deadhead subculture. Here are some comments from Deadheads:

> There's a certain philosophy in it, in the scene. It's just there's a real community spirit, it's a brotherhood. There's a lack of ego there definitely, not everyone's out for themselves. It's a big together thing, and that's really neat, that's something I have yet to find anywhere else, especially on that kind of scale.[16]
>
> When you're at a Grateful Dead show you get a definite feeling of oneness and belongingness that people in general are much nicer to you, much more open, much more trusting. . . . They'll smile at you openly without knowing you. And it just is a really intense feeling of belongingness that you fit in and you don't stand out.[17]

This sense of belonging certainly indicates a psychological mind-set, but it also might manifest itself in external forms that signified one as a Deadhead. Long hair was one example of a preferred style, among both men and women. Wearing tie-dyed clothing was another, so much so that, in many people's eyes, tie-dyed clothing became practically identified with Deadheads.[18] Other kinds of brightly colored clothing, often of ethnic origin, were also typical of Deadhead fashion. Many Deadheads adorned their cars, homes, or bodies with some form of the visual icon known as "Steal Your Face," or "stealie" for short. Taken from the cover art for the album *Steal*

Your Face (1976), a stealie consists of a stylized skull with a lightning bolt inside. Although the Grateful Dead own the trademark for this image, Deadheads have reproduced it in myriad unauthorized forms, and it has come to be an almost universal totemic symbol of Deadheads everywhere.[19]

As the Grateful Dead and the Deadheads continued full force into the 1980s, the tours and concerts coalesced into increasingly recognizable forms and began to take on an almost ritualized structure. What follows is a brief description of a typical Grateful Dead concert, an amalgam drawn from personal experience and countless aficionados' descriptions.[20] The announcement of the date and location of a show initiated the first activity associated with a Dead concert, the purchase of tickets. This would often involve spending long amounts of time waiting in line with other Deadheads, sometimes even camping out overnight. Getting to the show, for many people, would involve a form of pilgrimage, traveling some distance, often in an organized convoy. Once at the venue, there would be a tremendous "scene" filling the parking lot, with rows of colorful customized tourbuses, a main row of vendors known as "Shakedown Street" (selling or bartering food, clothing, drugs, drug paraphernalia, tapes, and tickets), and drum circles, in which conga players and other drummers and percussionists would jam and dancers would dance. The "parking lot scene" was an opportunity for old friends to reunite and catch up on activities since the last show. Many Deadheads would go just for the "parking lot scene" and not attend the actual concert.

The venues themselves would often be familiar gathering places for Grateful Dead shows. One example of such a venue was the Henry J. Kaiser Auditorium in Oakland, California, where the Dead played fifty-six times from 1979 to 1989. As Grateful Dead chronicler Steve Silberman put it: "I used to think of Kaiser as the living room of the tribe. . . . Kaiser was for lifers. It felt like home."[21] There were many other such venues across the country that Deadheads came to consider their home away from home. Once inside, Deadheads would set themselves up in particular spatial configurations. There were those who pressed up front near the stage to be within close proximity of the band. There were others who stayed further back to have more room. The tapers set themselves up behind the soundboard. And still others, known as hallway dancers, took to the halls outside the main auditorium, forsaking visual contact with the band to have even more room to dance. The sound crew actually set up speakers in the hallways so these dancers could have decent sound. In one account of the hallway dancing experience, a Deadhead wrote:

For those of us who are hallway dancers, the show is a completely different experience than for the vast majority of Deadheads who are inside the main arena. What the hallways lack in audio quality, they more than make up for in visuals and community. Instead of seeing the band, we see each other—dancing, swirling, laughing, spinning, loping, crying, zooming, bouncing, toddling, shaking, and smiling. . . . In the hallway, there is direct personal contact at every moment. The hallways can turn even the shyest Deadhead into a dancer, and many long-term relationships are engendered there.[22]

There was even a particular group of hallway dancers known as the Spinners, named for their characteristic whirling, who were actually members of a sect called the Family of Unlimited Devotion based on land in Mendocino County, California. Shenk and Silberman write:

The Spinners were a striking presence at shows throughout the late 80s and early 90s, young women and men whirling rapidly and gracefully near the hallway speakers in earth-toned cotton dresses, and dropping to the floor in supplication at the end of jams. The community supported itself by selling the handmade dresses in the parking lot and by mail order. Members of the church practiced celibacy, and took formal vows after living in the community for one year, after which they wore habits with roses and crowns of thorns embroidered on them. Church members maintained a daily schedule of prayer, communal work, and religious study; slept on the floor; did not wear shoes; and refrained from all meat, poultry, fish, and eggs, as well as intoxicants, including alcohol, tobacco, and caffeine.[23]

Jerry Garcia said of the Spinners: "They're kind of like our Sufis. I think it's really neat that there's a place where they can be comfortable enough to do something with such abandon. It's nice to provide that."[24]

Unlike the abstinent Spinners, a common practice among the majority of people at Grateful Dead shows was the consumption of mind-altering substances, marijuana and LSD chief among them. To a large degree, the purpose of taking drugs at Dead shows was not so much for fun (although some Deadheads took this approach) as to deepen one's experience of the music. Many Deadheads, in fact, preferred to use the word "sacraments" to characterize the substances they ingested, indicating the seriousness and respect of their approach, and also underlining its religious and spiritual implications.[25] Often, under the influence of psychedelics at these shows, the music would lead people on epic journeys through visionary landscapes, providing moments of peak experience, insight, revelation, and epiphany. Steve Silberman gives testimony to these experiences:

If you were tripping [on LSD], the music would pour forth celestial ar-chitectures, quicksilver glistening with might-be's, cities of light at the edge of a sea of chaos, monumental forms that could be partially recol-lected in tranquility, and turned into designs in fabric or clay, golden sentences, streams of bits. And some nights, the hair on the back of your neck would stand on end as a *presence* came into the room, given a body by the magnificent sound system.[26]

Deadheads had a number of words to describe these peaks—magic, groupmind, the zone, x-factor—and it is clear from their descriptions that these were states of consciousness that everyone experienced at one time or another in the course of a show. Deadheads bore witness:

When the Dead are in the zone, the humans onstage surrender their voli-tion to the Whole, and the venue is transported. It's as if the sound is going directly to my subconscious. The zone is hard to define, but un-mistakable when encountered, a sacred space that lies behind and be-yond the world we inhabit. It is where the Other lives, a place without time, but filled with consciousness. . . . When I enter the zone, trans-ported there by the Dead, . . . I am a consciousness without an I: the most awesome and liberating experience I have had the good fortune to live through. The zone is as close to pure Being as I have come.

The zone, however, is that place both within and beyond the music, something that lives beyond musical intention, that speaks directly to the soul of those listening, "a place of first permission," opening into the eternal.[27]

Such experiences are rare enough in our modern secular culture, but what made these peak psychedelic experiences unique was the fact that not only were they *shared* by a large group of people on a regular basis but that this was, in fact, the goal of the enterprise. Sociologist Shan Sut-ton, in arguing for the Deadheads as a religious community, has written:

It is based on a communal pursuit of the mystical experience centered around Grateful Dead concerts and featuring a combination of transformative agents: music, dance, and hallucinogens. In their ritual activities, Deadheads combine methods of achieving mystical states that are found in some practices of shamanism and spirit possession. Powerful emotional states, inspired by the aesthetic appeal of the music, differ markedly from ordinary states of consciousness and are enhanced by the emergence of *communitas,* the state of union among ritual participants.[28]

During the concert experience, Deadheads are no longer the unique individuals that exist in the everyday social structure. Instead, they become fellow parts of a brightly colored organic entity, with thousands of tie-dyed shirts swirling together. A Deadhead relates that "participation in each dance enables my spirit to transcend my body and mingle and rejoice and become one with the spirits of all the other participants."[29] In the next section, I will explore the dynamics of these "mystical" experiences in more detail. But for now, let me simply note their central importance in the Deadhead subculture, and the means used to attain them—music, dance, and hallucinogens.

Now that I have briefly examined the dance and hallucinogenic parts of the concert experience, I will discuss the music itself. Over the years, the sequence of musical events in Grateful Dead shows took on an almost formal structure that Deadheads came to rely on. There were two "sets" of music, each with a distinct feel. The first was generally regarded as the "warm-up set," in which the band would work out technical and musical kinks and play themselves into top form, generally sticking to the standard structures of the songs. Writes Sardiello:

> The first set is separated from the second set by a brief intermission or "break" that allows members of the audience to wander around and seek out friends with whom to share first-set experiences. Band trivia and set lists are often exchanged at this time. . . . Drugs are often taken or retaken at this time . . . in preparation for the second set, which is generally regarded as the highlight of the ritual performance.[30]

During the second set, the band would move into the highly exploratory jams that they were famous for, typically stringing together several songs seamlessly with extended improvisations that could last quite long. Often, it was during these jams that the peaks described above would occur. At a certain point, the guitarists and keyboard player would leave the stage and let the drummers jam together as a percussion ensemble. This section was known as "Drums." Drummers Mickey Hart and Bill Kreutzman would often be joined during "Drums" by guest drummers and percussionists like Brazilian percussionist Airto Moreira or Indian tabla master Zakir Hussain, as well as percussionist and sound designer Bob Bralove. Following "Drums," again usually in a seamless segue, the guitarists and keyboardist would return, while the drummers would drop out, and a highly experimental jam known as "Space" would ensue. Bralove writes of "Space" as entering "a musical environment without walls. . . . The song form is abandoned, and the very elements of music may be called into question. The only mandate is to explore new territory . . . where rhythm, tone, color, melody, and harmony can be explored without rules or predetermination."[31] Following "Space," the drummers would return, the entire band would play several more traditionally structured songs, and they would usually end with an uptempo rocker that raised the energy to a high level. Typically, the band would come back for an encore. Jerry Garcia noted that the second set "has a shape which is inspired by the psychedelic experience. It's like a wave form—it has a rise. It's taking chances, and going all to pieces, and coming back, and reassembling."[32] This temporal structure of the concerts was not a preplanned arrangement but an organic form that arose through trial and error over the course of decades of gigging.

The same was true for the social forms and practices of the Deadheads described above. As devotees of a band that stayed together for thirty years, the Deadheads demonstrated a unique combination of continuity and change that was perhaps most evident in their shifting demographics. Certainly, there were many Deadheads who had been following the Grateful Dead since the beginning. If they had been in their teens or twenties in the mid-1960s when the band started, then they would have been in their thirties and forties by the mid-1980s, and their forties and fifties by the mid-1990s. Of course, the Dead had also attracted younger fans but by rock music–industry standards, which primarily target teenagers and early twenty-somethings, the relatively older age of the Dead's audience was an anomaly.

However, an unexpected shift in the Deadhead constituency occurred in the 1980s with the release of the 1987 single *Touch of Grey* from the album *In the Dark*. This song actually made it to number nine on the *Billboard* charts, becoming the Dead's only top ten single. The success of

Touch of Grey spawned an MTV (Music Television) documentary on the Grateful Dead called *Day of the Dead,* and soon a new generation of young people became Deadheads. As Steve Marcus of Grateful Dead Ticket Sales put it: "When I started working for the Dead in '83, the median age group was twenty-seven years old. By late '87, it was down to about eighteen. That's a hell of a jump. But it's their band too."[33]

This influx of new, younger fans was unusual for an older band, and it enabled the Grateful Dead to expand their popularity and become one of the most financially successful bands of the late 1980s and early 1990s. It also enabled the Deadheads to renew themselves with fresh energy and to continue as a thriving, vital subculture. Even more remarkably, these developments occurred during the later history of the Grateful Dead, a period marred by Jerry Garcia's recurrent battles with drug addiction, attendant health problems, and numerous hiatuses for his recovery. While he won many of these battles and was to make several triumphant returns to the stage, Garcia eventually succumbed to heart failure and died on 9 August 1995. His death hit like a shock wave through the Deadhead community, shaking the very foundations of their existence. As Grateful Dead chronicler David Gans wrote:

> To those who feel that connection with the music—and the character—of Jerry Garcia, his death is much more than the loss of a favorite entertainer; it is a true life-crisis, more so than most cultural transitions, and more so than practically any political milestone. It is no exaggeration to say that in the world of the Grateful Dead, life as we know it has come to an end, and an immense social and economic network has been thrown into chaos.[34]

Twenty thousand people turned out several days later at a memorial for Garcia at Golden Gate Park in San Francisco, bringing the Grateful Dead full circle back to the place of their origins.[35] After nearly thirty years, the "long strange trip" of the Grateful Dead had finally ended.

The Religious Experience

> There was something about their music . . . that came to symbolize something more. They really seemed to open up some kind of interior space that was very refreshing and satisfying to have access to. Listening to their music I was able to lose myself to a greater extent than with any other

kind of music or any other experience. . . . The Grateful Dead symbolized some sort of nexus of expanded experiences of consciousness.[36]

In this quotation from a longtime Deadhead, the musical devotee touches on two of the major themes of the Grateful Dead musical experience in a concert situation—loss of self and expansion of consciousness. Another Deadhead put it even more succinctly: "It was like a loss of the personal, but a gain of the universal."[37] This loss of self did not literally mean losing track of who you were, but referred to one's ability to step out of the confines of the ego, the small personal day-to-day self, into some larger whole, which usually had some spiritual connotation.

For many Deadheads, the most immediately felt expansion led to a sense of connectedness with the people around them. "It's a lot of expansion of energy there. People opening up their fields. So it would be easy to go connect with people, and a fair amount of people, sometimes all at once. In a way, that was about recognizing something sacred in each other."[38] "A lot of the buzz of being at a show was that feeling that the other people around you get what you're getting, that if you're having a moment of ecstasy, it is a shared moment. It's not just your little personal moment, it's a moment that is including everyone in the room."[39] This connectedness was made possible by a quality of openness and acceptance not normally experienced in daily life.

> It was a quality of being with the people that was very very satisfying and very complete and kind of unconditional. The normal kind of judgments and reservations and day-to-day concerns that tied up your being that keep you from being with other people were just kind of blown out of the water . . . such a connectedness and openness and peacefulness. . . . It more closely approaches the sacred than anything else I've ever experienced.[40]

There was also a bodily component to this expansion of self and connection with other people, which Steve Silberman described as "a feeling of loss of boundaries of the individual body, flowing together into a collective being . . . one large happy organism."[41]

Often, this expansion of self went far beyond a feeling of unity with other Deadheads to a much more profound mystical union with the whole universe: "It's a melting of the ego and an allowance to enter into a space that feels complete, that feels oneness with the universe, oneness with yourself, peace, that's almost beyond words."[42] Some of these states of union went so far as to transcend even this unity with the universe into unity with the source of its creation:

> I had an experience of the most complete identity with the Creator at this one concert and experienced—it's hard to describe—but there was an underlying sensation of a giant wheel and sort of a picture of a mandala. . . . It was also a visceral sensation at the top of my head, opening up, and of just complete identity with all life and creation. . . . I felt the presence of the Creator of all, and identity with; in other words, immanence of the presence. And, you know, looking through my eyes.[43]

This type of epiphany, a visionary experience of mystical unity and identity much sought after in various esoteric religious traditions but seldom attained, was not unusual at Grateful Dead concerts. "A lot of people claimed to have religious experiences."[44]

The use of the word "presence" raises some interesting issues and calls for a more nuanced discussion of these religious experiences. Some Grateful Dead concert experiences refer to a unity with a larger whole, or being part of "the fabric of reality" and, in doing so, describe the divine in language that is impersonal in nature, suggesting a kind of monism.[45] Other experiences speak of "a direct feeling of the presence of the sacred," "what you might call an I-Thou experience, when I would feel a presence."[46]

> Part of the whole magic of conjuring the concert is conjuring up that connection and that presence which then hovers with us until it dissolves again at the end.
>
> The presence I associate with the kind of light that comes in from the music and the moment at certain times, a lot of the time, is kind of a familiar large affirming presence.
>
> There was an overarching, protective, life-affirming, loving, or accepting spirit which I would think of as . . . the Great Spirit.[47]

This is a very different language and model of religious experience, more personal and dualistic. Even so, terms like "I-Thou" or "Great Spirit" still seem to indicate a universal quality, albeit in a more personal way.

Some, however, took this notion of presence even further in speaking of a discrete entity or deity associated specifically with the Grateful Dead's music:

I had a distinct impression that there was an entity that could be accessed that wanted to teach me things, that was waiting for me inside the experience.

To say it ridiculously, it was as if something was saying hello, as if something was arriving in the music and making itself visible. And then it would disappear again.[48]

Deadhead author Steve Silberman was even able to describe this entity in very specific terms:

> The thing about the Grateful Dead deity, and I know I'm way out on a limb here, was that it was both wrathful and benevolent. . . . I remember seeing it with my mind's eye, and it was like a beast. It was partly lizard, partly mammal. It might have had more than two eyes. It definitely had big teeth. And it would just sit there and look out at you. . . . I would say that all serious, longtime Deadheads have had some experience of that creepy alligator in the nighttime sun that would look out at you from the music and was not altogether good.[49]

Silberman goes on to add the disclaimer that "what I say about the nature of that particular deity has everything to do with my personal past" and suggests that "each person would articulate what they had seen in completely different ways."[50] Nevertheless, here is a model of religious experience in which particular musics and group practices call forth particular deities. This model has some clear parallels to the West African musicoreligious complex we have discussed, although the Grateful Dead deity does not appear to take possession of individuals and incarnate itself in a human body.

Another interesting aspect of this description of the Grateful Dead deity is the combination of benevolent and wrathful aspects. A superficial reading of the predominant feeling among Deadheads at Grateful Dead shows would suggest a clichéd "peace and love vibe." Yet consistent reference to "the dark side"[51] by Deadheads suggests that the experience is "not just ecstasy and gratitude for being alive," but also "an acceptance of loss,"[52] "being so stripped down and lost and wasted and fucked up that you don't have anything left but the ability to smile."[53] For many, this process of being stripped down was not simply metaphorical, but involved having the actual experience of disintegration, death, and rebirth. One Deadhead described having a death experience, which was pretty common, where I would feel like I was disintegrating and dissipating, and it would be interminable, and it would be an eternity of losing myself. And then on the other side of it was always the Great Feminine, the Great Mother, the nourishment and the rebuilding. It was really reflected in the part of the Dionysus myth in which he gets torn apart by the nature spirits and then the mother Rhea, Zeus's mother, reconstitutes him. That was a pretty reliable part of the experience . . . [which occurred] between one and two dozen times. Completely disintegrating and then being reborn. Completely emptied out and then being filled.[54]

Another Deadhead used phrases like "resurrection" and "the phoenix rising from the ashes" in talking about the same type of experience: "It was a musical enactment of death and rebirth because you would start from structure, you would move to total chaos and disintegration, and then you would return to structure, but obviously not the same being that you were before you made the journey."[55]

There are a number of models for religious experience which are suggested in these descriptions. Two of them are directly mentioned: the Dionysian model of Bacchanalian frenzy and destruction, and the nurturing regenerative power of the Great Mother found in ancient goddess traditions. This sequence of disintegration, death, and rebirth is also widely found within shamanic traditions, often involving dismemberment and reconstitution from the bones.[56] The reference to the sequence of structure-antistructure-structure strongly echoes the ritual process model of Victor Turner discussed earlier. Here, the initiate moves out of the structures of daily life into a liminal state for an initiatic experience, often of a life-threatening nature, which is a symbolic death to the old identity, and then returns to society in a new social identity.[57] I will return to this point in the next section on ritual.

Any discussion of this sequence of disintegration, death, and rebirth would be incomplete without mentioning the central importance of psychedelics, particularly LSD and psilocybin mushrooms, to the Grateful Dead concert experience. While these psychedelics were not a necessary prerequisite for these experiences, and not everybody took them, a significant percentage of people clearly did, and numerous Deadheads reported that doing so "made a big difference"[58] and "changed everything."[59] The music and the psychedelics worked together synergistically to produce characteristic experiential states.

I realized that definitely the best music on earth to trip to was the Grateful Dead, that the Grateful Dead was somehow almost like the soundtrack of psychedelic experience. . . . There was something about the movement from structure, that is, fairly short songs with a fairly tight structure, more toward expansion and chaos, and then back to structure, that was perfect for psychedelic experiences. Because you'd start out in your ordinary mind and in your day-to-day self, you would take the drug, the drug would come on, you would feel the anchors of your day-to-day reality start to loosen and drift, sometimes accompanied by a slight feeling of fear. . . . You really don't know what's going to happen and it could be either cosmic or dreadfully terrifying. . . . This was something that was completely unpredictable and contained both heaven and hell in it.[60]

"The music and the drugs served as some sort of vehicle. . . . Sometimes it has a dark side, too, which means that you can't always take these vehicles and expect to be taken to a pleasant place. Sometimes it's really unpleasant."[61] This last quotation implies the idea of a journey, a metaphor often associated with the use of psychedelics. Grateful Dead drummer Mickey Hart often said: "We're not in the music business; we're in the transportation business."[62]

Another important aspect of the Grateful Dead concert experience is closely tied to the highly improvisatory nature of the music. For example, when questioned about how the Spinners conceptualized the sacred nature of Grateful Dead music, Steve Silberman gave this reply:

They did not believe that the persons in the band were divine persons, but they did believe that the *process* of Grateful Dead music was a channel of divine intelligence, which is basically what I came to believe. It's a very interesting question: is improvisation itself an access route to some kind of divine intelligence that reveals itself in a new form each moment? . . . I certainly found that to be the case.[63]

Here again are some echoes of West African musicoreligious practices, in which the music opens up a channel to the divine energies, but again, without actual possession. Some Deadheads expressed the spiritual nature of this improvisation in a different way:

It was like a reality read-out that was really instructive for me as a metaphor for other ways of both interpreting one's experience and expressing it. . . .

They improvised so much that their modeling was how to read that in the moment, how to be in real time and read the little signals, discover new ones even if they played the same song many times before, they had nuances they hadn't discovered before. I regard that as spiritual.[64]

These signals or nuances could also be seen as spirits and the Dead's improvisations as musical means of interacting with them:

> There are influences, whether you want to call them beings or not I don't know, that kind of come sailing in and out of the blue and that's where, to be a shaman, you have to be really good at recognizing that this has happened, assessing how to dance with them so that they come through and go out again. And that's where I would see the Dead do that sometimes and I think they'd get into some of that weird noodling when those negotiations were going on. And it would be just breathstopping to watch that happening and we would then go from being participants in openhearted spiritual communion to being observers of a really high level of shamanism.[65]

Here is another reference to shamanism as a religious model for the Grateful Dead concert experience.

Another phenomenon which supports this comparison to shamanism is that of healing, one of the primary tasks of a shaman. At Grateful Dead concerts, people would often experience "low-level faith healing" of physical ailments, all the way from colds being cured to healing lifelong chronic migraine headaches to correcting major misalignment in the spine.[66] As one Deadhead put it: "It actually got to where I knew every time I planned to go to a Dead show that I would have a healing experience, that it would help me be better afterwards and it was like entrainment. I was training myself to be in my body in a different way."[67] There were also powerful emotional healing experiences, in which someone might heal from the difficult circumstances of their life, such as a particularly painful personal relationship. One Deadhead talked about his realization at a concert about the need to separate from his wife for both their sakes, while another described healing from a particularly painful divorce. "That was such a big healing for me. It was just huge. There were only a few points for me that were that big."[68]

Finally, in this regard, it is important to note that these kinds of Grateful Dead concert experiences had a major spillover into people's day-to-day lives, a point to which I will return in more detail in the section on ritual. On the subject of this kind of spillover, Deadheads were emphatically clear:

> It turned me back on to life, because I had really kind of given up on the possibility of life being fulfilling and joyful and exciting, being completely alive. I felt so completely alive in a really unadulterated way that I remembered what I felt like, what I was here for. I remembered "Oh, okay. We're here to be like this."[69]

> It was like being recharged. Between Grateful Dead shows the feeling would kind of fade. And then I'd go to a Grateful Dead show and get recharged and turned on again.[70]

> It was as if you could recharge your spiritual batteries by going to a show, but eventually the day-to-day life would deplete that energy and then you'd have to go and recharge it.[71]

In addition to a general feeling of being recharged, there were also some very specific changes in daily life that the Grateful Dead concert experience engendered:

> One good gauge of a religious experience is: does it change your behavior in the mundane, day-to-day world following the experience? I can say that there were many many major changes in my life that I made immediately after a run of Dead shows.
>
> People would decide to break up a relationship that they were in, or get together with somebody, or move, like "I will take that job even though I have to move," or "I will quit this job." For me, Grateful Dead shows would remind me of my real self, as if I would get kind of caked and blurred by too much daily experience and I would lose the recognition of my original set of intentions about life. Then I'd go to Dead shows, and those would be stripped away by the music, by the dancing, by the psychedelics, and I would see my original face again. And I would say, "Oh yeah, that's what my life is about, that's what the core narrative of my life is. It doesn't matter that I'm trapped in this stupid position. What I have to do is this next thing." And then I would come away from the show and resolve to perform the day-to-day, concrete actions that would make that realization into a set of changes.[72]

This is a classic formulation of the transformative power of religious experience and I can think of no better way to end this section.

The Ritual Dimension

The forms which developed around Grateful Dead concert tours provide perhaps the most compelling evidence of classic ritual structures arising within popular music subcultures. As Grateful Dead chronicler Steve Silberman put it:

> What's so interesting about the Grateful Dead is that it ended up recapitulating or reifying or reiterating so many of the traditional forms of worship and initiation. Simply by improvising out of whole cloth, people came up with these forms as if they were inherent in the hardware of the human animal and I think that's one of the most powerful truths about the Grateful Dead.[73]

To begin with, going on "Tour" to get to the shows proved to be a particularly potent kind of initiation rite for young Deadheads.

> For many young Deadheads, I think the tour was, in a way, going into the wilderness for a vision quest. It was a wilderness in which there were many people, some of which were beasts of the wilderness, predators. It was a wilderness which occurred in, you know, Pittsburgh Stadium instead of in the mountains, but compared to where they were coming from, it was the wilderness. And with lots of privation. . . .
>
> To go on tour, you'd have to do without many of the creature comforts with which you had been coddled. You'd sleep on the floor of a Motel 6 with twenty other people. You'd have been taking often kind of Olympian amounts of drugs. And you'd be wearing down your baby self, the self that always likes to be comfortable. Sometimes you'd have to get by on your own, hitchhiking. Maybe you didn't have any money and you'd have to sell fruit juice in the parking lot to make the money.
>
> They were seeking a kind of, you could say, degradation, where they would be stripped down so that they could discover something essential about themselves. . . . They were seeking intensity and reality and the bones of existence, and they found it often.[74]

Here are numerous resonances with classic ritual forms—the removal from day-to-day life and normal social identity into a liminal state, the pilgrimage-like quality of being on the road, the ordeal-like aspect of physical privation and the vision quest analogy.

Yet the tour itself was just the initial component of an entire temporal sequence of activities which took place before the musical event had even started.

> There was a beginning and an end to it. There were certain things that al-
> ways happened. . . . Traveling to the thing is one. And the more weird of a
> way you travel, the better than if you just go there from your house and
> your car. Then you get to the outside part with the vendors. So, that was
> hours and hours hanging out there . . . eating, buying and selling, meet-
> ing friends. . . . And then getting tickets, that's a whole thing. And that's
> where the hierarchy of the community really came into play, too, back-
> stage passes. And then going into the show. Also, guessing what songs
> they were going to play . . . that was part of the ritual that would always
> happen. . . . Taking your drug of choice, whatever, dosing, coming on.
> And meeting old friends, that whole thing. There were a whole bunch of
> people who were like these other people.[75]

I have already enumerated how the structure of the musical sets evolved into an almost formalistic design: first set (traditional song struc-tures), break, second set (long jams, "Drums," "Space," climax). This tem-poral sequence closely matches Victor Turner's classic formulation of the ritual process's movement from structure to antistructure and then back to structure. In Turner's formulation, the crucial experiences and infor-mation of the ritual are imparted to the initiates during the middle phase of antistructure, and this was also the case in the Grateful Dead concert. It was almost always during the second set that Deadheads would experi-ence their religious epiphanies and usually in the course of some kind of extended musical improvisation, quite often in "Drums" and "Space."

> I often had the religious experience during "Drums" and "Space." . . . The
> Spinners were pretty into "Drums" and "Space" because they would have
> these big collective rituals in the hallways. . . . During "Drums" and
> "Space" the Spinners would be either bowing or they would be raising,
> body surfing, you know, levitating. Lots of stuff would happen during

"Drums" and "Space." I remember one time about thirty or forty people got naked and turned into this big human writhing sculpture.[76]

Deadheads were quite aware of the unusual power of antistructure as expressed in the musical improvisations at Dead shows: "You were out of the normal course of the thing. You were out of the melodic lyric-ed song part of it. So there's a difference between singing *Truckin'* and the whole "Drums" and "Space" thing, [which] was much more about building energy or getting very internal. It was a nonlinear thing."[77]

> There was something about the movement from structure, that is, fairly short songs with a fairly tight structure, more toward expansion and chaos, and then back to structure. . . . It was a musical enactment of death and rebirth. Because you would start from structure, you would move to total chaos and disintegration, and then you would return to structure, but obviously not the same being that you were before you made the journey.[78]

This is an almost perfect description of Turner's threefold sequence, including the final result of personal transformation to a new identity which is characteristic of most rites of passage. In this regard, it is helpful to recall the Deadhead who had the experience of "completely disintegrating and then being reborn" so many times that, for him, it "was a pretty reliable part of the experience."[79]

This type of reliability is the hallmark of an effective ritual, and the reliable, regular production of these experiences in a ritual context allows participants to make such rituals an important part of their ongoing day-to-day lives: "Between Grateful Dead shows, the feeling would kind of fade and then I'd go to a Grateful Dead show and get recharged and turned on again. And so it became a practice."[80] "It was as if you could recharge your spiritual batteries by going to a show, but eventually the day-to-day life would deplete that energy and then you'd have to go and recharge it. . . . There evolved, ad hoc, the notion that . . . Dead shows could be a path."[81] The use of words like "practice" and "path" indicate the ongoing nature of Deadheads' involvement with the shows. Many Deadheads came to regard this ongoing ritual practice as their form of church. "I know a lot of people who think of it as church. . . . I think of it that way. . . . I found it, it made me feel that way, and I went to it for many years."[82] And I showed in the last section just how much the impact of these shows spilled over into the activities and texture of their daily lives.

There is one more theme I would like to develop in this section on temporal sequencing, namely, the notion of the musical motto which I introduced in chapter 1. The motto is a brief musical phrase or theme loaded with semiological power which is capable of inducing altered states of consciousness, often to the point of possession. The same type of mechanism was also at work in Grateful Dead shows:

> Thousands of people at a Dead show . . . will not only know the songs very well, in many cases they will have in their minds thirty or forty other peformances of the same song. Thus, when the musicians make a musicianly craft gesture in the music, it will be appreciated in a universe of reference to other performances that will summon the most amount of meaning out of the gesture.[83]

More specifically, there was a particular musical gesture or motto that Jerry Garcia used consistently in Grateful Dead improvisations: "There was one little progression that Jerry played all the way through his entire career. It's just a little thing. Sometimes it came up during 'Space,' sometimes he would play it during the jams, it was like a little series of six notes, like his little signature."[84] And it was this signature line that was often the catalyst for some of the more profound religious experiences people had during the improvisations:

> He was going back and forth between two notes, and then the higher of those two notes and another note higher than that, and then repeated that four times. And these were all notes that occurred in the chords, like thirds and fourths. . . . It seemed to trigger the experience itself. . . . It was exactly at that point . . . I went from just being in kind of a positive, receptive, supportive state to the top of my head opening up and being aware of the kind of wheel.[85]

In this case, Garcia's musical motto triggered the incredible experience described in detail earlier in this chapter. The use of such musical mottoes to trigger these types of experiences is a central component of ritual practice in cultures all over the world.[86]

Turning our attention from temporal to spatial considerations, I would like to recall from the section on ritual in chapter 1 the work of Jonathan Z. Smith emphasizing the importance of place and spatial arrangement in ritual. Certainly, Grateful Dead shows demonstrated a very consistent spatial configuration over the years. I have already mentioned the pilgrimage aspect of going on "Tour," as well as the parking lot ritual outside the venue, each evincing a particular spatial structure. Because of the mass popularity of the Dead, the venues tended to be large arenas or stadiums capable of seating tens of thousands of people. These were often massive concrete and steel structures with large main floors and bowl-like seating extending upward. There were clearly delineated sections for groups of people with clearly delineated functions. As is typical of the Western spatial arrangement of musical and theatrical performances, the Dead performed on a raised stage in front, facing the audience. Bob Weir and Jerry Garcia, the guitarists and primary lead singers, were out front in the center of the stage, the most highly visible band members. The keyboardist and Phil Lesh, the bass player, usually framed them on either side, with the drummers at the back. Behind the band were their stacks of amplifiers, and various colorful decorations. To the sides and back of the stage, out of visual range of the audience, was the so-called backstage area, populated by technicians, road crew members, friends and family of the band, and those people connected enough to have procured a backstage pass.

The most fanatical Deadheads in the audience would try to get as close to the front of the stage as they possibly could to have optimal proximity to the band. If there were no seats on the main floor, as was often the case, this could entail physical difficulties because crowds at rock concerts have a tendency to push up toward the front, creating the dangerous possibility of being crushed. Others would carve out their space further back by laying out blankets. There was a specific section designated for people tape recording the show, usually in the center near the mixing board where the sound people were located, to get the optimally balanced sound. There were also projectionists responsible for the multicolored, multimedia light shows which were a standard feature of Dead concerts. Their location varied with the requirements of the venue. And then there were the hallways outside the main room, where special speakers were placed so the sizable number of hallway dancers could have good sound to dance to. While the majority of the audience was dancing during the shows, the press of the crowd near the front made it difficult to move freely, so the more dedicated dancers would be more toward the back, the sides, or out in the hallways. Those who simply wanted to listen tended to sit in the seats on the sides and in back.

In chapter 1, I discussed the importance of the body as the locus of integration of all the different levels of musicoreligious meaning and experience. In analyzing the ritual dimensions of these musical events, therefore, it is crucial to look at the body and how it is organized, not only as an object viewed from the outside, but also as a subject, with the somatic states experienced from the inside. I have already touched on several themes pertaining to the body with respect to the Deadheads. The first is simply the colorful neohippie style of dress and overall appearance. While there is clearly a connection between these styles and the psychedelic experience (that is, tie-dyes), there is also another aspect, which one Deadhead has called the Great Feminine: "It was completely evident everywhere you looked. There were so many men wearing skirts and had long flowing hair and dancing, you know it was pretty present and overt. . . . And, to me, that's the essential Grateful Dead vibe, the organic feminine energy of nature. All those colors in the tie-dyes, the twirling skirts on the dancers. . . ."[87] This organic quality could sometimes produce a dirty or disheveled appearance, often in stark contrast to one's well-manicured upbringing: "You'd see these kids who looked like they came from delicious, WASPy genetic stock, like these extremely handsome or beautiful kids . . . and many of them would be, for all their natural attributes, they would be dirty or have long hair or be unshaven or wearing rags. Even if they had a trust fund, they'd be wearing rags."[88]

This organic feminine quality also produced what one Deadhead called "utter characteristic movements."[89] These were primarily "really circular movements. . . . There was a whole lot of spinning, people were just spinning. There would be this whole scene of spinners. . . . Very snaky. And I do a lot of turning and stuff like that. Very circular. And this thing with the hands."[90] The spinning motion was not only a spontaneous movement for many Deadheads, but as I discussed earlier, also a specific form used by a specific group of hallway dancers known as the Spinners.

There were Spinners—very pretty young women who all seemed to be wearing the same kinds of cotton dresses, and also some rather androgynous-looking men—who would do spinning in the hallways. . . . It was kind of an exclusive cult. In fact, I discovered that the Spinners thought of themselves as an organized church. They were the Church of Unlimited Devotion, and they had land in Mendocino, they lived communally.

. . . They would have regular sessions of communal worship where they would spin . . . to Grateful Dead tapes, and that was their form of collective worship.[91]

There are obvious parallels here with the Whirling Dervishes of the Mevlevi Order, and such comparisons by Deadheads are too numerous to cite.

The reference to "this thing with the hands" is also a consistent movement associated with Deadheads. One Deadhead talked about an experience where "I was holding my hand in a particular way and this energy was just coming out,"[92] while another made reference to "dancing with my hands" and "really fine hand dancing."[93] The following quotation demonstrates how these movements were an external, physical expression of experiential states brought on by the music: "Really dancing to the music changes the music, changes the experience of the music. I loved it when there would be one of those moments where everybody would be moved to put their hands up and catch it and when they really jammed to a crescendo and everybody would be just like catching the rays with their hands."[94] Another Deadhead described an experience in which the music compelled him to move in a different way, in this case, to bow:

I had a direct feeling of the presence of the sacred, and I felt almost pushed down on the ground to do a full prostration. . . . You could literally feel the waves moving back and forth in the room, these huge sound waves. . . . I felt literally pushed down to the ground, like it was time for me, I had to bow right then. . . . Dead shows could include [such] direct experience of revelation and a physical enactment of the moment of revelation.[95]

The intense experiential somatic states which produced these kinds of spontaneous movements represent an entirely different mode of being in one's body. To begin with, the simple awareness of actually being in one's body, what one Deadhead called "an in-body experience,"[96] is already a significantly different state from most people's abstract, disembodied day-to-day experience. This in-body state was often characterized by feelings of happiness and ecstasy. "The dance itself was just . . . ecstatic, the freedom and the expression of joy and completeness with every moment, every movement."[97] But, going even further, Deadheads experienced much more profound somatic states:

Inexhaustible energy. Dancing for hours without tiring, to the point at which it approached the miraculous, of dancing at a fevered pitch for many hours. Colds cured, you know, low-level faith healing, really, in a way. Certainly a feeling of loss of boundaries of the individual body, flowing together into a collective being, a being that included the guy across the room. You were all dancing together; the dancing itself was dancing itself. . . . One large happy organism.[98]

In discussing her consistent experience of bodily healing at Dead shows, another Deadhead said: "I was training myself to be in my body in a different way."[99] And this different way of being in the body might even include "using the body to get to a place that's beyond the body. Not leaving the body, but accessing a bodyless place through the body."[100]

The reference to "flowing into a collective being" naturally leads to the last theme on the ritual dimensions of Grateful Dead concerts, namely, the aspect of social identity and communal bonding which these concerts engendered. Certainly, the deep kinesthetic connection through dancing just described is one example of this kind of bonding. But there are many more equally deep levels. The feeling of openness, acceptance, and connectedness is something I have already discussed. As one Deadhead put it: "I hadn't ever seen such a high level of collective group feeling and celebration and trust."[101] Moreover, this connection was not based simply on an absence of normal negative social conditions, but also on the fact that one was sharing profound religious experiences with these other people: "A lot of the buzz of being at a show was the feeling that the other people around you get what you're getting, that if you're having a moment of ecstasy, it is a shared moment. It's not just your little personal moment, it's a moment that's including everyone in this big room."[102] "In a way, that was about recognizing something sacred in each other."[103] "It's where I really got my biggest doses ever of live music making things happen on a spiritual level, where everybody would be astonished simultaneously because it was a collectively witnessed moment."[104]

One consequence of regularly practiced ritual in which this kind of bonding through collectively shared religious experience occurs over and over again is that the bonds deepen through repetition over time. An impressive statistic about Deadheads is that "there would be nearly a thousand people who went to every single show the Grateful Dead played, like, there would be a thousand people there every night, no matter where you were."[105] So, obviously, for these core Deadheads, the connections were very deep and very deeply imbedded in their social reality. But even for those Deadheads who regularly attended shows less frequently, the bonds were powerful: "It was amazing. I would meet people at Dead shows who[m] I hadn't seen for ten or fifteen years and there would just be this immediate connection. And then I'd meet people who[m] I'd seen at a Dead show somewhere else and a definite kinship would be there."[106] "There was, and in some sense there still is, a kind of instant mutual recognition of anyone who's ever gotten it about the Dead. It doesn't matter if you went to a concert with them or not, or if you ever went to the same concert or if you're the same age or anything."[107] Over time, these bonds deepened into what one Deadhead called "a tribal identity."[108] Another Deadhead described this process in more detail:

> Hanging around with people who would rave about various concerts or experiences, it became a matter of identity after a while. I identified myself with the Grateful Dead and what they stood for, with other Deadheads. . . . The Grateful Dead symbolized some sort of nexus of expanded experiences of consciousness which I then identified with them.[109]

While the Grateful Dead were still playing concerts regularly, this sense of identity and community spilled over into other arenas of life. For example, "they had AA meetings. They had Deadheads that were trying to save the whales."[110] Also, writes religious studies scholar Oren Baruch Stier, "cyberspace has been since the 1970s a place where the Deadheads could congregrate. . . , a zone of communal interaction."[111] There were, and still are, numerous virtual sites on the Internet devoted to the Grateful Dead and the Deadheads, foremost of which is the Well. As Steve Silberman notes, "the Grateful Dead community on the Well is one of the primary examples of thriving on-line community. It was thriving many years before any other on-line communities were."[112] These kinds of Deadhead affiliations continue in the wake of Jerry Garcia's death, along with a smattering of Grateful Dead dance parties and occasional performances by surviving members of the band. In fact, after Garcia's death, the Internet served as an important communication node for Deadheads to share their grief and mourn the end of an era.[113]

Yet it is clear that the lack of an ongoing ritual of Grateful Dead concerts has led to a major decline in the coherence and vibrancy of the Deadhead community. As one aficionado put it: "for me personally, there's a huge void," a feeling shared by many Deadheads.[114] Steve Silberman summed up the larger historical perspective: "It is now going to slowly die and dissipate into various forms, none of which are as magnificent and whole as the form which was able to maintain itself for thirty years."[115] This decline, while unfortunate for Deadheads, is a testimonial to the tremendous power the ritual form of Grateful Dead concerts had to create strong community bonds through shared religious experience over a long period of time. As Deadhead Gary Greenberg writes:

> A Dead show was not just a concert. It was a place of worship. The band was the high priest, the songs the liturgy, the dancing the prayer, the audience the congregation. Out of these simple ingredients, we created a tradition and enacted a ritual that was at once entirely familiar and thoroughly mysterious. . . . There are other gates to other sacred places. But this one door, this one that I have been through regularly for twenty-three years, is closed forever . . . and my life will always be impoverished for the loss.[116]

Worldviews, Philosophies, and Codes for Living

One of the hallmarks of the Grateful Dead musical experience was its highly exploratory, improvisational nature. This in itself was a primary template for the worldview of Deadheads, a model for approaching life.

> They improvised so much that their modeling was how to read that in the moment, how to be in real time and read the little signals, discover new ones, even if they had played the same song many times before. . . . When you're really looking at how it's all put together . . . there's a kind of acceptance . . . of loss and of the transitory nature of beauty and those kinds of things . . . and that I regard as real spiritual material.[117]

Earlier, I showed that the Spinners and many other Deadheads believed that "the process of Grateful Dead music was a channel of divine intelligence" and that "the process of improvisation . . . actually opens the door for some kind of transpersonal intelligence to reveal itself."[118] Certainly, this did not happen all the time, but it did happen often enough for the Deadheads and "the Dead [to] just trust that the process . . . would yield the goods." The following quotation is a good expression of how this trust in the musical process of improvisation as an access point to the divine translates into a philosophy and code for living:

In any given situation, if you put your heart into it and that X factor comes along, if you're lucky enough, the next thing you do can be the most ecstatic, the most meaningful, the most realized, the most fruitful, the most beautiful situation. And that the less preconceptions that you have, and the less attempt to pattern the experience with your conscious mind, the more open you are to what is in a situation, the better off you are and the more the possibility that something unexpectedly beautiful will reveal itself to you.[119]

Another Deadhead characterized the philosophy of living she had learned from her Deadhead experiences this way: "There was really room for adventure" and "opportunity for magic to happen."[120]

This magic, or X factor, or peak, or whatever name is given to it, is extremely highly valued in the Deadhead philosophy. Earlier, one Deadhead said that "the Grateful Dead symbolized some sort of nexus of expanded experiences of consciousness which I then identified with them." He also went on to describe the state of being

so completely alive in a really unadulterated way that I remembered what I felt like, what I was here for. I remembered "Oh, okay, we're here to be like this." We're not just here to play by the rules and be responsible. I mean, those things are important but that's only part of it. . . . It turned me back on to life . . . the possibility of life being fulfilling and joyful and exciting, you know, being completely alive.[121]

So this feeling of complete aliveness experienced at Grateful Dead musical performances becomes a goal in the rest of one's life as well, and important life decisions flow from the pursuit of this goal. I have already discussed some of these decisions, which include major changes in relationships, jobs, and living situations. The magnitude of these changes is strong evidence that Deadheads were more than willing to put their philosophy into practice with enormous consequences at stake.

This willingness to make major life changes applied to more than just their personal lives. There was a certain altruistic idealism Deadheads glimpsed in the shared peak musical experience which inspired them to take action to manifest their dreams in the larger social and political world. I have already mentioned some examples of this: the Deadhead Alcoholics Anonymous group called the Wharf Rats, Deadheads involved in environmental causes such as saving the rain forest, the on-line Internet

Deadhead conference on the Well, Grateful Dead DJ nights at various clubs, intentional Deadhead communities, and the like. As one Deadhead put it: "Wherever we go, there's always people who are Deadheads who are creating something that's fulfilling, and with a space for joy, and giving a present to the privilege of living on earth and the responsibility of taking care of the earth and each other."[122]

The Turnerian ritual sequence of structure-antistructure-structure is a useful analytic tool for bringing out certain nuances of these changes. It is clear that the magic experienced during the antistructure phase of the music inspired people to step outside the structures of their lives in a similar manner. For some, the goal was to remain indefinitely in the antistructure state:

> The Grateful Dead provided something that was kind of like what people did back maybe a hundred years ago. They'd run away from home and join the circus. Well, in the later twentieth century, they now were drawn toward the Dead, and it was a circus. You didn't have to have a job. You could be homeless. You could beg for tickets. You could beg for food and go from town to town. And it was this big tribe of people totally stepping outside of the structure.[123]

For others, however, the goal was to return to the day-to-day world in a new social identity and create a new structure which would more accurately reflect the ideals glimpsed in the antistructure experience. Many Deadheads were successful in achieving this goal.

It would be an innaccurate romanticization, however, to paint a simplistic portrait of Deadheads living in complete bliss and happiness, manifesting their dreams, and flowing from one peak experience to the next. Another critical aspect of the Deadhead worldview is that life is hard and one has to go through difficulties in order to reach the magic. Previously, I discussed one Deadhead's "death experience" of "disintegrating and dissipating" at shows, how this was "interminable . . . an eternity of losing myself," and how this happened "between one and two dozen times." He then went on to talk about how "on the other side of it was . . . the nourishment and rebuilding." He was very clear that these two sides are sequential stages in a unified process of "completely disintegrating and then being reborn. Completely emptied out and then being filled."[124]

The peak experience, then, does not come without a price of pain and suffering, and the same is true in life as well. Thus, rather than an "almost

Polyanna, just-keep-smiling kind of thing," "it's about being so stripped down and lost and wasted and fucked up that you don't have anything left but the ability to smile.... [It's] the phoenix rising from the ashes, I think, really, resurrection."[125] So the philosophy of being open to the magic of what life brings is not a naive optimism. Another Deadhead articulated it this way: "If we just try to act right and pay attention and be good, things will move forward in the way that they're supposed to, whatever that is, and it's also okay if it's hard because that's just part of how it is."[126]

There is another aspect of "how it is" which is perhaps best summed up by Robert Hunter's famous lyric from the song *Truckin'*, a line that has been and always will be associated with the Grateful Dead: "What a long strange trip it's been." When he wrote this in 1971, the Dead had been together for less than one third of their existence and yet it was already clear that longevity and endurance were central aspects of the Grateful Dead experience. Certainly, this was true in the sense that the Dead's career spanned over thirty years, a staggering accomplishment in the transitory world of rock stardom, especially given the challenges along the way, including the deaths of key band members. This was true for Deadheads as well, many of whom were affiliated with the Dead their entire adult lives, and many of whom went through numerous long strange trips just to get to the shows.

But this was also true in a musical sense. The Dead's trademark jams were of a length that was unheard of for a rock band, and they covered a vast musical terrain in the course of even just one song. Their sets were also of a length unparalleled by other rock bands, typically at least three hours long, and sometimes five hours or more. In addition, the Dead would often play several nights in a row at a particular venue, and many Deadheads would attend most or all the shows. As for how this longevity translates into a philosophy and code for living, one Deadhead reflected: "Something about their music really helped people see the big picture and the long picture. Something about endurance always came through."[127]

Throughout this study, I have made a deliberate choice not to focus on the lyrics of the music in question, not only because it is my opinion that this kind of approach is superficial and has been overdone, but also because I believe the major religious impact of the music takes place primarily at a nondiscursive level. Nevertheless, I think it is important to briefly examine the poetry of longtime Grateful Dead lyricist Robert Hunter in this section because it succinctly articulates key aspects of the

Deadhead philosophy. Two songs, *The Wheel* and *Stella Blue,* clearly illustrate this philosophy:

> The wheel is turning
> and you can't slow down.
> You can't let go
> and you can't hold on.
> You can't go back
> and you can't stand still.
> If the thunder don't get you
> then the lightning will.[128]

> It all rolls into one and nothing comes for free.
> There's nothing you can hold for very long.
> And when you hear that song come crying in the wind,
> it seems like all this life was just a dream.
> Stella Blue, I've stayed in every blue light cheap hotel;
> can't win for trying.
> Dust off those rusty strings just one more time;
> gonna make them shine.[129]

Deadheads took Hunter's lyrics very seriously as spiritual wisdom to guide them in their lives and make sense of the universe. For example, Steve Silberman talked about the lyrics of these two songs and his interpretation of them:

> The thing about both *The Wheel* and *Stella Blue* is, in the context of Hunter's lyrics, they are both very aphoristic songs summing up a transcendent perspective. *The Wheel* is literally about the workings of the universe and the nature of God. *Stella Blue* is about the workings of the universe and the nature of God from a very human perspective and involves statements like "There's nothing you can hold for very long," which is classic Dhammapadha Buddhism, and applied both to the immediate experience of whatever revelation you just had and also everything in your life. So I think that it was not only the instruments but also the patterning of the experience by the words that would deliver the message.[130]

Another Deadhead discussed how the messages in the lyrics of these songs could be applied to one's life in a more specific, personal way:

I often felt like Dead songs were talking about archetypal beings and we all could become archetypes. Even if it wasn't our story they were singing about, we became the archetypes they were singing about. And I would see them in my mind's eye on a big scale, these big beings acting out these stories of love and loss and absurdity and all of this wonderful stuff. . . . These songs were about selecting certain threads in the fabric of reality and kind of tugging on them and revealing them to all of us. . . . Each song seemed to have built into or woven into it some pathos and some humor and . . . it was like a reality read-out that was really instructive for me as a metaphor for other ways of both interpreting one's experience and expressing it.[131]

This quotation suggests a kind of mystical resonance between one's personal life and the larger world, between microcosm and macrocosm. Such a resonance is poetically expressed by Hunter in *Eyes of the World*:

> Wake up to find out
> that you are the eyes of the World
> but the heart has its beaches
> its homeland and thoughts of its own.
> Wake now, discover that you
> are the song that the morning brings
> but the heart has its seasons
> its evenings and songs of its own.[132]

Spiritual insight might thus come in the course of normal human affairs, as in the song *Scarlet Begonias*, in which the sudden appearance of a woman wearing "scarlet begonias tucked into her curls" leads Hunter to ruminate: "Once in a while you get shown the light in the strangest of places, if you look at it right."[133] Or on the other hand, it may come from an experience on a macrocosmic scale, as in the song *Dark Star*, in which a "dark star crashes, pouring its light into ashes." I conclude this section with the chorus of this song, which distills the Deadhead worldview into a simple invitation to the visionary journey:

> Shall we go, you and I, while we can
> Through the transitive nightfall of diamonds?[134]

4

The Dance Music Continuum

House, Rave, and Electronic Dance Music

Twenty-one years after the "Summer of Love" in San Francisco in 1967 marked a high point of the psychedelic hippie counterculture, there was another "Summer of Love" in England in 1988 that marked a high point of another psychedelic subculture—the rave scene. This subculture combined the rhythmically propulsive, electronically generated sounds of "dance music" genres like "house" and "techno" with the ingestion of drugs like LSD and Ecstasy (MDMA) at all-night gatherings called "raves." Beginning with a small committed British underground in the clubs and then in abandoned warehouses, raves caught on in popularity with young people, snowballing into huge outdoor gatherings attended by thousands. As the raves exploded from the underground into the mainstream in England in the summer of 1988, they displayed an uncanny resonance with their 1960s counterpart, sounding a new articulation of peace and love, psychedelics and ecstatic music for a new generation. Despite certain obvious similarities with the 1960s hippie counterculture, however, the rave subculture was clearly its own unique independent phenomenon, arising from a completely different set of sociocultural circumstances and musical influences.

To trace the history of the rave phenomenon, it is necessary to go back to the 1970s and the music known as "disco." The name is a shortened form of the word "discotheque," referring to the dance clubs at which this music was being played. New York City was the primary center for disco, and the original audience was primarily gay African Americans and Latinos. As disco became more popular, however, it spread throughout the United States into more mainstream demographic groups. One of the main catalysts for this surge of popularity was the 1977 movie *Saturday Night Fever,* starring John Travolta as a working-class Italian American who transcended the narrow restrictions of his blue-collar identity on the disco dance floor. This movie became hugely popular along with the sound track album of the same name, which featured disco music by the Bee Gees, a white group. The *Saturday Night Fever* sound track set numerous sales records, both for albums and for singles, becoming a pervasive influence in American culture in the process.[1] Mainstream Americans adopted disco fashion styles like the leisure suit worn by Travolta and flocked to their local discos to dance.[2] Many bands "went disco," adapting their normal musical style to the disco sound.[3] The disco craze became so huge that it spawned a backlash of venomous intensity, typified by the "disco sucks" campaign and the burning of disco records. As a popular cultural fad, it ran its course in a few years and retreated from public view. But the music and the underground club phenomenon continued as a strong subculture.

As a musical genre, disco drew on the influences of African American soul and funk, but because it was first and foremost a dance music its chief defining characteristic was its insistent, machinelike beat, which was foregrounded in the mix. The beat was in fact quite often produced by a machine; the first crude electronic drum machines were just being invented at this time, and disco record producers took advantage of the newly developing technology. Technology played a strong part in disco music in another respect, namely, the prominence of the DJ (disc jockey) as the master of ceremonies at clubs. Unlike the rock concert, which featured live music played by musicians, discos featured recorded music, usually on special twelve-inch records, played by DJs over large, loud sound systems. The DJ was responsible for the selection of music, and he or she would use a mixer to segue seamlessly from song to song, thereby providing a continuous sound track for the dancers with no breaks in the energy. A kind of symbiotic relationship between the DJ and the dancers developed, in which the DJ would monitor the energy of the crowd and, depending on the context, either raise it to a fevered pitch or bring it back down, creating several peaks in the course of an evening.

These musical and technological features continued to grow and evolve in the underground dance clubs of the 1980s. Catering to their core gay African American clientele, clubs like the Warehouse in Chicago and the Paradise Garage in New York pioneered the highly amplified, beat-driven music that came to be known as "house" (named after the Warehouse). One of the key figures in developing the distinctive sound of house music was the Warehouse's DJ from 1977 to 1983, Frankie Knuckles, who was so popular and influential that he became known as "the

Godfather of House." Knuckles's approach was creative and experimental, and he invented new musical and technological techniques that other DJs were to follow, "such as playing a Roland 909 drum machine under old Philly records—thus emphasizing the beats. He would also blend in rhythm tracks that he'd created on reel-to-reel tape recorders to link and boost the music."[4] Over time, certain recognizable components of the music began to coalesce: "simple basslines, driving four-on-the-floor percussion, and textured keyboard lines."[5]

As with disco, the importance of the beat was central to house music. Ethnomusicologist Kai Fikentscher writes:

> House music is most easily recognized by the character and presence of its pulse, which is pronounced by an electronically realized kick drum. This concept is known as four-on-the-floor and is borrowed from disco music, house's precursor. That pulse, seemingly ever-present and ever-constant, actually fluctuates, often in minute increments within a range from 115–130 BPM [beats per minute]. It represents the stable order, the structure against which individual freedom can be asserted.[6]

The driving beat of house music reflects its primary function as a dance music, providing a groove that serves as a rhythmic anchor for the dancers to lock onto. The dancers then express their own rhythmic articulation of the groove through their individual body movements. There are strong continuities here with several of the principles of African music discussed in chapter 2: the centrality of rhythm as an organizing principle, the groove generated from interlocking polyrhythms, the interconnection between music and dance, and the essentially participatory nature of the musical experience.

There are also strong continuities with some of the features of West African possession religion. Because of the high amplification and pounding insistence of house music beats, which are felt in the body as much as they are heard by the ears, the groove is often compelling to the point of trance induction for the dancers. One such dancer writes: "I get myself so worked up in the beat, I end up half-hypnotized. At times I have gotten so lost that my friends would swear I'm on something."[7] When a large group of dancers enter this state together, it often results in what DJs and dancers refer to as "peaks," palpable energy surges on the dance floor. The experience has been described as a peak of excitement and energy when the music is most stimulating, when the crowd is the largest and the most loosened up, most energetic. . . . The peak is like a sexual climax when everything and everyone flows together, a moment when time seems erased.[8]

an audience of thousands of dancers whose interconnected energy makes the main dance room feel like a rocket at the point of lift-off.[9]

Such peaks are one of the main goals of the house music dance club experience, and are sought after by DJs and dancers alike. There can be several peaks in the course of an evening of music and dance, each with its own distinct characteristic energy.[10]

The religious overtones of these powerful group experiences are not lost on the participants. As Fikentscher writes:

Awash in the sounds of house, the dance venue becomes a small version of . . . a social "utopia" where music and dance become vehicles of individual and collective affirmation and celebration. The social model of the church . . . in African American culture is adapted to a secular setting, which for many participants is comparable in style and dynamics to actual worship.[11]

DJ Frankie Knuckles, drawing from his many years of experience as a top house music DJ, has explicitly made this analogy: "From my particular end of it, it's like church. Because, when you've got three thousand people in front of you, that's three thousand different personalities. And when those three thousand personalities become one personality, it's the most amazing thing."[12]

House music continued as a thriving subculture in Chicago throughout the 1980s, with superstars like Knuckles, Ron Hardy, and Marshall Jefferson, clubs like the Warehouse and the Powerplant, and record labels like Trax Records and DJ International. At the same time, other local "scenes" also emerged, each with their own distinctive sound. In Detroit, for example, Derrick May, Kevin Saunderson, and Juan Atkins developed a style which came to be known as "techno," featuring strongly rhythmic drum machine programs and harder-edged synthesizer sounds. New York became known for its "deep house" or "Garage house" sound, named for the legendary Paradise Garage club and its DJ, Larry Levan. And in Chicago classic house music gave birth to subgenres like "acid house," which was built around the characteristic squelchy sound of the Roland TBR303 bass line machine that was used to compose the bass lines. Despite the growth and spread of these "dance music" genres, however, house music remained primarily an underground phenomenon in the United States, with only rare breakthroughs to mainstream chart success.[13]

In 1987, variations of house music, particularly acid house and techno, made their way across the Atlantic Ocean to England and became established in underground "scenes" there, setting the stage for a whole new series of developments. To begin with, it is crucial to understand that for a variety of reasons the club plays a much more important role in the lives of young people in England than in the United States.[14] Thus, when acid house and techno music hit England, young people flocked to the clubs to be part of the newly developing scene in unprecedented numbers and percentages that would not have been possible in the United States. The acid house clubs quickly developed their own unique subcultural identity, which was strongly tied to the psychedelic experience.

Although there is some debate about what the "acid" in acid house refers to (some say it is the squelchy bass sound; others say it is short for "acid burn," a slang term for stealing a DJ's tracks), many adherents took it to refer to LSD. While some ingested it, however, LSD was not the drug of choice. The preferred drug was 3, 4-methylenedioxymethamphetamine, MDMA, commonly known as Ecstasy. Although not technically a hallucinogen because it has an amphetamine base, this drug does induce states of consciousness similar to those of psychedelics. In addition, MDMA is often classified as an empathogen, a drug that has the effect of increasing feelings of empathy and connectedness, both to other people and to the world. Another effect that MDMA has, because of its amphetamine base, is keeping people awake, useful in dance clubs where the music and dancing go on into the early hours of the morning. For young people seeking freedom and novelty, adding these drugs to the already potent combination of highly amplified beat-driven house music, trance dancing, and pyrotechnic light shows made for intense experiences.

These wild all-night gatherings attracted thousands of enthusiastic adherents, who developed their own distinctive forms and fashions. In the hands of British musicians and DJs, the music itself began to shift away from its American roots toward a more characteristic British sound, exemplified by groups like 808 State. This process was enhanced by advancing digital musical technology like samplers and sequencers.[15] The same was true of visual technology, progressing from the basic dry ice and strobe lights to programmable lasers, fractal animation, and video effects units. Special spaces called "chill rooms," with soft cushions and relaxing music, were set up for people to temporarily escape the sensory overload of the main dance floor.[16] A new class of beverage called "smart drinks," often featuring some combination of amino acids or exotic herbs, became standard fare at these gatherings. Club goers began to dress in an identifiable acid house look: baggy, fluorescent, brightly colored clothing with psychedelic patterns, sometimes accompanied by visual paraphernalia and gadgetry. The so-called "smiley face" became the totemic symbol of this new psychedelic subculture (strangely paralleling the "Steal Your Face" symbol of Deadheads), adorning T-shirts and posters alike. Numerous "pirate" radio stations sprung up, playing acid house and techno music and serving as information clearing houses, along with a proliferation of acid house "fanzines."

Acid house became so popular in 1988 that it crossed over to the mainstream, as songs like D-Mob's *We Call It Acid* hit the top of the record charts and tabloids like the *Sun* began to run sensationalist headlines and stories on the new subculture, emphasizing its drug use and bacchanalian nature. As acid house exploded into mainstream awareness, its psychedelic associations began to trigger a backlash from authority figures that some scholars have called "moral panic."[17] *We Call It Acid* was banned by the British Broadcasting Company, along with all other songs with any reference to the word "acid." The police began raiding clubs, shutting them down, and arresting people for possession of drugs. Such tactics forced the acid house subculture to develop more elaborate strategies in order to continue. One such strategy was to move out of the established legal clubs into abandoned warehouses or other large structures, where the acid house gatherings would continue illegally, becoming known as "Warehouse Parties." This strategy worked for a time, until the police became aware of it, figured out the locations, and closed down the gatherings.

These cat-and-mouse games between underground organizers and the police gave birth to the next major development in the British dance music subculture, the "rave." This appellation was originally given to the wild acid house gatherings described above, referring to the crazed activities and states of consciousness the participants engaged in, and used as both a verb and a noun. However, as the trajectory of these gatherings moved them out of legal dance venues into abandoned warehouses, aircraft hangars, municipal pools, and, ultimately, into open fields and other outdoor locations that could accommodate even more people, the term "rave" began to be applied more specifically to all-night events in these new contexts. The sheer logistics involved in organizing these raves gives an indication of the degree of fanatical dedication ravers had to their subculture and its ritual form.

> During the day, organisers would prepare the secret venue, setting up the required sound systems, lighting, lasers, refreshments, merchandise, etc. In the evening, via a mobile phone, they'd dial a computer that would record their spoken directions to a special meeting point. . . . Prior to this, tickets or flyers would have been sold for the event . . . with the special phone number printed on them. Party goers would ring this number to get directions to the meeting point and within minutes of the pre-recorded message being made available, thousands of people would be driving in their cars to the rendezvous. . . . A member of the Rave organizers would be at the meeting point with instructions on how to get to another one. . . . After getting to the last meeting point you had the option of being herded onto buses to be taken to the venue . . . or just joining the convoy of cars, the atmosphere like that of a Carnival procession. The sheer amount of party goers descending on the site would prevent the police from stopping the Rave.[18]

Unlike the clubs, the largest of which could accommodate two to three thousand people at most, these raves at secret illegal locations, particularly the outdoor events, could, and did, attract even larger numbers of people, often from five to ten thousand. There were two motivations for this on the part of the organizers. One was simply good old-fashioned profit. The money generated by ten thousand people at twenty pounds per person was enormous, making the logistics and legal risks well worth the effort. The second motivation was a strategy to thwart police intervention by sheer numbers. If thousands of people were already present at a rave, it was impossible for the police to shut it down. From the point of view of the participants, the cat-and-mouse tactics, the novelty of new locations, and the illegality of the raves made them even more attractive.

In the summer of 1988, the illegal outdoor rave became wildly popular, with dozens of events attracting tens of thousands of young people. Unencumbered by any external constraints, these raves took the wild energies of the acid house club gatherings even further, going all night long into the daylight hours, creating intensely powerful group experiences along the way. For many of the participants, the raves were nothing short of a religious experience:

> For a lot of people, it was equal to a religious experience, but they didn't have to follow a religion. . . . For me, it was on the level of being in this situation of healing, very safe with a community of people. On a ritualistic level, going into something and coming out feeling different, or feeling that you had become enlightened in some way. . . . I really feel that the rave parties definitely had an element of ritual to them. I suppose in other circumstances people would say it would be like a religious ritual. . . . You felt very connected to yourself and connected to other people. There was an incredible amount of energy, feeling that you were energized when you left and this feeling of being very happy for a few weeks.[19]

Some ravers took these ritual metaphors a step further to the level of practice. For example, in Sheffield, England, in 1993, there were a number of experimental ritual gatherings organized by Reverend Chris Brain, which combined aspects of rave music and dance with weekly Episcopalian church services. It was called the

> "Nine O'Clock Service," a.k.a. Rave Mass or Planetary Mass. The services, produced by and largely for a young working-class group, incorporated elements of rave-ambient house music, large video screens playing computer generated images and video clips with ecological and social themes, nightclub-style lighting and the freedom to dance.[20]

Although these gatherings were to end in allegations of sexual misconduct that forced Brain to resign and the rave masses to discontinue, the innovative combination of raves and Christian liturgy inspired other such experiments in England, including one Anglican version called "Rave in the Nave."[21]

The utopian feelings glimpsed in the heat of the peak rave experience were eventually articulated as a coherent ideology symbolized by the acronym, PLUR, which stood for peace, love, unity, and respect.[22] Such ideals, shared by the tens of thousands of young people who were attending the raves, are what led some to call that time period "The Summer of Love." Like "The Summer of Love" of the psychedelic hippie counterculture twenty-one years before, it was probably the high-water mark of the rave subculture, attaining a critical mass in terms of sheer numbers and purity of shared experience.

The mainstream authority figures did not share this sense of love and community, however, and responded with more forceful tactics to try to shut down the rave phenomenon:

> A special police unit was set up to deal with the parties. . . . (A combined intelligence unit drawn from 12 police forces, the Home Office's most powerful computer system, sophisticated radio scanners, monitoring of underground magazines, light aircraft, road blocks and arbitrary arrests.)
>
> . . . phone companies were pressured into halting the use of their systems by organizers, and pirate radio stations promoting raves were shut down. . . . A new law was passed enabling a promoter to be jailed for six months with the confiscation of all profits.[23]

These tactics did eventually begin to have the desired effect of slowing down the momentum of the illegal raves. By 1990, faced with a virtual police state siege, most promoters chose to work legally and negotiated agreements with local authorities to hold licensed raves. Although the rave phenomenon continued to be huge in the early 1990s, spreading to continental Europe and the United States and developing new articulations in these new locations, its character in England changed considerably. It became more commercial and more superficial, losing the sense of love and extended community that had characterized the "Summer of Love." Within a few years, the British raves had degraded and, although still quite popular in sheer numbers, were no longer vibrant utopian centers of the subculture.

Interestingly, however, as the rave phenomenon spread to the United States for the first time, attracting a whole new audience, it seemed to carry some of its original authentic flavor with it. Los Angeles became a particularly important center for raves in the early 1990s, with British DJs and artists like the Orb and 808 State helping to reproduce the music and the feeling of the British raves. Raves developed in most major cities across the country, with Ecstasy-fueled gatherings taking place in clubs, warehouses, and outdoor locations. Young Americans were able to have the same type of revelatory experiences as their British counterparts, and they developed their own indigenous versions of the subculture, complete with clothing and accessory fashions, fanzines, pirate radio, Internet web sites and bulletin boards, and so forth.

The rave subculture even followed a similar trajectory in the United States as in England, beginning as an underground phenomenon with a wild utopian sensibility and strong feeling of community and, as it gained in popularity and spread to the mainstream, gradually becoming more commercial and superficial. Organizers in the Los Angeles area, for example, rented the Knot's Berry Farm amusement park facility to hold a particularly large commercial rave, demonstrating the mainstream legitimacy of raves and unintentionally drawing a parallel between raves and corporate entertainment. But perhaps the best indication of the rave subculture's penetration into the mainstream was an article in *Time* magazine in August 1992, entitled "Tripping the Night Fantastic." Wrote author Guy Garcia, in the typical breathless *Time* style: "Fueled by techno music and neo-hippie vibes, a wave of 'raves' is putting a new spin on the pop scene."[24] For young ravers who saw themselves as part of an authentic underground movement, receiving coverage in *Time* magazine was like the kiss of death.

Despite the mainstream media coverage, however, the rave phenomenon and subculture continued, and still continues, in a myriad of musical forms and social configurations throughout the United States and Europe and, indeed, the entire world. In Berlin each year, for example, one and a half million ravers attend the Love Parade in the central Tiergarten Park, as well as countless smaller rave parties scattered throughout the city. Since 2000, the Detroit Electronic Music Festival has attracted a comparable number of ravers to Hart Plaza in downtown Detroit for three days of nonstop techno music and dancing. And each year in the desolate Black Rock Desert in Nevada, far from any major metropolitan area or infrastructure, tens of thousands of people attend the Burning Man gathering for a week of wild revelry, creative artistic expression, outrageous performance and ritual, and dozens of nightly raves. Yet, for every such megagathering that retains a feeling of the original rave spirit, there are dozens of commercial events that are simply large and impersonal, filled with kids who are unfulfilled, confused, disconnected, often wacked out on drugs, and have never experienced that feeling. On the other hand, many cities in the United States and Europe have thriving underground scenes with close-knit groups throwing small, intimate parties where generating that magic is still the central goal.

The Religious Experience

The first theme that stands out as nearly universal in the dance floor experience of the rave subculture is that of trance. The trance state is inducted through the high-volume insistence of the continuous beat and the accompanying continuous dance. One veteran of the Chicago house music scene put it this way: "You would definitely get rather hypnotized by the constant rhythm, the continual motion of the music. . . . You can get into a trance state without being high [on drugs]. . . . So much of it is repetitive dance, repetitive motion; you're getting into such a groove that you put yourself into a trance state."[25] A San Francisco raver described it as "a really powerful experience. It transports you. The volume, the sheer volume of the music, and just the repetitiveness of it is hypnotic. You're dancing, you're moving in time to the music and, after a while, you don't know what your body is doing. . . . You just kind of have this sense of your own motion and it goes with the music."[26]

This connection between the music, the rhythm, the dance, and trance induction is consciously recognized by ravers, and induction of the trance state is a specific goal of the music.

> Rhythms have a real powerful influence on the mind. . . . The music definitely definitely definitely caters to this trance, trying to put your mind into it. When it starts getting these really regularly looping patterns, it goes into a state which is kind of hard to describe. . . . You start achieving some really unusual states of consciousness, which I think people really like. The music attempts to manipulate that sense of consciousness. It tries to take you to a place, tries to sculpt your experience in some way, by manipulating those mechanisms in your mind.[27]

It is important to note that this is a *deep* trance state induced over a long period of time, one that "completely alters your state of consciousness."[28] As one veteran San Francisco raver put it: "The periods of pure trance have been profound raving, simply because . . . raving's about eight, nine hours nonstop."[29]

The trance state, however, is not of a uniform texture. Another nearly universal theme in the house-rave dance floor experience, noted in the last section, is the notion of gradually building the energy to a peak. "A well-structured, a well-done DJ set really builds a flow and an ebb, builds it up and takes it back down again, and can bring you to the peak of something and then take you back down gently."[30] Reaching these peaks is a conscious goal of both the DJ and the dancers, and DJs have developed specific strategies for how to get there.

> I will move the crowd up to a high level of energy by gradually increasing the beats per minute over time and then I will take it to a peak if I can, to some ecstatic peak where I'll just keep going as long as possible. And then, when the crowd seems to fade, or have enough of that, then I will gradually take it down again, rest them for a while, and then bring them up again. . . . As a DJ, I see myself as taking the crowd on a journey and through a number of different emotions and feeling states. And, at some point, letting all that break open into an ecstatic state. And, over the course of the night, doing this a number of times. And the feeling in the room grows.[31]

Another DJ put it more succinctly: "I like to definitely build up a crescendo and let it all explode."[32]

One of the primary feelings associated with the peak experience on the dance floor is that of joy or happiness. "I've had what I might term, and not facetiously, religious experiences when I've been dancing. You just get incredibly happy. You get filled with a real sense of joy."[33] And this sense of joy is not just a private, personal feeling, but one which is shared by almost everyone else present at the rave. An aficionado talked about an ongoing event he helped organize that "was positively notorious for this group joy that would happen. . . . They would walk into the space and they would just feel it. . . . They became truly joyful, truly ecstatic."[34] For many ravers, this sense of joy is the main goal of the rave. One stated that "it's all about happiness,"[35] while another went so far as to call music "the ultimate bliss."[36] This is not to say that there aren't other emotions and feeling states experienced in the context of raves but simply that the feeling of joy and happiness is central. One former Deadhead who became immersed in the rave subculture noted that at the raves, "you just are not exposed to that really negative, hard, dark side that you would be with the Dead," thus implying a relative absence of those emotions at raves.[37]

It is probably more than just simple coincidence that MDMA, the drug most often ingested at raves, goes by the common name of Ecstasy, because the feeling states induced by this drug certainly can be described as ecstatic. It is clear that the use of MDMA in rave contexts is a major contributing factor to the feeling states described above. At the same time, however, many ravers were emphatic in stating that these states were easily accessed *without* using MDMA, that the tremendous combined power of the music, the rhythm, the dance, and the visuals was more than sufficient to produce such states. One raver talked about experiencing profound altered states of consciousness at raves long before she ever took MDMA, and that MDMA "just confirmed the way I already felt about it, just enhanced it more."[38] Another described the opposite sequence—after taking MDMA and having ecstatic experiences, that state became accessible without the drug, solely through the music: "The connection I had with the music was real because I felt it when I wasn't high."[39] I will discuss the impact of MDMA on the dance floor experience and the rave subculture in general in more detail as I continue my analysis.

MDMA or not, in discussing the peak experience and trance state on the dance floor, with the accompanying feelings of joy and happiness, it is important to emphasize that this is not simply a psychological phenomenon, but one which also has a very strong *bodily* component. One raver summarized it succinctly by saying that "it's all about being in your body and out of your head."[40] "What you have to do is get out on the dance floor and just get into your body and feel the groove. And once you allow that to happen, I find that most people are able to make that connection and suddenly they get it."[41]

> There is a point that, when you achieve it, it's truly wonderful and it's kind of a mystical thing where the music literally—I mean, this all sounds so trite—where the music really sort of sinks its teeth into you and my boyfriend always says, "It's got you" or "It's got me." And it's that kind of thing where the music just completely—it's in you, it's around you, and your body is moving despite yourself.[42]

These kinds of accounts suggest a trance state very similar to possession, in which the music becomes the rider and the body becomes the horse, but without reference to any specific possessing spirit.

However, in talking with DJs about their experiences, the comparison with possession becomes much more closely analogous in this regard. One DJ described her experience of being

> completely in a trance state. . . . It seemed like I could just do no wrong. . . . And, in those times, I feel like, seriously, the spirit's taking over. . . . I

definitely feel like there is some spirit force that comes over my body.... Someone, some thing is assisting me. . . . And I don't really know who that spirit is that's inside me. I've talked about it with a couple of friends. They agree that something just sort of takes them over.[43]

This same DJ talked about selecting the music in her sets by moving her hand over the records and feeling the heat emanating from them: "I feel like there's heat actually coming out of the records, like my hand goes closer to certain records that are speaking to me and it seems like they are the most perfect records at the time. And I don't know what is guiding me that way. I can just assume that it's a great mixture of my talent and a spirit that's taking over the set."[44]

Another DJ also discussed the music selection process of a set in terms that strongly echo possession:

I do have a sense of opening to something larger than myself when I play. . . . I do have a sense of being divinely guided in the choices of the music and, when I'm truly in a flowing place, the sense of what to play is just coming. That's the place where, as a DJ, I like to get to, where each piece of music is just flowing from one to the next. And I believe that I can most help people enter that state of flow when the music is happening that way, when it's just coming through me.[45]

There is a sense of transmission here, in which the possessing spirit comes over the DJ, who then transmits it to the dancers through the vehicle of the music. "You can get sometimes just a vortex of energy coming . . . out of heaven into the DJ, out of the turntable and into the speakers and into the people. And you can just see this energy, you know, almost a physical wave downloading into everyone."[46] Thus, the transmission of energy seems to flow along specific spatial pathways which the participants recognize, harness, and consciously participate in.

I will explore the spatial dynamics of this flow of energy further in the next section on ritual dimensions, but for now I would like to return to the idea that the dancers experience this energy through the body. One dancer said: "I experience it as a universal force that is present in every one of my cells and that moves through me."[47] The goal, then, is

to really inhabit the physical body from another space, so that you're feeling your own consciousness participating with physical matter, so that consciousness starts to rest within physical matter. What I experience is that then I feel like, just as there's no separation between myself and a tree or another person, there's also no separation with my hands or my elbows, etc., so that I can rest in those areas and have a direct experience of moving from inside them. And the more I do that, the more those areas open and they literally begin to conduct energy in a new way. . . . The energy of the earth can come through the body in a very unimpeded way, the energy of anything, another person's energy. . . .

I feel that dancing permanently alters my perception and also alters my body and that my body opens more and more. The alignment shifts and so the energies can flow through more clearly, more quickly, without resistance.[48]

Thus, when the energies flow through the body in this way, there is also a greater connection to the external world—other people, the earth, even the spiritual world. What is being described here, then, is a kind of *bodily* mysticism, in which mystical union is experienced at a physical, kinesthetic level. "When you dance with people in this way over time, one of the things that becomes totally evident is the oneness, that we're all moving in this field, this vibrational field. . . . What I feel occurring is a sense of global consciousness, a sense of one moving world, one enormous dancing body that is felt in a physical sense."[49]

The bodily aspect of these experiences is definitely amplified and enhanced by the use of MDMA. As one raver described it:

It changes the way you hear things. It gives music and the things you hear a powerful substance. It binds music more directly to emotions than anything I've ever experienced in my life. When you hear something that is emotionally evocative, when you're under the influence of MDMA, your whole body feels it. . . . It's like an almost physical reaction you have to the music. So, it has a tendency to make music a very substantial experience.[50]

When MDMA's amplification of the bodily dimension of music is added to the already intense peaks on the dance floor, it makes for some extraordinarily powerful experiences, particularly because the music is specifically designed with these experiences in mind.

That's definitely something that I always felt with MDMA—you get this sense of these waves of abstract feelings washing through your entire body. . . . The music just pandered directly to that portion of the experience you would have. In fact, a lot of the best music that you would hear on the dance floor understood what it was like to be under the influence of MDMA. . . . It really is sort of like teetering on the edge of an orgasm for a very long time.[51]

With or without MDMA, the rave experience can produce some very unusual states, such as synesthesia, where the senses cross over with each other into a unified whole. An even more unusual state is what I have termed bilocation, in which one is simultaneously in one's body, dancing, and yet, at the same time, also floating high above the dance floor, looking down at oneself. "I was outside myself looking down at myself. . . . I was above myself looking down, sort of in a helicopter if you will, looking down at all these people dancing."[52] "I talked with other people about this particular subject and that's a pretty common perception, to see yourself as if you're looking down on yourself."[53] One might dissociate from the body altogether and merge into some other level of reality.

> I was subtracted from the individual and became part of the whole, blending into the field which binds all of the molecules of the universe, . . . the energy that binds the entire world together. . . . I checked out of my body in some way and experienced things from a higher plane of existence. . . . There were definitely times where I felt like I was existing . . . as everything all at once. . . . I would blend into the cosmic mind. I felt like I was a part of that and not part of an individual consciousness, an individual experience with a sense of self.[54]

This merging into a larger whole, whether experienced in the body or out of the body, is widespread almost to the point of universality among ravers. I will return to its implications shortly.

For now, however, I would like to explore how it is possible for ravers to have such a wide range of experiences, from being deeply in the body to journeying far outside it, and many combinations in between. One interesting model proposed by insiders posits some kind of a causal relationship between types of music, areas of the body (which roughly correspond to the Indian system of chakras, or energy centers), and experiential states.

> Music introduces different vibrations. It introduces different rhythms that my body then moves with. . . . Different musics open up different

parts of the body. You know, salsa will move a certain area of my body and techno will move it in a different way. . . . Some music, the African, seems to affect the heart center. Other music seems to affect the lower chakras.[55]

"To me, it's all about chakras. . . . The higher the chakra, it starts to look trancy . . . so people look like they're in a trance, whereas people that are dancing more of a groovy, funky stuff with house or acid jazz, they look more sensuous, like they're in their lower chakras."[56] According to this model, then, some musics affect the lower chakras and produce a more earthy, sensual experience. Some affect the heart chakra and produce more of an experience of love. Some affect the higher chakras and produce more of an out-of-body spiritual experience. But the interesting thing about techno music, according to some ravers, is that it seems to affect all the chakras along the entire vertical axis at the same time. "I experience it [techno] actually affecting chakras above the head and all the way through to the earth. . . . Some of the techno is affecting the whole vertical dimension, so that the body will get a sense of both grounding and being very connected to the transpersonal. I'm getting that sense of both with techno."[57] Therefore, techno music appears to open up the whole range of experiential states, from the earthy to the cosmic, including some unusual and extraordinary combinations.[58]

As with the Deadheads, these types of powerful experiences can have a profound impact in the day-to-day lives of ravers.

> The music made me feel both just free and inspired and more in touch with myself. . . . The music was so powerful to me that it just highlighted all the beautiful things. . . . I found myself getting reconnected with myself, just picturing what I needed to do and what I wanted to do and how I wanted to enjoy myself, all in the course of an evening, just from the music, you know, losing myself on the dance floor. . . . It definitely gave me a larger sense of the world and how I fit into it and what I needed to do for myself.[59]

Here is a description of the recharging of oneself and one's life. But more than that, there is also an awareness of the larger world and one's place in it, accompanied by a strong sense of one's purpose. This is an extremely common theme among ravers and it ties in to their sense of spirituality. One raver said: "It's definitely a spiritual experience. And I never had any spirituality before, so this was my first time that I had ever experienced that."[60] Another described how

> at that point in my life, things really transformed in me. I really started feeling like I had a more noble purpose in life. . . . I consider it to be a very spiritual experience. In fact, I can say that prior to doing that, my sense of spirituality was pretty weak, pretty undeveloped, pretty dormant in me. . . . I definitely felt a very strong sense of spirituality and mostly the spirituality was kind of a personal transformation into just understanding that oneness, the concept of the one. . . . My spirituality attained the understanding that it really isn't about the small world I live on; it's about the bigger scheme.[61]

It is important to emphasize that these are not simply superficial changes at the conceptual level, but ones which affect people's behavior. Many ravers talked about changing jobs or relationships or other important aspects of their lives. Yet the changes went beyond simply making external adjustments. As one raver put it, the raves "actually I think make people kinder and gentler and more compassionate."[62] These kinds of changes reflect an even deeper shift at the epistemological level which penetrates to the core of one's being:

> There was one particular experience I had at a party that was almost like a revelation as far as, not specifically what I wanted to do with my life, but like the general direction of it. . . . It really was a momentous occasion. I remember very clearly it was a dramatic change in the way I perceived what I should be doing with myself. . . . It had pretty profound effects in my life. . . . The basis, the foundation of it all, just kind of shifted.[63]

There is also a powerful social dimension to the changes in ravers' daily lives, some of which bears an uncanny resemblance to the conversion experience. One veteran put it succinctly in describing his first exposure to the San Francisco house music scene: "I had come home."[64] Another raver used similar terms to describe his first rave experience: "We felt like 'Yeah, this is our thing. We finally feel at home.'"[65] A big part of this feeling of being at home has to do with a sense of being connected with other people in a way that transcends normal social barriers. "I was really impressed with the vulnerability that everybody showed to each other. . . . That really shook me at the time because it didn't occur to me that it was possible to be so unguarded with complete strangers."[66] One raver described this as "instant community," and talked about how "it helps you feel part of something and to feel like you were part of a bigger network of people than just yourself."[67]

In this regard, one of the themes almost universally mentioned was how the raves broke down racial, ethnic, and class barriers. One veteran of the original British rave scene put it this way: "In Britain, I think it is so much about who you are in terms of what class you come from and how you talk and what clothes you wear. I think this was the first time in our contemporary history that this was broken away and it really gave this opportunity for people from all different classes and races just to be to-gether."[68] This coming together of different groups has also been strongly evident in raves in the United States. "It was a composition of a lot of dis-parate groups of people—gay, straight, men, women, black, white, His-panic. It was a polyglot of a lot of cultures and races and mind-sets and orientations coming together in a very positive way. . . . Everybody was getting off on it."[69]

This phenomenon is so central to the rave experience that it is often consciously articulated as an ideology of unity: "The concept that I love about it the most is the concept of the beat as something that unifies dance floors and that unifies people. That has always been my goal in music because, on the dance floor, you can break down color barriers, sexual barriers. . . . It becomes universal and it brings a lot of people to-gether."[70] I will explore this ideology further in the worldview section of my analysis, but for now I return to the topic of how the dance floor ex-perience has changed people's lives in terms of their social context.

Following their initial conversion experience, many people plunge them-selves completely into the rave subculture, going to raves once a week or more, and making the rave community their primary social context.

> It definitely, for a good number of years, was all I did and all of my friends were doing the same. My friends were in the scene. We were the scene. Everything we did revolved around going out to parties and going out to clubs and stuff like that. . . . There was a time where it was several nights in a week, you know, five, six nights in a week, we'd be going out somewhere and just dancing and carrying on.[71]

On the one hand, a raver talked about how his "friends changed" because "the friends I had before really didn't understand the drug dance culture at all."[72] On the other hand, the new social group confirmed a transformation and led to further spiritual developments: "The people I started meeting were a whole different group of people from what I had ever known before. People were more open-minded and spiritual and much more holistic. They were much more loving and caring. . . . It definitely changed me and filtered into the rest of my life."[73] Another raver recalled:

> It [the rave experience] blew me away and suddenly I found myself going to parties every weekend and meeting new people that blow my mind. I mean artists and dancers and visionaries and people that were creative and doing all kinds of things with their energy to promote this great vibe. . . . I started meeting all kinds of people that were very spiritually inclined and doing all kinds of spiritual work in all different levels.[74]

I would like to conclude this section with a few short quotations from ravers that make clear the religious implications of the rave experience for them:

> It was what I always thought that religion was supposed to be, the community lightening of yourself, and to come out of a party and just be so filled with pure love and leaving the frustration of the week behind at the rave. It showed me true spirituality, from within flowing out of myself and joining it with other people. Undoubtedly the most spiritual feeling I've ever had.[75]

"The music is a religion. . . . If you've got a keyhole somewhere, that's the thing that puts the key in and turns the lock and opens you up."[76] "For a lot of people, it was equal to a religious experience but they didn't have to follow a religion."[77] "It's food to the soul. It's like church out of control."[78]

The Ritual Dimension

While the rave subculture has not produced ritual components with the same formal coherence and structure as Grateful Dead concerts, nevertheless, raves clearly have ritual components which are powerful and striking. To begin with, as I just showed, ravers often become part of the subculture through an experience akin to conversion which combines the deep religious trance of the dance floor with a sense of home and belonging. Following this experience, ravers will often immerse themselves completely in the subculture by going to raves once a week or even more frequently. Considering that raves are typically all-night affairs which require enormous outputs of physical energy (and, for many, the ingestion of consciousness-altering drugs), this kind of temporal frequency and regularity of practice is strong evidence of the central importance of the rave as an ongoing ritual in their lives. "We started doing ritual . . . every week together and going to parties on weekends. And this thing just continued to blossom and blossom and blossom. Basically, it hasn't stopped in three years since I got involved."[79]

> There are people that take their house music and their club time very seriously. I hesitate to use the word "revere," but they do, in a way. They plan for it. They aim for it. And then they go out and have the best time that they possibly can, because the next day, they feel wonderful. Speaking from personal experience . . . the next day, I would feel great. . . . It absolutely would carry over into the rest of my life. . . . Definitely, it was a recharge.[80]

For many ravers, the ritual aspect led to comparisons with church: "Raving was Saturday but, suddenly, raving was Sunday morning too. We used to talk about [how] we should just find an old church and throw a rave every Saturday night on into Sunday. It was my first hit of religion as far as something organized."[81]

> We were all sitting around at the end of one [Saturday night] Sunday morning tweaking our brains out. And we were going, "Yeah, we really should start a Sunday morning thing and keep the vibe going." And my friend Frank said, "Yeah, and we should call it Church because that's what it is. I mean, I go to a club on Sunday morning for my church." And so we did. . . . We actually started another one-off kind of thing that went on intermittantly and we called it Church. And it started out at six on Sunday morning and it ran all Sunday. And Carefree [the main club] kind of bled into Church.[82]

These comparisons are largely based on the regular weekly temporal sequencing of raves on Saturday night going into Sunday morning and the religious significance of such sequencing for the participants.

In addition to this regular weekly sequencing, there is also a strong temporal sequencing of events which occurs within the raves themselves. First of all, there may be a period of time spent just tracking down the location of the rave through phone calls and driving to a series of informational checkpoints. The raves usually begin no earlier than nine or ten o'clock in the evening and often the dance floor(s) will not really get full until eleven or twelve or even later. DJs will typically spin two- to three-hour sets, starting slowly and then building to the peaks described earlier. A good set will include several peaks which take the dancers up and bring them back down over and over again, leading them on a musical journey. Because of the strenuous nature of the dancing, it is necessary sometimes for the dancers to take a break to recuperate physically and psychologically. For this, there are especially designated spaces called "chill rooms," which I will describe in more detail in the next section on spatial configuration. In the chill room, one can relax with friends in a relatively quiet, safe, comfortable environment. In the course of the evening, there is a rhythmic temporal oscillation between the intensity of the dance floor and the relaxing break of the chill room.

Generally speaking, the overall peak of the rave, in terms of density of crowds and intensity of dancing, will typically happen between twelve and three in the morning. This is the most highly coveted DJ time slot and the headline DJs are usually scheduled during this time. The dancers have been dancing long enough to be well warmed up and inducted into deep trance states, and those who are taking drugs are already feeling the effects. During this time, DJs tend to keep the musical peaks going for longer periods of time and, therefore, the dancers tend to have their most powerful experiences of the night. One of the musical techniques used by DJs to produce these prolonged peaks, which I have already noted, is to gradually increase the beats per minute in a sequence of songs over a period of time: "The speed of the music is one thing that the DJ uses to control the peak of the set. You start out playing slower music and it gradually speeds up with each song. . . . If you start out slow and then build it up, then definitely people are kind of forced to go along with it, you're forced to higher levels of exertion to keep up with it."[83] As another DJ put it: "I like to definitely build up a crescendo and let it all explode."[84] This is a good example of Rouget's combination of accelerando and crescendo as a trance-inducing technique.

There is also the skilled use of the musical motto, another trance-inducing musical technique noted by Rouget, to inject a quick jump in energy.

There's definite motifs in electronic dance music you can use for a desired effect. If you want to build a peak, you bring in a sixteenth note snare roll and you change the pitch of the snare roll up as it quickens and that just all of the sudden gets everyone's attention and everyone's waiting for the payoff. Then you drop out the pounding kick drum and just have one long bass note, and it's like "boom!" And everyone, all of the sudden, it's like they hit a bump in a car and they're floating in the air and they're about to hit the ground. . . . It's like the whole room has just opened up. It's like the floor fell out from under you and you're just floating in space all of the sudden. And when it comes in again, it's like a big kick in the ass. It just sends you flying down this tunnel.[85]

Sometimes, this peak time on the dance floor can go on for many hours, keeping the intensity going until dawn. In many raves, however, there is an energetic scaling back in the pre-dawn hours, when the crowd thins out somewhat and the music becomes more ambient and downtempo. This time can be very sweet and intimate, in which the energy and connections that have been established over the course of the night can be more personally expressed and savored. Finally, for those who stay all night, the onset of dawn and the light of the new day provide another kind of peak which wraps up the whole experience with a sense of upliftment and completion. There is a feeling of having gone on a collective journey together and arriving at the end transformed, renewed, and unified. One may even continue to dance into Sunday morning or, at least, continue to be with other ravers who have also gone all night.

Inevitably, however, one must return home and sleep in order to recover from the high level of intensity and exertion. The nocturnal nature of the rave, followed by daytime recuperation, leads to a lifestyle in which the daily rhythms of ravers are nearly the opposite of the mainstream world—up all night and sleeping during the day. This nocturnal lifestyle contributes to the liminal, betwixt-and-between state that Turner has identified as central to the ritual process.

In some rave communities, the ritual aspect has been brought to such a level of consciousness that specific times are set up in the course of the night to practice more traditional ritual elements. For example, I have attended raves where such rituals occurred after the first DJ set, in which people were smudged with sage (a Native American–derived practice), the four directions were called in, verbal prayers were offered, and people were led in guided visualizations. Other raves might begin with the collective chanting of the Hindu seed syllable Om. In one rave around the time of May Day, there was even a multicolored May Pole with streamers, and people participated in a circular May Pole dance to the sound of especially written techno music. One San Francisco rave veteran talked about how

> that kind of off-beat spiritual interest in the Bay Area just naturally took hold within the rave community. So, there's a big part of the rave community that's taking the new age movement and moving it into the next century with a whole new technology built around dance. . . . They do want to have a transformative experience. And so there's a lot of people who have been in the rave culture for ten years now. They're not kids anymore, and they're throwing these pretty sophisticated parties that have . . . ritual with intention.[86]

There are many more examples of the experimental integration of traditional ritual forms with a rave or the converse, integrating rave forms with traditional rituals, including the Techno Cosmic Mass put on by excommunicated Catholic priest Matthew Fox and his University of Creation Spirituality in Oakland, California, in which techno music and rave dancing are integrated into an unorthodox liturgical mass and communion. As I conclude this section on temporal sequencing, let me simply note that traditional ritual forms often occupy a prominent place in the temporal sequence of activities at certain raves.

Turning our attention now to spatial configurations, the first theme that stands out is the unique nature of the spaces in which raves are held. While it is true that many such events take place at established clubs, arenas, or outdoor locations, the primary underground rave tradition has demonstrated a consistent preference for the warehouse as the space of choice, particularly the illegal, abandoned warehouse. In many cases, organizers go to elaborate lengths in order to set up such spaces and elude authority figures in the process. This contributes to a certain renegade ethos, a feeling of going on a pilgrimage, and a strong liminal sense of being removed from the normal spaces of day-to-day life. As one raver put it: "For me, it was just kind of that thrill of going places that were also dirty warehouses. I think it was just being out of a pristine environment and going into a probably more dangerous environment that was important."[87]

The warehouse spaces are often very large and dark, with an almost cavelike atmosphere and an urban, postindustrial ambience. Bright multicolored decorations and light shows enhance the visual field, giving it a strong psychedelic and cybernetic feel. Just as DJs invest time, energy, and money to hone their musical craft, decorative artists and light technicians do the same with their visual craft. For many ravers, this visual element is just as critical in their experience as the music: "The lights and visuals are really important to me. It definitely alters my consciousness. It's crucial to have visuals and lights for me."[88]

In many cases, altars may even be set up throughout the space, containing fabric, figurines, paintings, candles, incense, and various assorted sacred objects. One San Francisco raver estimated that "75 to 80 percent have altars or try to at least have a few candles, tapestry around the DJ or in front or on the bar or on the table or wherever, somewhere to keep the element."[89] The altars, decorations, and lights are sometimes organized around particular spiritual themes. For example, there is a subgenre of electronic dance music called Goa Trance, which originated in Goa, India, and subsequently spread to England and the United States. Visuals at Goa raves are likely to include images of various Hindu deities like Vishnu, Krishna, Ganesha, Kali, and others. The May Pole mentioned earlier is another example of a specific religious theme.

A number of raves have multiple rooms with dance floors, each decorated in a different style, with DJs spinning different types of music. At such raves, one can move from room to room, depending on which atmosphere one is most drawn to at the time. Another option at most raves is the chill room, a quiet space where one can escape from the sonic assault of the dance floor music. The chill room is usually filled with couches, beds, soft cushions, or carpeting, where ravers can recline and relax. The lighting is low and often there is soothing ambient music being played. People can have conversations here because it is possible to actually hear what is being said. It is a space where more intimate personal interactions can take place or people can just lie down and catnap. Most raves also have some sort of a bar area, where water is available, and often chai tea, so-called smart drinks with amino acids, other beverages, or even fruit or other solid foods.

The dance floor at a rave is configured in a very different spatial arrangement from that of a rock concert in that there is no stage with a performer as the main focal point of the crowd's attention. There is also no bank of speakers facing unidirectionally; instead, speakers are distributed equally throughout the space. Therefore, for the most part, the dancers' attention is focused primarily on the dance floor as active participants and cocreators.

"When you're on the dance floor, who you're looking at, if you're looking at anybody, is each other, and that's really a big difference. You're not watching the stage; you're looking at each other."[90] Sometimes, one focuses on friends and other dancers who are in close proximity, and certain kinds of movement interactions can develop. But to a large degree most of the dancers are deep within their own interior trance states, not directing their attention outward at all.

If there is any reliable external focal point, it is often the DJ, who has a special space for her equipment and records which is off to the side or slightly raised or even in a small, self-contained booth. Sometimes a significant percentage of the dancers are paying attention to the DJ, with their bodies facing in her direction. One key characteristic of the house and rave traditions is a high level of interactivity between the dancers and the DJ.

> Dance music is something that's really keeping that interaction with the DJ, as opposed to going to a rock concert and seeing someone up on stage performing. I think that's a very different interaction. . . . You do have a navigator, and I think a lot of people feel that with the DJ—the tribal connection to the shaman guiding you through and bringing you where you go to experience what you need to experience for your own personal thing.[91]

A good DJ pays close attention to the dancers to see how they are responding to the musical flow she is creating and where she can take them with that flow: "I'm basically interacting with the crowd and trying to feel where their energy is that night, where the room can go as a whole, how I can have the most bodies dancing at once, and experiencing the most ecstasy at any one time."[92] Likewise, the dancers are paying attention to the DJ, especially to let her know when she is in a good flow or creating a peak, often through vocal exclamations or bodily gesticulations.

This dance floor interaction naturally leads into the next section on the body in the house and rave subcultures, a subject I have already touched on in the section on religious experience. To briefly recapitulate, I mentioned the central importance of getting out of one's head and into one's body, how the rhythmic groove is key to that process, and that the groove can actually take over the body in a manner similar to possession. I discussed the ability to feel energies flowing through the body and how this allows one to connect both to other people and to a larger field. I talked about the power of MDMA to amplify this bodily dimension of the music to an incredible extent. I noted unusual bodily states such as synesthesia, bilocation, and out-of-body expansion into higher planes. I also introduced the theory that there is a relationship between type of music, its effect on different chakras, and corresponding feeling states and bodily experiences, speculating that techno music is capable of simultaneously stimulating centers along the entire vertical axis. All these points should make it abundantly clear that the body occupies a central position in the rave subculture, and that these distinctive modes of somatic experience are one of its primary ritual technologies.

More than any other subculture in this study, the rave subculture is about dancing, and dancing is the ritual activity which opens the doorway to whole universes of experience which are qualitatively different from our normal consciousness.

> It feels like it is coming through from this deep vast place. It feels endlessly creative, so creative and so beautiful that in a sense like I'm falling in love with myself, and not just my small personal self but a larger sense of self. That also spreads out to the room in the sense that other people are included in that. . . . It's as if I'm flowing with different bodies in this vibrational space and . . . we all know that we are at some very deep level of communion. . . . At those times, my sense is that I'm really glimpsing how spirit is.[93]

> I find everything inside of it. I can be anything. I can go anywhere. . . . The reason I find dancing is such a beautiful and deep experience is because it's completely letting go of, forgetting that you walk. I think it's a form of swimming or flying, it really is. It's a form of releasing in me. It's a form of entering a place that you can't [enter] just walking around and observing the normal everyday. And it's a form of going inside the music. It's a relationship that you have with the music. And, once you come in harmony, you're in bliss, really.[94]

Thus far, I have looked at the internal somatic experiential states of dance. But what do these movements look like from the outside? To begin with, the movements tend to vary with the subgenre of music and contextual factors. For example, one fairly universal movement form with standard rave techno music is what some ravers have called "directing traffic":

One thing actually I think is pretty common is what we call the "directing traffic," where you have really dramatic rhythmic gestures with your arms. There must be some weird correlation with how you feel when you're on Ecstasy and doing that stuff because everybody does it. . . . The open arms, the extended arms, is you're kind of opening yourself, you're moving rhythmically to the music.[95]

The house music subgenre, on the other hand, produced a different characteristic movement known as "jacking the body":

In the early Chicago house music scene, all the parties were in really tight spaces. So, people were jacking their bodies, the whole concept of "jack your body". . . . Jacking your body is all about . . . imitating sexual movements, you can take off your clothes, you're jacking yourself to the beat. And it's all in this really close environment where you are touching someone but you're not making love to them. And you're touching anybody around you. . . . And that was what a lot of the rhythm and motion was, in a really tight environment, where it was just like the sway of the ocean almost. That's how people danced. But now everyone has a lot more room in the raves, so they're like jumping around more, and it's a different type of trance.[96]

So one factor in these different movement forms is itself a spatial consideration—how much room there is to dance. Another factor is the rhythm and BPM, beats per minute.

When you have a very high BPM [135–150], that tends toward the techno genre, more ravey kind of stuff. And as you move down the BPM, you start moving into the house genre. . . . House runs in the 110 to 120 BPM range. . . . House music has a tendency to get you into this kind of pelvic trance thing, whereas techno or rave music tend to get you more into an upper body trance thing.[97]

The "jungle" subgenre, also known as "drum and bass," has a different characteristic movement: "There's definitely more footwork in dancing to jungle . . . more of a foot thing that goes on with jungle that you don't see in standard techno. . . . When you see people dance to jungle, there's definitely steps."[98] Again, one of the factors in this different movement has to do with the rhythm, which has less of the pounding "four on the floor" kick drum and more complex, multilayered polyrhythms: "If you listen to jungle, most of it, the bass line is half time from the drums, so it's usually 80 or 85 BPM for the actual perceived time of the music. . . . You hear these breakbeats that are totally sped up, you hear this crazy snare drum and cymbals and shakers going all over the place."[99] "What you do is dance half as fast you would normally dance to regular techno, even a quarter as fast, because you've only got a pulse in one place, you've got it one quarter of the time that you do in regular techno. And so actually you have to totally dance a different way."[100] Overall, then, as one raver put it: "Rave music comes in a thousand different flavors. And, depending on the scene you're in, it dictates the kind of dance you're going to see."[101]

The body is also organized according to a certain fashion and style aesthetic. As with the Deadheads, brightly colored psychedelic-patterned clothes are de rigueur, but the designs have more of a high-tech, cybernetic edge to them. Hairstyles also reflect this aesthetic, with brightly colored dyes, dreadlocks, and unusual shaved patterns quite commonplace. Ravers often have little high-tech accessories such as glow-in-the-dark wands or flashing lights. Actual modification of the body occurs in the form of tattoos and multiple body piercings. The pain involved in such procedures closely parallels the ordeal aspect of traditional initiation rites. In this regard, the phrase "future primitive" is a pretty accurate summation of a lot of the rave fashion aesthetic. There are some rave circles where this aesthetic is important: "Once you adopt the look of a raver, it definitely can open doors later. If you look like a raver, people are going to not be suspicious of you. They're going to tell you all kinds of crazy things."[102]

On the other hand, it is critical to note that there has always been a strong element of the rave subculture which has consciously devalued the importance of any particular fashion aesthetic and judging people based on external appearance. One veteran of the original raves in England said: "In Britain, it's so much to do about what you're wearing and how you're talking and who you know, etc., etc. It just wasn't like that at the raves. You could go in designer clothes or you could go in a T-shirt and nobody cared. It was very nonjudgmental."[103] This element has carried through to the present-day rave subculture in San Francisco: "I could dress the way I wanted, which was very casual, jeans and T-shirt."[104] So, in addition to the future primitive fashion aesthetic, there are also plenty of ravers dressed in nondescript clothing, as well as in many other eclectic styles.

This sense of inclusivity and unity-in-diversity is a hallmark of the social ethos of the rave subculture, a theme I touched on earlier, when we looked at how different races, classes, and ethnicities all came together as one on the dance floor, creating a sense of community and home. But this unity-in-diversity goes beyond people's backgrounds to their internal experience on the dance floor as well.

> The party may be common, and the vibe is common, and everybody's on the same dance floor, but if you pull all those people off the dance floor and ask each one of them individually exactly what they believe and what their cosmology is about God, you'd find every one of them have a different answer. . . . There's a little saying that "We are one in the dance," so if you get out on the dance floor, and you're all in that vibe, we suddenly become one regardless of cosmology. And what seems to be so transformative is that people aren't hung up on any particular dogma, like religion. It's more about sharing this spiritual nature that we all have with each other, and an understanding that we all do have it.[105]

"Here was a place for me to go and dance with other people, to share love with people who are openly giving love. I never ever found that anywhere else, at least not that amount of love and nurturing."[106]

The ability to share in this unguarded yet profound way with other people is a classic example of what Victor Turner has called "communitas," the spontaneous community which forms in the liminal stage of the ritual process outside the constraints of normal social roles.[107]

> So you're able to incorporate a lot of diversity. Maybe some people don't even have a high school education. Other people have three Ph.D.s. And they're all dancing together and dance is a great leveler in that we're all simply moving our bodies in a vibrational field. . . . What I've seen over time is that a community has developed that is very loving and heartful and very interconnected. . . . A community based on love and this ongoing spiritual experience, shared spiritual experience. . . . But that power of the group united in that way is something that we haven't seen much of on the planet. Mostly it's been led by a cult figure or some guru or something, but this is more of an organic process that's occurring. I think the potential is endless.[108]

This quotation shows how the type of communitas which occurs on the dance floor can serve as a model for an alternative to mainstream society. This is true for many ravers not just as a concept, but because the experience of communitas spills over into their day-to-day lives. I have already mentioned how some ravers' entire social context changes to the point where they are primarily socializing with other ravers. Many ravers live together in group households or large collective warehouses and participate in a variety of rave-influenced social activities.[109]

In the rave subculture, the word "tribal" is an important aspect of this alternative model of community:

> The dance music experience, ritual, and community are essential, especially when our culture is so devoid of that. . . . They want to be part of a tribe that isn't the dominant one. . . . They're going back to a much more communal, tribal way. It's because they're not happy the other way, they're not healthy the other way. . . . People who are part of this culture are willing to explore spirituality maybe that they weren't allowed to. But they really look toward tribal traditions.[110]

> Tribal is a dominant word because if you are in wonder with music that has rhythm and a number of you feel the rhythm and you move to the rhythm at the same time, it's a way of coming together and that's what being tribal and ritualistic is all about.[111]

> I felt like I really was part of some quasi-religious cult: The shaman-DJs in conjunction with nature's energy and the altered states of consciousness of the participants created a religious atmosphere. . . . The roots of raving are really intertwined with ageless tribal rituals of music, dance, trance, and the partaking of mind-expanding sacraments, where reaching a oneness with our inner nature links us to a oneness with the forces of nature around us and in each other. You don't have to watch many National Geographics to see the obvious similarities between parties such as these and the religious ceremonies of more "primitive" cultures. Ritualistic ravings will remain viable because it appeals to the sense of spirit in us that has been viable since the dawn of human consciousness. . . . On Sunday we were a tribe of the Universe, of the basic essence of life and energy, body and mind.[112]

Finally, in concluding this section, it is important to note that this idealistic communitarian impulse within the rave subculture also has a very strong global scope to it: "People are literally listening to it in every corner of the planet and it's wonderful because it unites a planet in a language that is beyond language. It really isn't about lyric music, it's about a beat, and everybody can dance, so that's what's really great about it. I think that's what gives it hope to unify people in a way that maybe hasn't happened before."[113] "Ultimately, on a larger scale, that's what this is all about—just bringing together all these different families, all these different people, and building it into something new and going somewhere else with it. That's always been my goal."[114]

Worldviews, Philosophies, and Codes for Living

The hallmark of most electronic dance music is the pounding, trance-inducing repetitiveness of the beat, coupled with the soaring visionary textures of the keyboards. The beat keeps one grounded in the body, while the harmonies and melodies transport one to higher realms, producing some of the incredible musicoreligious experiences I have already examined at length. Because of the profound nature of these experiences, members of the rave subculture, more than any of the other musical subcultures we are studying, articulate a philosophical perspective of the deep transformative power of music both at a personal and at a universal level.

> The feeling that music gave me was higher than anything. . . . And it's the only thing that links me to all my deepest feelings and connections and ideas. Things that words could never say, music can. Music can be anywhere, anytime, in that same form, and fill the entire atmosphere and bring what it needs to bring, and connect people. . . . To me, that's the ultimate bliss, is music. Everything is music. If we really said what we really wanted to say, if we really said everything that is our deepest feeling within our soul, we'd actually be singing to each other, I think. And I'm only here for that reason. I'm only here to see that. And I can't survive on anything else. That's the only thing that I hope for as far as the future goes. Nothing else can feed me life. As far as I'm concerned, I'm pretty much dead right now until that happens. That's the only thing that's going to bring me to life. And I thank God for music every day. Nothing else that can get me there, absolutely nothing.[115]

This philosophical perspective is true for dance as well, particularly because, in the rave subculture, dance is the primary means of entering deeply into the music. I repeat part of a quotation I used earlier to illustrate ths philosophy:

> It's a form of entering a place you can't [enter] just walking around and observing the normal everyday. And it's a form of going inside the music. It's a relationship that you have with the music. And, once you come in harmony, you're in bliss, really. . . . I think that every beautiful approach inside of life, every gesture can be a musical gesture. And it is, but it's so on the surface that we don't see it. . . . If you look at the leaves, the way they go in the wind, they're dancing! That's all they're doing, is dancing. It's all anything does that's natural. It's all dancing. . . . If we cut down the bullshit, we'd be dancing. That's what I see.[116]

The picture that emerges from this perspective is of a universe made up of music, where everything is dancing.

> We start to feel that the earth is dancing with us, and the trees and the wind and the sky. . . . One of the senses I get when I'm dancing, when I'm most in that flowing place, is that sense of "I am the Creator." . . . At those times, I'm really glimpsing how spirit is . . . that spirit is this endlessly moving, creating, playful energy that the dance has made very apparent to me.[117]

By participating in this dancing, musical universe by dancing to music themselves, ravers feel they can see the grand scheme of things and how they fit into it. "I got the big picture. I got a picture of the universe as a whole and my involvement in it. . . . I finally put it all together and I began to realize . . . exactly where I'm supposed to be."[118] "I felt like I would blend into the cosmic mind, this layer of energy that binds everything together. . . . Things really transformed in me. I really started feeling like I had a more noble purpose. . . . I realized what it was I wanted to do with my life."[119]

These realizations naturally create a momentum for making changes in one's life. "It definitely teaches a whole new perspective in terms of that what you do comes back to you and that you can make change."[120] For many ravers, this change translates into specific choices:

> I had to make decisions about how my life was going to be. . . . And the only person who could make them quite right was me and I had to do

that all for myself. . . . I think this is part of all the things that coalesced during this one time where I was just dancing, is that you're not independent, you're interdependent and you have to recognize what effects you're going to have on other people. But, at the same time, you have to be an active part of that chain. You can't just be sitting there being pushed and pulled around because you're not being truly part of it, you're going with the flow or whatever, you have to actually be an active part. And so I started realizing all of this, I've got to make my choices, I've got to do this, I've got to do that, and this is how I will live, I won't live scared.[121]

For other ravers, "it wasn't specifically like 'you have to do this.' . . . It was just like, there was no reason why this openness can't carry over to the rest of my life."[122] Or, to put it even more simply: "I could act like however I wanted to act."[123] There is an element of faith in this approach of completely being yourself and living your life accordingly, the sense that if you "just keep following your heart, do what you know is right, you're going to find enlightenment. You're going to find the pieces you need."[124] There is also an element of living one's life by a higher set of spiritual values. "People were more open-minded and spiritual and much more holistic. They were much more loving and caring."[125] The raves "actually, I think, make people kinder and gentler and more compassionate."[126]

Another central feature of the rave experience which provides a template for the worldview of this subculture is the sense of unity achieved through the music and the dance. "There was something unique about a rave and that unifying experience that helped you on that path to just feeling like you were part of the big whole."[127] "You see that it's all made up of goodness and love and life, and it's all part of one. . . . So music, it's just a reminder of that."[128] An important aspect of this unity which I have explored in detail is that it brings diverse groups together, cutting across ethnicity, class, education, race, gender, sexual orientation, nationality, age, and other socially constructed barriers. I showed that this is even true of diverse cosmologies as well. This unity, therefore, is not some naive or superficial idealism, because the rave subculture actually does incorporate diversity with an applied praxis of openness and inclusivity.

The rave philosophy which eventually became codified into PLUR (peace, love, unity, and respect) was thus an articulation of social relations that had already been attained to some degree. While there are certainly many cases where the rave subculture falls short of these ideals, nevertheless, over the course of more than ten years, in numerous countries, there is also an impressive track record of instances where they have been realized.

I have already touched on another aspect of this unity and the philosophy of PLUR, which is that many in the rave subculture consider it to be an alternative to the lifestyles and values of mainstream culture. "Tribal" is one term frequently used to describe this alternative. Another paradigm for this alternative links it to the New Age movement. And while these rave communities are local phenomena in which intimate ongoing face-to-face relationships are forged, at the same time there is also a strong global perspective:

> We want to be connected and this is our wire. Music is our link and always has been, but never in this way, never on the equal level between everything involved. I think it's the true music in the world, it's just going to feel like more of a together place. Closer connections, really. It's hard to specify because it's really large. . . . It will go anywhere and everywhere and it'll make just more and more connections and bring more things together to make them one. In reality, that's all we really map to, that's all we are, we're all one. I deeply believe in that and see it clearly and live it and breathe it. . . . And music is our link. This is what's going to work for us more and more in the future, more and more and multiplying every year. And it's going to move really fast.[129]

5

Stairway to Heaven, Highway to Hell

Heavy Metal and Metalheads

Not all popular music subcultures are based on the values of peace and love, a positive outlook on life, and the consciousness-expanding mindscape of the psychedelic experience, as are the Deadheads and the ravers. One of the most enduring, fanatical, and commercially successful popular music subcultures is that of heavy metal, and its stance is almost diametrically opposed to peace and love and a positive outlook on life. Heavy metal music and its adherents, known variously as headbangers or metalheads, exhibit some obvious and powerful religious dimensions, albeit with quite a different orientation from the subcultures we have already explored. Heavy metal's orientation is much more toward the dark side of life—alienation, chaos, violence, depression, anger, hate, power, powerlessness, and Satanism. Its sound reflects this darker orientation—extremely loud, primarily in minor keys and gothic-sounding Aeolian and Dorian modes, with distorted electric guitars, rough vocals, and pounding rhythm sections. It is a male-dominated domain that celebrates an aggressive, testosterone-based, biker-style masculinity (even heavy metal's female adherents tend to adopt this characteristically masculine stance).

For these and other reasons, heavy metal has been demonized and attacked from many sides—by fans of other rock music genres, by popular music critics, by right-wing moral crusaders, and by left-wing social activists. Despite such attacks, however, as heavy metal musicologist Robert Walser writes, "Heavy metal is perhaps the single most successful and enduring musical genre of the past thirty years."[1] Cultural sociologist Deena Weinstein puts it more colorfully, characterizing heavy metal as "the beast that refuses to die."[2] Thus, while heavy metal may cause certain people to respond with revulsion and disgust, it is clearly an important and significant popular music subculture not only in the lives of its fanatical adher-ents, but in the larger landscape of popular music in general. In order to understand how heavy metal came to occupy this strange position of being incredibly popular and intensely reviled at the same time, it will be useful to briefly sketch the historical and cultural background of its emergence as a distinct musical genre and subculture.

As in most popular music genres, there is some debate about its ori-gins. Most aficionados agree that heavy metal got its start in the late 1960s and early 1970s with the archetypal British heavy metal bands Led Zeppelin and Black Sabbath. But the roots of heavy metal go back further. One strong influence, in terms of attitude and fashion, was the motorcy-cle/biker subculture that emerged in the United States in the 1950s. Typi-fied by Marlon Brando in the movie *The Wild One,* this subculture joined a stance of youthful rebellion and outsider status to a black leather-clad style of masculinity. This style carried forward into the 1960s with the Hell's Angels motorcycle gang as the most visible representatives of the biker subculture. In the late 1960s, a particularly important point of in-tersection of biker subculture with rock music that was to become heavy metal was the Steppenwolf song *Born to Be Wild,* featured in the classic 1960s movie *Easy Rider.* This movie told the story of two hippie bikers' search for freedom and transcendence within the confines of a hostile and repressive mainstream America. The song itself became both a biker and hippie anthem and arguably contains the first use of the phrase "heavy metal" in its lyrical reference to "heavy metal thunder" to describe the biker experience.[3]

Both the song and the movie point to another major influence on heavy metal, both attitudinally and musically, namely, the psychedelic hippie counterculture of the 1960s. Musically, the blues-rock style of mid-1960s British bands like the Yardbirds, Cream, the Jeff Beck Group, and the Jimi Hendrix Experience laid the groundwork for the heavy metal sound. Interestingly, just as heavy metal musicians were to imitate blues-rock guitarists like Eric Clapton, Jimi Hendrix, Jeff Beck, and Jimmy Page, these guitarists were imitating classic African American bluesmen like Muddy Waters, Robert Johnson, Howlin' Wolf, and B. B. King. In fact, Walser argues that "a heavy metal genealogy ought to trace the music back to African-American blues," not just in terms of the obvi-ous blues-based musical structures, but thematically as well.[4] For exam-ple, he finds the roots of heavy metal's "occult concerns" in "Robert John-son's struggles with the Devil and Howlin' Wolf's meditations on the problem of evil."[5] I will return to these thematic concerns later. For now, I note the musical contribution of the mid-1960s blues-rock bands: a psychedelic-influenced sound that featured "heavy drums and bass, virtuosic distorted guitar, and a powerful vocal style that used screams and growls as signs of transgression and transcendence."[6] It also included the use of "power chords" and extended exploratory guitar solos.[7]

Attitudinally, heavy metal also has strong roots in the psychedelic 1960s hippie counterculture:

> Heavy metal carried forward the attitudes, values, and practices that characterized the Woodstock generation. It appropriated blue jeans, marijuana, and long hair. It put rock stars on pedestals, adopted a distrust of social authority, and held that music was a serious expression and that authenticity was an essential moral virtue of rock performers.[8]

However, as the 1960s counterculture splintered and declined in the late 1960s and early 1970s, some factions of youth turned away from an emphasis on peace, love, and utopian ideals. I have already discussed the importance of Woodstock and Altamont as key events in this process, and Altamont can be seen as the dark side of Woodstock. Altamont strongly foreshadows central heavy metal themes, and it is not simply coincidental that these violent events were instigated by a biker gang. In fact, Weinstein sees the incipient heavy metal subculture as arising from a combination of the hippie counterculture and the biker subculture, claiming that this new group

> found in the styles and hedonistic pursuits of the 1960s youth culture a means of justifying and enhancing their normal rebelliousness. . . . They adopted the long hairstyle, the casual dress, the drugs, and the psychedelic music of the prevailing youth culture, but they preserved their traditional machismo and romance with physical power, which were epitomized by the images of the outlaw biker gang. This hybrid youth subculture [was] a melding of hippie and biker.[9]

> Woodstock, the utopia of peaceful hedonism and community, and Altamont, the dystopia of macho violence, exemplify the polarity of the 1960s youth culture. The heavy metal subculture borrows from both of them, never affecting a genuine reconciliation of the utopian and dystopian oppositions, but creating, instead, a shifting bricolage of fash-

ion, ritual, and behavior, which includes elements of each partner in the binary opposition.[10]

Thus, Weinstein argues that the heavy metal subculture "is a legitimate offspring of the 1960s youth culture."[11]

As the late 1960s gave way to the early 1970s and the idealistic youth counterculture splintered into many pieces, heavy metal emerged as a distinct musical genre and subculture. The classic exponents of this emergent heavy metal sound and style were the British bands Led Zeppelin and Black Sabbath. Led Zeppelin was the brainchild of guitarist Jimmy Page, who was already famous for his blues-rock guitar work in the influential British band, the Yardbirds.[12] He teamed with vocalist Robert Plant to form the nucleus for his new band. Their early work was very blues and blues-rock influenced, including versions of classic Willie Dixon and Howlin' Wolf songs. Over time, however, their sound evolved into a unique identifiable style.[13]

> Led Zeppelin's sound was marked by speed and power, unusual rhythmic patterns, contrasting terraced dynamics, singer Robert Plant's wailing vocals, and guitarist Jimmy Page's heavily distorted crunch. Their songs were often built around thematic hooks called riffs, a practice derived from urban blues music and extended by British imitators. . . . In their lyrics and music, Led Zeppelin added mysticism to hard rock through evocations of the occult, the supernatural, Celtic legend and Eastern modality.[14]

This innovative sound and style struck a responsive chord with audiences, and Led Zeppelin attained increasing popularity which vaulted them to stardom. Their first album made the top ten of the record charts in Britain and the United States. Their second, third, and fourth albums all went to number one, and the band toured extensively to sold-out crowds in progressively larger venues. Onstage, the band's flamboyant stance came to embody the archetype for the heavy metal rock star style. Plant, with his long wild blond hair flying and shirt unbuttoned, sang with wild abandon, exuding a raw, untamed sexuality in his movements. Page was his counterpart on lead guitar, displaying intense distorted virtuosity with his extended solos, and also developing stylized gestures that came to be identified with heavy metal lead guitar. This dual leadership of singer and lead guitarist became the template for many heavy metal bands to follow. Offstage, the band became famous for their hedonistic lifestyle while on tour, consuming vast quantities of drugs and engaging in lurid sexual exploits with willing young female fans.[15]

With the release of their fourth album (sometimes known as *ZOSO*, a rough alphabetical translation of the runes which appear on the cover), Led Zeppelin firmly secured a preeminent place in the history of heavy metal and rock music in general. The song *Stairway to Heaven* was a huge hit and went on to become one of the most played songs in the history of radio. Even today, fledgling teenage guitarists still cut their teeth on this song, learning it as an initiation rite. *Stairway to Heaven* and the whole album abound in occult and mystical references, and both were seminal in linking heavy metal with a dark, ambiguous, vaguely spiritual sensibility.[16] Led Zeppelin continued to be one of the most influential, popular, and commercially successful rock bands throughout the 1970s and on into the early 1980s, even after the first wave of heavy metal had waned. The death of drummer John Bonham, however, proved to be a setback from which the band never fully recovered, and they never reformed except in rare temporary contexts. Nevertheless, their influence on rock in general, and heavy metal in particular, cannot be overestimated, not only musically but stylistically as well.

The other seminal band in the creation of the heavy metal genre was Black Sabbath, a group that came out of the working-class town of Birmingham, England. Musically, Black Sabbath's sound was denser, darker, slower, and less obviously virtuosic than Led Zeppelin's, "using dissonance, heavy riffs, and the mysterious whine of vocalist Ozzy Osbourne to evoke overtones of gothic horror."[17] Thematically, the group delved even more deeply into the dark side of life, blazing the trail for heavy metal's preoccupation with violence, destruction, depression, death, and Satanism. Their dark orientation is reflected in the band's name, taken from a Boris Karloff horror movie, which they chose in a deliberate attempt to subvert the hippie values of peace and love after initially calling themselves Earth.[18] This dark orientation is also reflected in the title of their classic 1970 album *Paranoid,* and early songs such as *Evil Woman, Electric Funeral, Sabbath Bloody Sabbath, War Pigs,* and *Iron Man.* Said guitarist Toni Iommi: "If we come across doomy and evil, it's just the way we feel."[19] While Black Sabbath did not attain the superstar status and megacommercial success of Led Zeppelin, they did develop their own devoted audience, sold millions of records, and toured productively in England and the United States. More importantly, they created a heavy metal sound and style that was to become at least as influential as that of Led Zeppelin, if not more. Even today, as a solo artist Ozzy Osbourne continues to be a popular heavy metal act, serving as a kind of elder statesperson of the genre.

Black Sabbath and Led Zeppelin broke ground for a host of other groups who followed their lead in establishing this new sound and style. Bands like AC/DC, Deep Purple, Judas Priest, Motorhead, the Scorpions, and a host of others all attained success in the 1970s.[20] They continued the loud, pounding, heavily distorted musical approach as well as the dark, violent, occult thematic orientation, which became the distinguishing features of an identifiable genre which rock music critics had begun to call "heavy metal."[21] On the thematic side, Jeffrey Arnett has written that "heavy metal songs are overwhelmingly dominated by themes and moods that express the ugly and unhappy side of life. The world according to heavy metal is nasty, brutish, dangerous, corrupt. Nothing escapes this taint, not even sex and love. Moreover, there is no prospect, no hope even, that things will ever be any better."[22] Arnett analyzed a hundred and fifteen heavy metal songs and found the most frequent themes, in descending order, to be: violence, angst, protest, myths/legends, hatred, the heavy metal life, Satan, sex, and love. The first three categories comprised over 80 percent of the sample. Weinstein, for her part, has divided heavy metal themes into two categories, Dionysian and chaotic. The first category is endemic to rock music in general, but the second, she argues, is specific to heavy metal and is strongly tied to religious imagery, references, and terminology.[23] These religious aspects are obvious in band names like Black Sabbath, Judas Priest, Armored Saint, and Grim Reaper, and in album titles like *Sacred Heart* (Dio), *Sin after Sin* (Judas Priest), *Heaven and Hell* (Black Sabbath), and *The Number of the Beast* (Iron Maiden). Religious iconography along these lines is often utilized in cover art, band logos (which are functionally equivalent to the Deadheads' stealie and the ravers' smiley face), and concert stage sets. I will return to consideration of these religious dimensions in a more detailed discussion later.

For now, I turn to the way these heavy metal themes are expressed on the musical side of the equation. Arnett comments that "these grim lyrical themes are reinforced by the music. The drums pound thunderously, the bass guitar rumbles like the growl of an angry beast, the lead guitar races madly as it piles dozens of notes into each measure, the vocalist shouts, screams, and roars with rage and agony. The combination of these sounds gives the music an apocalyptic quality."[24] As I noted at the outset of this section, heavy metal music is extremely loud, almost deafeningly so, and the songs are primarily in minor keys and gothic-sounding Aeolian and Dorian modes. Contrary to some critics' perception of heavy metal as a crude, primitive music, however, there is a high level of skilled musicianship among its practitioners, particularly the guitarists. The song structures can be quite complex, with many complicated changes, while virtuosic soloing ability on the guitar is highly valued.[25] Most metal bands, in fact, give the lead guitarist and vocalist equal emphasis, both in the music and onstage, underscoring the importance of the guitar.

It was also during the 1970s that the heavy metal audience began to coalesce as a distinct subculture with its own styles, activities, and social forms. To characterize this subculture in very broad general terms, the prototypical heavy metal fans are white, male, blue-collar teenagers.[26] Moreover, most of these adolescent males are also likely to feel an acute sense of unhappiness and alienation in their lives. Human development and family studies scholar Jeffrey Arnett conducted extensive interviews with more than one hundred self-proclaimed metal fans and found that "many of the adolescents who like heavy metal are unhappy with their family relationships, express negative attitudes toward school, and tend to be cynical about politics and religion. . . . The alienation that is characteristic of metalheads is striking."[27] This bleak view of the world and one's own life is what draws metalheads to heavy metal's dark, violent lyrics and music. It is not that they are violent criminals or practicing Satanists (although they may be), but that these dark themes accurately reflect the grim reality of their contemporary situation. In refusing to ignore the dark aspect of life by courageously acknowledging it, the heavy metal adherent sees himself as an outsider rebelling against the strictures of mainstream society.

Heavy metal fashions reflect and codify this rebellious stance. The characteristic heavy metal look consists of black T-shirt with band logo prominently displayed, boots, black leather or jean jacket, pins or rings, tattoos, and long hair.[28] The tattoos and long hair are particularly potent symbols of dedication to the subculture as the former is permanent and the latter not easily hidden, thus irrevocably setting the metalhead off from mainstream culture. Designs for the pins, rings, and tattoos tend to be icons like skulls, skeletons, snakes, dragons, daggers, and maces. There is also a strong element of leather and metal (that is, studs or chains) in heavy metal that borrows as much from S & M (sadomasochism) style as it does from biker fashion. These elements of heavy metal style have become so codified as to verge on being an identifiable uniform, thus creating a paradoxical and ironic tension between rebellion and the conformity of its mode of expression.

As with the Deadheads and the ravers, heavy metal adherents also have their totemic symbols. Each band has its own distinctive logo, usually incorporating the band name in some ornate typeface, often Teutonic or runic in design. Some logos, like that of AC/DC for example, are accompanied by icons of power like lightning, again strangely similar to the lightning in the Grateful Dead's "stealie."[29] These logos appear on album covers, T-shirts, pins, hats, patches, and tattoos, and they are displayed by metalheads as a badge of loyalty to their favorite band. Metalheads also have a distinctive movement style in which they vigorously shake their heads up and down in time to the beat while their long hair flies in accompaniment. This movement is the origin of the term "headbanger." There is also a characteristic gesture of thrusting one's arm in the air, often with the thumb and little finger extended, again in time to the music. In some of the more recent hardcore styles, like thrash and speed metal, there is slamdancing in the mosh pit in front of the stage, in which dancers deliberately bang into one another.[30] In terms of consciousness-altering substances, the drugs of choice among metalheads are beer, marijuana, and downers (usually Quaaludes), with beer occupying a place of prominence. Unlike the Deadhead and rave subcultures, psychedelics or other consciousness-expanding drugs are almost never taken. The primary objective of metalheads in using drugs is to "get wasted," to lose themselves in a chaotic catharsis.

In fact, in this regard, Arnett has characterized the basic orientation of metalheads as "sensation-seeking," an impulse which is particularly strong during the hormone-drenched period of adolescence:

> Part of the appeal of heavy metal for the metalheads is the astonishingly high level of volume and force that characterizes the music, particularly in the concert experience. Metalheads love the grinding, pounding sensations of the music, they love the *intensity* of it. . . . It is the ultimate in sheer skull-pounding, body-wracking, roaring sensation, and to them it is an ecstatic experience. The love of such intense sensations is . . . generally more acute during adolescence than at other stages of life. . . . Enjoyment of these types of experiences is a reflection of the personality trait of *sensation seeking*, which is the degree of *novelty* and *intensity* of sensation a person prefers.

... The musical combination of speed, roughness, and volume that is characteristic of the heavy metal sound makes for an orgy of auditory sensation, and the metalheads find it thrilling.[31]

Contrary to the perception of some of its detractors, argues Arnett, heavy metal does not cause violence. Rather, it deters it by allowing metalheads to satisfy their sensation-seeking impulse in heavy metal music. Metalheads are quite articulate on this point. "Sometimes I'm upset and I like to put on heavy metal. It kind of releases the aggression I feel. Instead of going out and getting all mad at somebody I can just drive along, put a tape in, and turn it up. It puts me in a better mood. It's a way to release some of your pressures, instead of going and starting a fight with somebody, you know?"[32] The live concert, attended by thousands of fellow male adolescent heavy metal fans and featuring extremely high levels of sonic volume and visual spectacle, is the preferred medium for this kind of release: "To me, at a concert, that's your time, it's your place, to release yourself from all the anxiety and troubles."[33] Slamdancing at the concert is a more extreme way of effecting this release. One headbanger described slamdancing as "mainly a release of aggression, tension, stress. Trying to get as wild as you can without killing yourself."[34]

If the concert attains a certain high level of intensity, this wildness goes beyond the mere release of tension into a more transcendent state of ecstasy, a hierophany:

At its best, when it realizes its ideal, it is an ecstatic experience, a celebration of heavy metal where the metal gods rule from stage as culture heroes. When the emotion reaches a peak ... the concert becomes an awesome experience. At the point of perfection, time stands still and one feels that one belongs to a higher reality, far away from the gray, everyday world. To see the dazed and confused, happily exhausted, faces of the crowd as it files out of the venue into the night; to hear the terse, whispered reviews—"Awesome, man," "That was really something!"—is to understand that a great heavy metal concert is not, or is not merely, an entertaining diversion. The fans have been "wasted," have been taken on a physical and emotional journey that leaves them satiated, satisfied, spent.[35]

Here is a strong parallel with religious experiences engendered in traditional ceremonial contexts. In the next sections of this chapter, I will offer a more detailed comparative analysis to bring out these religious and ritual dimensions in greater nuance. But for now I return to the chronological account of heavy metal's history.

Heavy metal went through a decline in popularity at the end of the 1970s, leading many critics to predict its demise and to characterize it as an outmoded "dinosaur." Such critics were forced to recant, however, when heavy metal enjoyed a resurgence in the 1980s, which saw a variety of metal bands attain huge mainstream success. In England, for example, from 1979 to 1981 there were so many new heavy metal bands, led by popular groups like Iron Maiden and Def Leppard, that the period became known as the New Wave of British Heavy Metal, or NWOBHM.[36] In the United States, Los Angeles emerged as a center of the new wave of heavy metal, with bands like Quiet Riot, Dokken, Motley Crue, and Ratt attaining prominence in the clubs and on the charts. Van Halen was another Los Angeles–based band that became hugely popular in the early 1980s, landing four albums in the top ten of the record charts. Although there is some debate as to whether the group was really heavy metal or simply hard rock, there was no denying Eddie Van Halen's virtuosity on guitar, with an innovative style that influenced a whole new generation of heavy metal and hard rock guitarists.

The big commercial breakthrough for heavy metal, however, came with Def Leppard's 1983 album *Pyromania,* which sold an unprecedented 9 million copies.[37] This album had much more of a catchy "pop" sensibility than early heavy metal, and the photogenic good looks of the band members also aided in its marketing, particularly on the newly influential music television station MTV. The success of *Pyromania* alerted the major record labels to the mainstream potential of heavy metal, and they flooded the market with metal bands, creating a commercial boom. From 1983 to 1984, heavy metal's share of all recordings sold in the United States increased from 8 percent to 20 percent.[38] This boom accelerated with the success of Bon Jovi's 1986 album *Slippery When Wet,* which sold 12 million copies, also on the strength of the band's "pop" sensibility and photogenic good looks.[39] By 1987, heavy metal had become enshrined in the mainstream of popular music, with huge album sales, concert tours, radio play, and MTV video rotation. With this mainstream success, the demographics of the heavy metal audience moved beyond its core of male teenagers. There were now older college-age fans, younger preteen fans, and most significantly, increasing numbers of female fans.[40]

As a result of its huge success, heavy metal began to experience growth pains, a development that led to a splintering into at least two camps, "lite" metal and "speed" or "thrash" metal. The former is a somewhat derogatory appellation given to the more "pop"-oriented, photogenic bands like Bon Jovi who attained chart success in the 1980s. These bands were also called "glam" metal, a reference to their emphasis on a glamorous image achieved through big hair, makeup, and flashy clothing (often spandex). They were the bands primarily responsible for helping heavy metal break through to a female audience, enjoying very high percentages of female fans.[41] However, they were also an anathema to the original, core heavy metal subculture, which saw them as "posers" selling out authentic heavy metal music and ideals for mainstream success.

These core metalheads, disgusted by the mainstreaming of metal, took their music and subculture in the opposite direction, back to the underground, with a harsher, more aggressive sound. This sound and style, which came to be known as "thrash" metal or "speed" metal, had a strong punk influence, which was evident in its faster tempos, underground sensibility, and the newly incorporated punk practice of slamdancing. Thrash metal bands like Metallica, Megadeth, and Slayer gained devoted followings in the club scenes of San Francisco and Los Angeles in the mid-to-late 1980s, where the subculture flourished outside the glare of mainstream media attention. Ironically, however, even these bands began to attain mainstream commercial success in the late 1980s and early 1990s, after lite metal had run its course of popularity and grunge had proven that "alternative" music could sell.[42]

As the popular music industry continued to gobble up innovative and rebellious metal bands and market them to the mainstream, co-opting their "alternative" stance in the process, newer metal bands continued to seek niches that had not yet been corrupted. Thus, in addition to the splitting of heavy metal into the "lite" metal and thrash metal camps, metal has also splintered into a number of smaller subgenres. One of these is death metal, featuring bands like Rigor Mortis and Post Mortem, whose songs focus on grisly violence and death. Another is white metal, sometimes known as Christian metal, whose most popular band is Stryper. White metal bands attempt to subvert the heavy metal paradigm by inserting a positive, Christian message into the music. On the other side of the spectrum, black metal, typified by bands like Vengeance and Mercyful Fate, has an exclusively Satanic-demonic orientation.[43] Here is a series of articulations of the pattern of subcultural innovation and mainstream appropriation I discussed earlier, using punk as the template. In the case of heavy metal, however, the pattern has repeated itself several times, as the mainstream appropriation has led to further subcultural innovation that in turn has resulted in further mainstream appropriation that in turn has spawned further subcultural innovation.

From the mid-1990s to the present day (2002), this process has continued apace. Established superstar metal bands from both the "lite" and thrash camps, as well as older "classic" heavy metal bands, continue to be popular, although not at the watershed levels of the 1980s. Niche metal subgenres also continue to thrive subculturally, and some have broken through to mainsteam popularity, such as metal-rap hybrid bands like Korn, Limp Bizkit, and Kid Rock. Metal remains one of the most enduring forms of rock music to this day, occupying a prominent place in the popular music market and attracting legions of new fans. And the current generation of metalheads does not lack for the devoted enthusiasm characteristic of the heavy metal subcultural tradition. As one metalhead puts it: "I listen to my music every single day. It's an addiction to me. If I go without it, I miss it."

It is not only the music, however, but an entire meaning system and way of looking at the world, a surrogate religiosity if you will, that explains the enduring power of heavy metal. Arnett summarizes:

> Metalheads find a crucial source of meaning in their involvement with heavy metal, not just from the way they resonate to the lyrics of the songs but from their admiration of the performers, from their participation in the collective ritual of the heavy metal concert, and from becoming part of a youth subculture that shares not merely music but a way of looking at the world. It may seem strange that adolescents would look to something like heavy metal music as a source of meaning, and it *is* strange, it is a reflection of the uniqueness of our time. Perhaps the most explicit and obvious source of meaning in most cultures is religious beliefs. . . . That heavy metal could also be one such source demonstrates that the human propensity for finding sources of meaning is highly flexible and that there is tremendous variability in the sorts of experiences and ideas and symbols that may serve this yearning.[44]

The Religious Experience

Although scholars like Arnett are able to clearly identify heavy metal as a source of religious meaning, the specifically spiritual and religious implications of the musical experience in heavy metal are often not so explicitly recognized and consciously articulated by metalheads. Nevertheless, there is strong evidence from their testimonials that metalheads do have such experiences, and that these experiences are also very powerful and life-changing. However, the qualitative tone and texture of their experiences are quite different from those of the Deadheads and ravers. In contradistinction to those subcultures' feelings of peace and love, heavy metal is characterized by its aggressive feel, which allows participants to release anger and tension. One metalhead said: "I always considered heavy metal as a great release of tension, a great way to get aggressions out. . . . I think the reason why there is a heavy metal is because it is an aggressive art form, it's an aggressive music, because it kind of fills a gap for people that have that gap that they need to fill."[45] Another concurred: "Metal is just more aggressive. It makes you just feel better. It's the only music I ever listened to that made you feel good, you know, you were happy. It was aggressive, yeah, it just feels good."[46]

This release of aggression through the music is particularly intense in the live concert experience. Here is a good description of how it works: "I found a release when I went to concerts. You know, I went in there angry. I did my moshing. I did my stage-diving. I did my screaming. I did my metal signs. I did my headbanging. I did everything to let out whatever was bothering me that day. When I walked out of that club, and I was straight, I felt great."[47] Thus, when one finds an outlet for one's anger and aggression through heavy metal music, the result is that it feels good.

> I think it brings up something in the unconscious. . . . There's things you're dealing with and you just kind of keep them all down as you're going through a normal day. You have to act like a normal person. You can't lose it all of a sudden. So, the adrenalin, it's more of a push on the unconscious just bringing things up, letting them get out there. . . . It's not blind. It's more of just an uplifting feel that you get. It's a release.[48]

For metalheads, the most universal phrase used to describe their musical experience is that of the "adrenalin rush": "I think that's the one thing about metal music that was appealing, was the adrenalin rush. . . . That was the big thing that I got from metal was the big adrenalin rush."[49] The adrenalin rush is an intense, high-energy experience. Metalheads often used the words "exciting" and "excitement" in talking about this experience. One metalhead said that "I get goosebumps at concerts" and that the "hair on the back of my neck will stand up."[50] The term "rush," in fact, is borrowed from the language of drug subcultures and describes the rapid and powerful effect that occurs when a drug first impacts one's nervous system. This analogy between the drug experience and the metal experience is commonly used by metalheads. As one aficionado put it: "It's like doing a drug. It's like a high."[51] Another metalhead talked about needing his "correct medication of adrenalin" and that, with metal music, his "medication was filled."[52]

Interestingly, although the drug analogy is widespread and many metalheads have an extensive history of drug use, several of my interviewees reported that they do not use drugs at all. One metalhead claimed that "I never did drugs at a concert," that he was "totally sober, always."[53] Another stated outright that "I'm straight. I don't even drink. I don't smoke. I don't even do caffeine, nothing."[54] While I would not go so far as to extrapolate from these statements and argue that they are representative of a high percentage of metalheads, they do suggest an interesting angle on the metal experience, which is that metal music can be a substitute for drugs. One metalhead suggested as much when he said: "It was filling a void that I guess drugs were a nice fill for me."[55] In this regard, it is important to point out that the druglike high engendered by heavy metal music does not lead to the same kind of loss of sense of self experienced by the Deadheads and ravers. On this topic, metalheads are quite clear: "I was always myself. I wasn't like a zombie. I mean, I wasn't mesmerized."[56] Another metalhead concurred: "I'm always who I am. I don't think I changed any."[57]

The initial experience of this type of adrenalin rush at a heavy metal concert is especially powerful. Time and again, metalheads recalled their first concert in terms that strongly parallel the conversion experience:

> When Judas Priest came on, they had the whole black leather image and the real high energy, you know, the floor attack was like thrash and speed metal. And we'd just be like totally blown away. You'd just go, "Oh my God, this is incredible." Like, that was really our thing. . . . That's the thing that really lit the fire underneath our asses. I really wanted to pursue it. You know, it was special.[58]

"I went and saw a band in a small club where they were standing two feet away. . . . I was floored. . . . That's where I built my definite structure on 'this is what it's all about' and it was a great night. I'll remember it for the rest of my life."[59] Usually, this type of initial experience becomes the entry point for full immersion into the heavy metal subculture, particularly in terms of going to concerts. "I started just going to shows once a week. . . . I started seeing anybody I could get my hands on, anybody I could hear about. . . . I loved going to concerts."[60]

Certainly, the music is the most powerful component of the concert experience, but the larger ethos of the elaborate stage show contributes to a multileveled, multisensory assault:

> You're very impressed by the whole scheme of things. . . . The whole ex-
> perience was a little bit more of an art form. . . . You'd go there and you'd
> get the whole experience and you're really impressed by the grandeur of
> it. . . . The music was one thing, but you also had the show on top of it
> that made a big impression on you. . . . It was pretty much the energy, the
> imagery, the total concept of what the music was about, you know, lyri-
> cally, visually, what they were trying to say as far as a complete package.[61]

There is a sense here of many dimensions of experience coming together in a synergistic way. The crowd also plays a big part in this synergy: "People are screaming the songs. People are singing along with the lyrics. People are into the music. No-holds-barred stage show. Elevated audience roar. . . . Just the volume, the vibe, the vibration, the words, the lyrics, everything must come together."[62]

And when everything comes together in this way, there is a unitive experience which even some metalheads have identified as religious:

> There's this completion. We have the same tie-in, which is you sink into
> this one thing and you become, you feel your humanity . . . and you're re-
> ally connected. . . . There's that one connection where you feel the whole
> thing come together. You feel the whole experience come together and
> there's nothing that can top it. It is like a religious experience. I imagine
> it's just like some people say that they're finding God.[63]

Some other interesting phenomena occur within this heavy metal concert peak which also parallel the religious experience. One aficionado talked about how "time stops. You know, when you have a good concert, you have no perception of time."[64] This timeless, eternal quality is a common characteristic of religious or mystical experiences. Another metalhead talked about feeling an energy in language that almost suggests a presence: "I think there was something there. There was an energy. And an energy would be a force, or another thing, or something. So, definitely, you could feel it. I think you could walk next to someone and feel the energy. I'm not into the holistic thing where you can touch their energy. But I think a group of people can generate something."[65] This account is the closest parallel I found in my interviews within the heavy metal subculture to a description of possession.

Although this same metalhead immediately added the disclaimer that "I never thought of it as something with higher meaning," he did go on to say that the concert experience impacted his life.[66] So, regardless of whether the experience is specifically seen as religious or not, it still has the same kind of spillover into day-to-day life that is present in the other subcultures. Another metalhead discussed his transformation in no uncertain terms:

> I let it shift me. . . . My life did shift, I would say, to the positive. Because, I mean, if I had kept going the way I was, I would either go and kill people or I would kill myself or both, at that point, because I was so angry. . . . I found a release when I went to concerts. The feeling was an arrangement of excitement, self-love. Being myself means I love myself. Being involved in the music brought me to other people who like that style of music, so there's my social life, my family. I found a love. . . . It made me a stronger person. It made the depression go away. . . . I would have to say it's a positive religion, what I believe in. . . . I live a pretty positive life.[67]

One would be hard-pressed to find a more positive transformation in any classic account of religious conversion.

Moreover, because his starting point was filled with anger and destructive rage, the distance this metalhead traveled to come to his "positive religion" was far greater than that of participants in other musical subcultures. The feeling tone of metalheads' musical experiences has a strong quality of psychological catharsis because they have to work through and release so much more negative emotion before they can arrive at the uplifting religious aspects of the experience. Therefore, in comparison to the experiential states of the other musical subcultures, there is a greater emphasis on the discharge of negative feelings and less conscious articulation of the positive spiritual qualities latent in these states. So even though the religious dimensions of the heavy metal experience function primarily at an unconscious level or are consciously articulated in a rudimentary fashion, nevertheless I think it is clear from the evidence that they are powerful and transformative.

I would like to conclude this section with the ruminations of one metalhead who explicitly saw the religious implications of heavy metal in his life and eloquently expressed them:

> I think that any kind of music ends up being a religious experience for the people involved in it. . . . There's a lot of religious symbolism, a lot of religious context brought into these art forms. . . . It's a way for us to interpret our lives. Music, to me, is an interpretation of what we're all about. . . . Whether playing music or going to a church, you always form your own god. . . . With religion, it's not tangible. . . . I think that music is more tangible. . . . It's an art form that you can take a listen to, you can go experience.[68]

The Ritual Dimension

Although the ritual dimensions of the heavy metal concert are not nearly as consciously articulated by metalheads as those in the Deadhead and rave subcultures, they are nevertheless quite powerful and pervasive, as several scholars have pointed out:

> The ideal heavy metal concert bears a striking resemblance to the celebrations, festivals, and ceremonies that characterize religions around the world. . . . Ideal metal concerts can be described as hierophanies in which something sacred is revealed. They are experienced as sacred, in contrast to the profane, everyday world. The sacred takes place in its own sacred time and place, where the *ens realissimum,* the greatest reality, is found.[69]

> A heavy metal concert can be seen as a substitute manhood ritual. . . . As in other manhood rituals, adolescent boys at a heavy metal concert are gathered together in one place and bound together by a common enthusiasm. As in other manhood rituals, high sensation is central and is delivered in part through the use of music. As in other manhood rituals, the response to this high sensation is active, visceral. . . . As in other manhood rituals, adolescent boys at a heavy metal concert subject themselves to an imposing physical test—in the case of the heavy metal concert, the

test is to withstand the immense volume of the music as well as the battering of bodies in the slamdancing pit—and are challenged not just to endure it but to glory in it.[70]

In this section, I will articulate these dimensions in more detail, using metalheads' own testimonials to demonstrate the temporal sequencing, spatial structuring, somatic organization, and social bonding that are distinguishing components of the ritual process.

The first aspect of temporal sequencing in a heavy metal concert often takes place well before the show itself. If the concert is by a nationally known band on a major record label, it is often part of a tour tied in to the release of an album, and so there is usually a push of publicity in the weeks preceding the show. This push may include heavy radio airplay of the album and its designated single, print and broadcast reviews of the album, interviews with band members, advertising in a variety of media, and various promotional activities like contests for free tickets or in-store record signings with band members. Similar but smaller-scale activities take place for less widely known, more underground bands in the underground equivalent of these media. All this contributes to a sense of anticipation which is already a powerful feeling for metalheads: "You'd get really psyched for it, especially if it was a good band. It was like, wow, you were just talking about it for weeks. . . . You have that feeling right before the show, you know? It's just, you're ready, you're ready, it's going to be exciting, it's an excitement."[71] "It was a beautiful feeling. It was anticipation. Who's going to be there? What's going to happen? What's not supposed to happen that's going to happen? Are they going to do four encores? You know, there's so much that goes through your head."[72]

Metalheads will make sure they dress in the appropriate heavy metal clothing and rendezvous with their friends to go to the show. Whether the concert is at a large arena, stadium, or a small club, one often has to wait in line to get in. This contributes further to the feeling of anticipation and also creates a context for socializing, which usually consists of discussions about the band, the music, and other concerts. This socializing will continue once inside, particularly as friends and acquaintances spot each other. Quite frequently, there is a less prominent opening band (or bands) and, unless they are exceptionally good, one does not focus one's attention on them in an undivided way. There are breaks between bands while musical equipment is broken down and set up. Finally, when the main band is ready to come on, there is a marked energy shift as the sense of anticipation and excitement reaches its peak. The lights are brought down to darkness, and some sort of musical theme is often played over the PA system as the band takes the stage. At this time, the crowd will press forward toward the stage in a surge, emitting a loud roar. Many bands begin their sets with a visual flourish of smoke and lights to enhance the initial rush of the music. Sometimes the lead singer will acknowledge the audience with a stock line like "Hello Seattle," which will draw an enthusiastic audience response. Then the musical set begins in earnest.

Like Grateful Dead concerts or raves, there are particular times in a heavy metal concert where one can expect a peak to occur. These peaks are an important part of the metal concert experience. The temporal sequence within the song itself usually follows a fairly standard structure of introduction, verse, chorus, verse, chorus, bridge, guitar solo (these two may be reversed), verse, chorus, conclusion (often a crescendo with repeated chorus and/or guitar solo). For different people, different parts of the song stimulate the peak. One metalhead, for example, said that "my favorite part of the song was always the chorus. That's what's supposed to be catchy about the song. That's supposed to be the hook."[73] Given that metalheads typically know the lyrics well enough to sing along, the chorus can be a particularly potent musical motto, especially with the added power of the repeated lyric.

For many others, however, it is the guitar which is most powerful. As one aficionado put it: "The guitar has just really changed the face of music. Incredible. It's that sound. People really respond to it."[74] Heavy metal guitar uses two kinds of musical mottoes which produce powerful effects. One is the power chord, which musicologist Robert Walser explains in more detail:

> If there is one feature that underpins the coherence of heavy metal as a genre, it is the power chord. Produced by playing the musical interval of a perfect fourth or fifth on a heavily amplified and distorted electric guitar, the power chord is used by all of the bands that are ever called heavy metal. . . . The power chord can be both percussive and rhythmic or indefinitely sustained; it is used both to articulate and to suspend time. It is a complex sound, made up of resultant tones and overtones, constantly renewed and energized by feedback. It is at once the musical basis of heavy metal and an apt metaphor for it, for musical articulation of power is the most important single factor in the experience of heavy metal. . . .

Its overdriven sound evokes excess and transgression but also stability, permanence, and harmony.[75]

In many ways, then, the power chord is the signature feature of a heavy metal song, and is certain to produce a powerful response anytime it is played, which is often.

The second musical motto of heavy metal guitar is the solo, in which the lead guitarist steps out from the simple power chord to a virtuoso progression of single note lines, usually improvised, which builds to a crescendo. "Metal guitar solos typically take the form of rhetorical outbursts, characterized by fast licks and soaring, amazing virtuosity that can create a sense of perfect freedom and omnipotence; they model escape from social constraints, extravagant individuality."[76] Various techniques are characteristically used—string-bending, distortion, trills, and tapping—which function as musical mottoes within the solo. The skilled sequencing of such techniques is almost certain to elicit a powerful response from the audience. Perhaps more than any other part of heavy metal music, then, the guitar solo is designed almost expressly for the purpose of raising the energy and bringing the song and the concert to a peak. In this regard, ever since Jimmy Page of Led Zeppelin, the lead guitarist has been regarded with awe and reverence as a kind of magician capable of taking the music to a high level.

In terms of the sequence of songs within a set, heavy metal bands tend to save the most popular and powerful songs for the end of the show so as to end on an energetic upward trajectory. These last songs are often more drawn out and intense, perhaps with longer, more extended guitar solos, repeated choruses where the audience may be invited to join in, and various musical and visual flourishes which build the energy of the whole night to a climax. The band leaves the stage in the midst of this peak and, if the climax is effective, the audience responds with thunderous applause and vocal appreciation. This will continue for several minutes until, inevitably, the band returns to the stage for an encore of one or several more songs. The same type of musical and energetic intensification characteristic of the climactic last part of the set is carried over into the encore and, ideally, amplified further into one last crescendo, after which the band departs triumphantly to the roar of the crowd.

Once a metalhead has experienced the epiphany of the live show and become part of the heavy metal subculture, he or she will probably begin attending concerts as frequently as possible: "I went to shows very frequently, as much as I could."[77] "I started seeing anybody I could get my hands on. I saw King Diamond, Candlemas, all these bands. I saw anybody I could hear about. . . . I saw Slayer. I saw Testament. I saw Iron Maiden. I loved Motley Crue. I pretty much saw everybody. I started just going to shows once a week, I'd be going somewhere."[78] Having this type of intense concert experience on a regular basis definitely has a spillover effect in a metalhead's day-to-day life, although perhaps not to the same degree as with Deadheads and ravers. As one metalhead put it: "It had repercussions on things I did later. And it always affected my life. You acted a certain way, and it was probably shaped somewhat by doing that."[79] And again, just as with the Deadheads and the ravers, this temporal rhythm of going to shows once a week invites comparisons to the weekly ritual practice of going to church:

> In a sense of a concert, it is kind of like going to sermon or something in a church and getting preached upon. Because no matter what you might say, the information you're getting from that person, they're speaking to you in a language, they're communicating on some basis, they're communicating with the music. You're listening, you're responding with your response. You do have that tie-in there.[80]

The spatial configurations of the heavy metal concert follow a pretty traditional stage show structure—the band onstage facing the audience, with amplifiers behind them. The lead singer is generally located center stage, and the lead guitarist tends to have a place of prominence as well. The venue can range from small, crowded clubs to large arenas and stadiums. With the bigger bands in the larger venues, there are often very elaborate staging elements, including digitally triggered lighting, huge decorative backdrops, various props, and costumes. These visual elements make an important contribution to the power of the concert experience.

> The staging and the light show definitely had to be a key to everything. Specifically, bands like Iron Maiden had a big backdrop, theatrical thing, that was part of the show as much as the costume. The music was one thing, but you also had the show on top of it, you know, that made a big impression on you because you got that feeling.[81]

The audience itself follows a traditional rock concert spatial configuration, with the more fanatical pressed up to the front so as to get as close as possible to the band. The mosh pit also tends to be toward the front of the audience and in the center, often taking the form of a large circle.

The ritual aspect of moshing in the pit naturally leads us to an examination of the body in heavy metal, its identifiable movement forms, dress, and somatic experiential states. To begin with, the first movement forms identified with heavy metal are headbanging (vigorously swinging one's head up and down to the music), arm thrusting, and air guitar (mimicking playing the guitar with one's hands): "In the earlier eighties, it was just headbanging. If you were an advanced headbanger, you'd pretend you had a guitar or bass in your hands and you'd headbang. Other forms of headbanging would be up front, to the stage, with your hand on the rail, or your hands extended out on the stage, and you'd headbang."[82] In the mid-eighties, with the advent of thrash and speed metal, the mosh pit began to appear at metal concerts: "There was this thing called the circular pit . . . and it was just called moshing or going around in a pleasant circle."[83] Initially, the activity of moshing, though a more aggressive movement form, was primarily noncontact, with distinctive body structuring and movement forms:

> It was swing your elbow back, definitely hands are clenched, you make like a rowboat with your arms and extend forward with your feet, and kick your heel on the floor, like a robot going out of control. A temper tantrum robot is what you kind of look like. And there was no physical contact between anybody in the whole mosh pit. . . . I did not get hurt. There were no elbows hitting me or teeth getting knocked out or anything. . . . It was another higher level of getting your aggressions out. Quicker.[84]

As moshing became more popular and the mosh pits more crowded, contact began to occur and the form began to resemble that of slamdancing.

> It was just something in the music that made you want to go and you wanted to run around and hit and run into people. I never saw it as too much violence . . . but it was more, just the music, all of a sudden, you had adrenalin going. . . . It was fun. It was not hurting anybody. You're just running around pretty much in a circle having a good time. . . . It's a release and you don't necessarily understand it but you have to kind of act upon it in some certain way and this seems how it manifests, in the mosh pit.[85]

I have already noted some of the characteristic fashions of heavy metal: black T-shirt with band logo, boots, black leather or jean jacket, pins or rings, tattoos, and long hair. One metalhead referred to this look as the "full-on metal uniform."[86]

> It became kind of a lifestyle, kind of a look. I remember at school, thinking everybody kind of picks their uniform and their associations that they have with people based upon their uniform, they're easy to untangle. It came to the point, like, we were the kids into black leather. I remember sitting in class with a spiked belt on and leather jacket, you know, that whole gimmick.[87]

"I had Levi jackets and I had a big patch over that . . . and the pins and I put the little spikes up on the collar, let my hair grow long."[88] In addition to the external fashions, there tend to be characteristic heavy metal body types as well.

> The metal subculture also fosters the ideal of a specific body type, even if that type is not achieved by the majority of the subculture's members. Muscle building is a hobby of many metal fans; their concentration on their arms creates the look of the idealized blue-collar worker. . . . The people who stand near the stage, moshing and slamdancing, are generally skinny, gangly. . . . Those off to the sides, headbanging or merely standing there, have far more muscle mass, and tend toward the beefy.[89]

These body types exemplify a certain rigidity and armoring which in turn reflect central heavy metal attitudes. One metalhead summed up these attitudes, describing one of his first experiences of being exposed to heavy metal when he saw Lemmy Kilminster and Motorhead on television: "He looks really big, powerful, nothing can penetrate him. He's loud. He's obnoxious. He stands his ground. Nothing can penetrate to hurt him emotionally. That's what I saw when I first saw this. And I went 'That's what I want to be.'"[90] To extend this point further and relate it to the larger discussion, I would add that nothing can penetrate *but* the high-volume sensory assault of heavy metal music and the intense adrenalin rush of slamming in the mosh pit.

This ideal of impenetrability is one key to understanding the kind of social bonding that takes place within the ritual context of the heavy metal concert. On the one hand, as I will explore further in the next section on philosophy and worldview, this impenetrability is one aspect of a larger theme of individualism which runs strongly through the heavy metal subculture. On the other hand, when individualistic metalheads go to concerts, they become part of a collective group which shares many common styles, values, and experiences, including that of individualism. One metalhead expounded on the paradoxical tensions of the dialectic relationship between these two polarities:

> When you're into heavy metal and it's not a mainstream art form, people look at you with long hair and earrings, whatever you want to say, it's kind of a different uniform, they think of you as kind of being ass backwards. One of the things it gives you is that you're just trying to be an individual. . . . But you end up being a collective in that genre of music. You associate with people. You actually are your own little society, your collective, even though to the mainstream you seem as an individual. You try to set yourself up as an individual, but I think that you really end up just associating with a group just like everybody else does.[91]

The heavy metal concert is the key ritual form which brings metalheads together as a community. First of all, most metalheads do not attend concerts alone, but "usually go in a pack." Then, once at the venue, "you automatically have something in common. . . . You're sharing something with all these different people."[92] As another metalhead put it: "There was a certain, you know, metal thing. There was a bond, a sense of belonging. . . . Being involved in the music brought me to other people who liked that style of music, so there's my social life. Family, my social life, my family. I found a love. I found attention. I found positive attention . . . when I went to concerts."[93] And the bonds that form in the ritual communitas of the concert tend to be powerful and long-lasting: "To this day, most of the friends that I have, you know, just my personal friends from work and people in the past, most of my friends are people I deal with in music that happen to like the same kind of music that I do."[94] Finally, there is also an aspect of social identity tied up in the music and the subculture: "Music tended to be what I would find my friends with. The people I would want to be with and hang out with would be people listening to the same music. . . . I wanted my friends to see me as cool. If you listened to heavy metal and you had all these things, you were cool, if you went to the concert. So, I think it was an identity thing."[95]

In the heavy metal subculture, then, although the ritual experience of communitas bonds metalheads together in a kind of community, it does not necessarily produce the same idealistic philosophies of social change as with the ravers. This is not only because of the strong individualistic bent of metalheads but also because of metal's concern with the dark side of life and its pessimistic outlook on the state of the world. In a classic Turnerian sense, heavy metal may in fact be a truer expression of communitas, in that the experience takes place primarily within the ritual context of the concert and the liminality of the antistructure phase. Once metalheads reemerge from this context into the structure of normal life, they understand that these two contexts are distinct and separate, and they do not suffer any delusions that their experience can somehow change the world.

However, this does not mean that the ritual experience of the concert does not change their *lives*. To repeat the words of a metalhead describing his first concert epiphany: "It was a great night. I'll remember it for the rest of my life. . . . That's where I built my definite structure on 'this is what it's all about.'"[96] This is a perfect testimonial to the transformative power of the ritual of the heavy metal concert.

Worldviews, Philosophies, and Codes for Living

> I think that there's definitely a philosophy. There's definitely a kind of mode that you're in. I mean, you definitely assume a certain lifestyle. You base your philosophy, base your opinions, base what you are as a person related to your music. I think there definitely is a tie-in there. I still base a lot of my opinions on how I feel within what my music will tie in, what it makes me feel as a person. I think the music has an enormous impact on people. I think it has more of an impact than we like to admit. It definitely had an impact on me.[97]

One of the reasons I have selected the particular musical subcultures in this study is because of the diversity and range of their religious expressions. There is definitely a stark contrast, for example, between ravers and metalheads that powerfully illustrates this diversity. Heavy metal's worldview, philosophy, and code for living are almost exactly the opposite of those of the rave subculture. Where ravers emphasize unity, metalheads emphasize individuality. Where ravers proclaim a message of peace and love, metalheads are fascinated with anger and death. Where ravers optimistically see their music as a force for positive social change, metalheads have a grim cynical view of the realpolitik of the world.

Despite these sharp contrasts, however, it would be a mistake to overlook certain important similarities. Both subcultures highly value the release they experience through their music. Both subcultures share a strong interest in non-Christian religions. And they also both share a powerful critique of mainstream culture, encouraging adherents to step outside the proscribed norms of how to live one's life. In this section, I will explore several of these themes in greater detail.

Earlier, I showed that heavy metal music tends to feature the lead singer and the lead guitarist (although usually not at the same time) and their highly individualized forms of expression. This musical approach is the template for an individualism that is the cornerstone of metal philosophy and its code for living. As one metalhead put it: "I think that heavy metal's message, as much as anything, is to do for yourself, have your own mind, do your own thinking. . . . I think there's a little bit more of a teaching there of being a little bit more of an individual."[98] Along these same lines, another metalhead remarked that "the vibe is more isolated. The vibe is more yourself. The vibe is individualism."[99] One aspect of this individualism is that of stepping outside the norms of mainstream society:

> One of the things that [metalheads] do is try to become more of an individual, try to separate themselves from things that seem normal to them. I think that a lot of the things they do to separate themselves are some bad things, you know, being involved in drugs, like assuming that kind of lifestyle. . . . I think that really relates to the kind of music that you play because the music has those sounds and there's a definite direction, lyrically based, that kind of fits in. For my lifestyle, I am more attracted to that, in that direction than I am in the other direction that I think you would consider just a normal life, you know, going to church, everything else. I think the music has definitely formed some religious opinions in myself in the sense that I always believed religion was a form of control and its basis was to control people and put their rules and regulations on people so that you would end up doing things in a certain way that higher up people in power want.[100]

Interestingly, this kind of individualistic nonacceptance of normative religious and social control is very strongly tied to one particular articulation of Satanism, that of Anton LaVey (or at least one metalhead's interpretation of LaVey):

> You know, a lot of people look at Satanism as being this form of evil, but Satanism in its purest teachings, say like Anton LaVey, say it's a belief in yourself. . . . Anton LaVey, in *The Satanic Bible,* his basic teaching, when you get through all the crap that's related to it, is to work for oneself only, which means pursue what you want to pursue for yourself at the expense of others, if that's what you need to do to make yourself happy.[101]

This interpretation of LaVey's Satanism can be considered a strong expression of individualism because it places such a high value on the individual and the pursuit of his or her agenda. In this stripped-down philosophical form, it can be appealing to a broad spectrum of metalheads who might otherwise view the Satanic posturing of metal bands as a metaphor at best or a marketing ploy at worst. Although the scholarship on heavy metal tends to downplay the Satanic element, the Satanic imagery in heavy metal is too pervasive to ignore.[102] While it may be true that most metalheads are not practicing Satanists, they are obviously drawn to Satanic imagery for other reasons. I would argue that these reasons include heavy metal's individualistic philosophy, its rebellion against normative authority, and its connection with the supernatural.

Of course, there are many metalheads who prefer not to discard "all the crap that's related to it," and take their Satanism far beyond a simple philosophy of doing for oneself. In this regard, there is quite a bit of confusion as to what Satanism really is and a number of different religious traditions and mythologies tend to be indiscriminately lumped together. One of these is the occult Western magical tradition, whose connection with heavy metal can be traced all the way back to Led Zeppelin. Lead guitarist Jimmy Page was rumored to have been a follower of the controversial British occult figure, Aleister Crowley, and to have indulged in shocking rituals within that tradition.[103] Certainly, there are many metalheads who practice these traditions. One metalhead talked about his involvement in this way: "It's just like a different belief, a different power. I'm into the occult, black magic. Just private rituals. Meditation, transchanneling, automatic writing—things like that. You just kind of channel your energy source."[104]

Another aspect of this polyglot mixture is a fascination with the religious symbolism, mythology, and practices of pre-Christian European folk traditions like the Vikings or the Druids. This fascination can also be traced back to Led Zeppelin, whose music, lyrics, and cover art contained numerous folk allusions. In the 1990s, this was updated in a much more extreme way with the emergence of death metal and black metal:

> Now the music has definitely taken on more of a violent aspect, taken on a little bit more of a tie-in with religion. And that's mostly because of death metal and black metal, which is pretty popular in Europe. Scandinavian countries like Sweden and Denmark, they're really into this black metal movement. And these guys really tie a lot of music into the religious aspect—anti-Christian, anti-Catholicism, anti-Judaism teachings. And they base a lot of their stuff on ancient folklore, stuff like the Viking gods. . . . These people take it really seriously. They've formed their own religious cults and stuff like that. And there's like the church burnings and murders.[105]

Frighteningly, death metal and black metal are a powerful example of a popular music subculture with obvious religious dimensions that provides a worldview, philosophy, and code for living which its adherents follow in a disturbingly literal manner. However, although these groups have taken the Satanic aspect to a horrifying extreme, no one would claim that this sector of heavy metal represents anything more than a tiny minority of metalheads.

Nevertheless, all this points to another major theme of the heavy metal worldview, which one metalhead has identified as a "fascination . . . with death and the dark side."[106] This fascination is evident in "its emphasis on the images of death, satanism, sexual aberration, dismemberment, and the grotesque."[107] There is also a strong element of chaos, which heavy metal sociologist Deena Weinstein has identified as

> a distinctive attribute of the genre. Chaos is here used to refer to the absence or destruction of relationships, which can run from confusion, through various forms of anomaly, conflict, and violence, to death. Respectable society tries to repress chaos. Heavy metal brings its images to the forefront, empowering them with its vitalizing sound. It stands against the pleasing illusions of normality, conjuring with the powers of the underworld and making them submit to the order of the music.[108]

Again, the template for this orientation is found within the music itself: the minor keys, the gothic modes, the distortion of the electric guitars, the screamed vocals, the assaultive rhythms. Yet, while the music expresses this worldview of darkness and chaos, there is also an element of empowerment contained within this expression. "Distortion functions as a sign of extreme power and intense expression by overflowing its channels and materializing the exceptional effort that produces it. . . . As one successful heavy metal producer puts it, 'Distortion gives that feeling of ultimate power.'"[109] Or to put it in nonacademic metalhead terms: "The real over-the-top either overboard Satanic or overboard distortion vocals or overboard eeriness to the music—that's when my medication was filled, as being 'yeah, this is good.'"[110]

This notion of "medication" being "filled" ties in with one final theme in this discussion of the heavy metal worldview, philosophy, and code for living, namely, the paradoxical notion that by releasing their anger through the music, metalheads can transmute the darkness into a positive outlook:

> You know, you've got those hormones going when you're fifteen or sixteen years old. It's great to release them somehow. Like, in the concert, people are in the pit slamming, listening to the music and banging your head, that's a great release of tension because, if you didn't have that, you'd end up getting into situations where you're a criminal, you commit crimes. That's why a lot of people think it pushes kids to do that, but I think it's actually the opposite. I think a lot of kids use it as a release.[111]

In this regard, the following quotation is worth repeating:

> The vibe is a relieving of an anger. . . . I found a release when I went to concerts. You know, I went in there angry. I did my moshing. I did my stage-diving. I did my screaming. I did my metal signs. I did my headbanging. When I walked out of that club, I felt great. . . . It made me a stronger person. It made the depression go away. . . . My life did shift, I would say, to the positive. Because if I had kept going the way I was, I would either go and kill people or I would kill myself or both, at that point, because I was so angry. . . . I live a pretty positive life. . . . I would have to say it's a positive religion, what I believe in.[112]

So although there is no sense of heavy metal as a force that can change the dark, chaotic nature of the world, there is definitely a sense of it being a force for positive change in the lives of metalheads. Using the Turnerian ritual sequence of structure-antistructure-structure, one can say that some metalheads are transformed in the ritual experience of antistructure and this enables them to return to mainstream society in a positive frame of mind. Deena Weinstein puts it another way:

> Heavy metal's insistence on bringing chaos to awareness is complex affirmation of power, of the power of the forces of disorder, of the power to confront those forces in the imagination, and of the power to transcend those forces in art. . . . That judgment is presented with all the power of the music behind it, fostering a sense that one is at least momentarily saved from despair by identifying with the truth of things.[113]

6

The Message
Rap Music and Hip-Hop Culture

Thus far in this study, I have been examining musical youth subcultures that are almost exclusively white. This is no coincidence; as I showed in chapter 2, once rhythm and blues had crossed over from its African American context to become rock and roll, its audience became primarily a white youth market. The great tradition of brilliant African American secular music that began with the blues, however, did not disappear with the advent of rock and roll. On the contrary, it continued to grow and evolve in a number of important directions, particularly with the great efflorescence of soul music in the 1960s and funk in the 1970s, each of which produced a myriad of hit records and stars.

But even though artists like the Supremes, James Brown, and others crossed over to attain popularity with white audiences in the rock era, the popular music market was, and still is, largely segregated. In other words, soul, funk, and other African American popular music genres which carried the blues tradition forward were almost exclusively the province of African Americans.[1] African Americans were the artists who created the music, and African Americans comprised the market that supported it. One result of this segregation, or "ghettoization," of the African American popular music market was that new styles and innovations occurred in a separate context cut off from white America. So, for example, while a musical genre like funk was hugely popular among African Americans in the 1970s, it barely made a dent in the white mainstream market. Thus, to a large degree the history of African American popular music in the rock era is a marginalized one, moving along a parallel track that rarely intersects with the white mainstream.

All this was to change, however, with rap, a new style of music that emerged in the South Bronx in the late 1970s. Rap music was just one component of a new street culture known as hip-hop, which also included graffiti and break dancing as important forms of expression. The music for rap was put together by DJs mixing stripped-down, bass-heavy, polyrhythmic beats from turntables and samplers, drawing heavily on its roots in soul, funk, and disco. This new style of sonic collage quickly became the sound track for street parties and "ghetto blasters" (portable tape players) throughout the Bronx. But the term "rap" actually refers to the rhyming poetry that the lead vocalist would improvise on the microphone in rhythm to the beats. Raps were spoken as well as sung, and they featured the rapper's prowess in turning a phrase. This prowess could take the form of innovative rhyming, rhythmic dexterity, boasting, humor, narrative storytelling, or even truth-telling and preaching. The subjects of the raps reflected the grim reality of young African Americans' life in the ghetto: racism, poverty, broken families, substandard housing, unemployment, violence, drugs, gangs, police brutality, arrests, incarceration, and a short life expectancy.

Before I follow rap's progression forward from its Bronx African American and Hispanic communities of origin to its breakthrough as a chart-topping national phenomenon, it will be useful to examine its ancestral roots in greater detail. Because it is firmly grounded in the unbroken tradition of African American secular music, rap displays more continuities with the characteristic features of this musical complex and its African origins than any of the other subcultures I have explored so far. Musically, one finds the centrality of rhythm as an organizing principle, with the elements of harmony and melody stripped down almost completely. The groove is generated from interlocking polyrhythms, and even though the constituent elements are sampled or prerecorded, they operate in the same way as live drumming. The interconnection between music and dance is also central, as is evident from the importance of break dancing in the early hip-hop subculture. Interestingly, the circular form of break dancing, and even some of its dance moves, show a striking similarity to African American musicoreligious dances like the ring shout, the Afro-Brazilian martial art Capoeira, and traditional West African dances.[2] Call and response is also a key feature of rap music, with the rapper's exhortations of "everybody say wo" punctuated by the audience's vocal response, or instructions to "put your hands in the air" followed by hand waving. These interactions demonstrate the participatory nature of the medium as well.

What is especially distinctive about rap music's continuities with West African and African American musical principles, however, is the rap itself and its prominent foregrounding of an oral mode of expression. The roots of the oral tradition can clearly be traced back to West Africa, not only in the coastal forest belt cultures like the Fon and the Yoruba, whom I have already discussed, but also in the Sahelian areas of modern Senegal, Gambia, Guinea, Mali, and Burkina Faso. These cultures, primarily Manding, but also Wolof and Peul, have a long and distinguished lineage of men's societies of court poets and musicians called *jalis,* also known as griots in the West, who maintained complex oral traditions of praise, lineage, and celebration. Many of the *jalis'* pieces were extremely long and had to be memorized, while others were improvised on the spot for the specific occasion. In either case, a high level of oral skill was required.[3] In these West African cultures, the spoken word was seen as potent and sacred, having the power to evoke that which was being spoken about. The supernatural power of the spoken word was called *nommo.*[4]

This emphasis on the potency of the spoken word and the oral tradition was to continue after the slave trade brought many West Africans to the Americas. During slave times, in the context of plantations especially, the oral tradition manifested itself in more secular forms such as the work song and the plantation tale (that is, Brer Rabbit or Stagger Lee), as well as in rhyming jokes and singing games. Yet, as African American scholars Albert Raboteau and Lawrence Levine have shown, these secular forms preserved elements of the sacred traditions in a way that allowed them to continue, albeit in a significantly transformed context.[5] The Christian church, as the only officially legitimized context for religious expression allowed to the slaves, was also an important repository for the oral tradition. This was particularly evident in the preaching style of African American ministers, who relied heavily on rhythm, rhyme, and the skillful use of other rhetorical techniques to raise energy and to give the message greater potency.

The oral tradition continued to evolve in the postemancipation era, becoming a significant component in both major forms of African American secular music—blues and jazz—not so much in the music itself as in the lingo of the subcultures. As African Americans moved from rural southern areas to northern cities, oral expression took the form of urban street talk, which had a more boastful, aggressive quality. Thus, practices like sounding, woofing, jiving, signifying, rapping, telling toasts, and playing the dozens were raised to high levels of prowess on the city streets in a friendly but competitive atmosphere. Some high-water marks of this oral artistry include the Harlem Renaissance and the poet Langston Hughes, black radio DJs in the 1940s and 1950s like Philadelphia's Jocko

Henderson, and the game of ritual insult called "the dozens," of which H. Rap Brown was the acknowledged master.[6] The Reverend Martin Luther King, Jr., captivated the nation in the 1960s with the visionary fervor of his preaching style, and Malcolm X also had a powerful oral style which strongly impacted the African American community in the 1960s. And the flamboyant and controversial boxing champion Muhammad Ali, widely idolized among African Americans, exposed the whole world to his boastful, humorous rhyming.

But perhaps the most important trailblazers for contemporary rap were the poet Gil Scott-Heron and the ensemble the Last Poets. Active during the late 1960s and early 1970s, the Last Poets were a group of black militant storytellers and poets who used the rhythms of conga drums to accompany their spoken political raps. Scott-Heron's brilliant work, including famous pieces like *The Revolution Will Not Be Televised* and *This Is Madness,* was innovative and influential not only on account of its marriage of spoken raps with rhythmic grooves, but also because of its unabashedly hard-hitting political message. Scott-Heron and the Last Poets were a source of inspiration for many key figures in the first generation of rappers, so much so that some consider them to be "the godfathers of message rap."[7]

Developments during the late 1960s and early 1970s strongly influenced rap from the musical side of the equation as well. Soul, funk, and even disco musics were to have a huge impact on the construction of rap music. Soul music, pioneered by the likes of Louis Jordan in the 1940s and Ray Charles in the late 1950s, fused two of the major strands of African American music, namely, gospel and rhythm and blues. Aretha Franklin, the daughter of a minister and revered as the queen of soul, started singing in gospel choirs. James Brown, the godfather of soul, had more of a rhythm and blues background. Between the two of them, they influenced a whole generation of African Americans who grew up in the 1960s to the sound of soul music. Soul music, with anthems like Brown's *Say It Loud I'm Black and I'm Proud,* was critical in helping to fuel the black power and black pride movements. The complex of associations of the word "soul" including the "unspeakable essence" referred to in chapter 2 by Keil, underscores its considerable religious dimensions.[8]

While it is beyond the scope of this work to go into a more detailed history of soul and the multitude of soul artists, it is important to note the centrality of Berry Gordy's Detroit record label Motown in bringing soul music to national prominence. Motown not only brought together an impressive array of recording artists and songwriters, and produced an unprecedented number of hit singles that crossed over to white America, but it also did so as an African American–owned and –run enterprise.[9] The explosion of African American musical creativity and commercial success in the 1960s was inseparable from the civil rights movement; both played a crucial role in empowering African Americans and helping them stake their claim to equal opportunity. As James Brown said: "Soul music and the civil rights movement went hand in hand, sort of grew up together."[10] In the latter part of the decade, soul music touched on a wide variety of other social issues affecting the African American community—the Vietnam War, economic hardship, urban degradation, the emerging underground drug culture, and racist political structures, to name the most important.[11]

During the 1960s, Brown's musical sound began to shift, and he is widely credited with giving birth to the style known as funk. This music was more strongly rhythmic than soul, with an emphasis on the first beat of the 4/4 signature, and powerful syncopations and accents provided by the vocals and the horns. The harmonies and melodies were stripped down to a minimum, the bass was foregrounded, and the polyrhythmic grooves made funk irresistible dance music. Brown's hits, like *Papa's Got a Brand New Bag* and *I Got You (I Feel Good)*, and his dynamic performances, which earned him the title "the hardest working man in showbiz," helped make funk the next big African American popular music.

However, it was George Clinton and his bands Funkadelic and Parliament that took funk to its fullest development. Not only did Clinton add his own quirky signature to funk with weird electronic colorings and humorous vocals, but he literally created an entire mythological system with his African American *Chocolate City* and the science-fiction-style interplanetary *Mothership*. These mythic themes were evident not only in Parliament's lyrics, but also in their cover art and especially in their elaborate stage shows, which featured a large ensemble dressed in outrageous spacesuit costumes and an enormous flying saucer. He also developed a notion of black nationhood that was perfectly expressed in the title of the 1978 album *One Nation Under a Groove*. Following Brown and Clinton's lead, a host of African American bands flooded the market with dance-oriented, groove-heavy funk music in the early- to mid-1970s, including artists such as Kool and the Gang; Earth, Wind, and Fire; Chic; and the adult Stevie Wonder.[12] One popular offshoot of funk was disco music, which took the polyrhythmic dance groove of funk and stripped it down to its basic 4/4 pulse for the dance clubs.[13]

Rap emerged out of this lineage of African American popular musics in the late 1970s. The influence of soul, funk, and disco can be clearly discerned in rap, particularly its early articulations. Soul's impact was evident not only musically but also in terms of thematic content, particularly its concern with social issues and black pride. Funk was the most influential musically, as the rhythmic grooves created by Brown and Clinton were widely sampled to form the foundation of countless rap songs. Rap musicologist Tricia Rose writes:

> The quality of sound found in these 1960s and 1970s soul and funk records [is] as important to hip hop's sound as the machines that deconstruct and reformulate them. . . . The sound of a James Brown or Parliament drum kick or bass line and the equipment that processed it then, as well as the equipment that processes it now, are all central to the way a rap record feels; central to rap's sonic force. . . . Soul and funk drum kicks—live or recorded—are almost always the musical glue that binds these samples together.[14]

In many important respects, then, rap music can be seen as an extension of soul and funk. Disco music's influence was evident in two of the first singles that helped bring rap music to a wider audience, the Sugarhill Gang's *Rapper's Delight* and Grandmaster Flash and the Furious Five's *The Message*, each of which featured raps laid over what were essentially reworked disco grooves. Soul and funk's influences, however, were deeper and longer lasting and can still be found in today's rap music, while the disco influences quickly faded.

There is one more important influence on rap music that must be mentioned in this discussion, and that is the blues. This influence is more social and cultural than musical, particularly in the ways in which both blues and rap artists have responded through their music to the repressive circumstances of African Americans' marginalized status in the United States. Just as the great bluesmen refused to take refuge in an otherworldly spirituality by squarely facing up to the harsh reality of their oppression, so too do today's rappers. Just as the great bluesmen sought whatever measure of this-worldly redemption could be achieved through embodied sexuality and the solidarity of the African American community, so too do today's rappers. Andre Craddock-Willis has characterized

188 | *The Message*

this aspect of rap, "which calls into question the existing social order, puts forth vision, and inspires critical engagement" as its "visionary, blues, or prophetic wing," and argues that it is "a profound extension of the . . . blues tradition."[15] I will elucidate these aspects in greater detail shortly.

Now that I have explored the African and African American roots of rap, I return to the survey of its cultural and historical development. As noted at the outset, rap originated in the tough neighborhoods of the South Bronx in the late 1970s as part of a larger hip-hop subculture that also featured graffiti and break dancing as major modes of expression. Hip-hop chronicler S. H. Fernando, Jr., has written:

> It is difficult to describe New York's South Bronx without invoking a host of clichés: "America's worst slum," "the epitome of urban failure," "a city of despair," "the ghetto of ghettos," "a blemish," "a cancer," "a constant re-minder of neglect." On a 1980 campaign visit, Ronald Reagan likened it to the firebombed German city of Dresden after World War II. Many res-idents . . . simply call it "Vietnam." To try to put such intense poverty, crime, and drug infestation into words may evoke extremes, but the South Bronx is an extreme place.
>
> In the midst of this overwhelming negativity and decay, an explosion of creativity—an earnest expression of the sufferers—rose above and conquered this seemingly insurmountable environment. . . . The cul-tural movement known as hip hop spread with the ferocity of the fires, proving that the South Bronx was not some land of the lost. The cur-rency of youth, hip hop transformed a ghetto into a gold mine—not tangibly, but in the spirit and pride it ignited in every kid who ever at-tended the early "jams."[16]

The music was to come first, with innovative DJs like Kool Herc and Afrika Bambaataa using their turntable mixing skills to create the first beat-driven sonic collages that form the foundation of rap music. These were originally dance mixes for neighborhood parties in houses, parks, and community centers. These pioneering hip-hop DJs were pushing the edges of musical composition in a parallel track to house music DJs of that time, drawing heavily on soul and funk recordings, but also using the new technologies of the cross-fade mixer, the sampler, and the drum ma-chine. Songs were segued seamlessly into each other for a continuous dance mix. At the same time, the breaks in each song and between songs—those places where the instrumentation would pull back to highlight the rhythm section—were emphasized and extended in a collage of peak dance beats. These became known as "break beats" or "b-beats," and DJ Kool Herc was their acknowledged master.[17]

The wild athletic dancing which accompanied these break beats became known as "break dancing," and the male break dancers became known as "break-boys" or "b-boys" for short. Hip-hop DJs also developed new skills on the turntables which strongly contributed to the distinctive rap sound. Foremost among these was "scratching," a technique in which the DJ used his hand to quickly spin the record back and forth under the needle, thus producing a quirky staccato rhythm. Another technique was "backspinning," in which the DJ isolated a short verbal or musical phrase on a record, and repeated it by quickly spinning back to the beginning. One of the early creators and masters of both the scratch and the backspin was Grandmaster Flash. Both these techniques produced cross-rhythms on one turntable while the other supplied the main groove, a clearly polyrhythmic approach to musical composition. Samplers also allowed DJs to bring a wide assortment of sound sources into their eclectic pastiches.

Tricia Rose has argued that the sonic architecture of rap music is based on the organizing principles of flow, layering, and rupture. Flow is the aspect of seamless segue and continuous mix. Layering refers to the aspect of sonic collage in which disparate musical snippets are layered one upon the other. Rupture refers to the breaks, that aspect that foregrounds disjunction and discontinuity. Rose goes on to suggest that these three organizing principles are also found in graffiti and break dancing, hip-hop's other major early forms of expression.[18]

Groundbreaking DJs like Kool Herc and Afrika Bambaataa each had his own group of neighborhood friends, known as their "crew" or "posse," who spent time with them and accompanied the DJs to all their jams. Rap music grew out of specific neighborhoods and local communities, each developing their own distinctive styles. Often, there were competitions between DJs and their crews for territory, both physical and sonic, in which DJs would exhibit their mixing prowess and b-boys would display their dance moves. These competitions closely paralleled the territoriality of street gangs, but with one notable difference—there was no violence. Instead, the crews channeled their competitive energies into artistic expression, choosing a creative outlet rather than a destructive one. Afrika Bambaataa was a pioneer in making explicit the connection between these hip-hop crews and a sense of African identity and spiritual pride. Bambaataa, whose name means "affectionate leader" in Zulu, called his crew "Zulu Nation," and created an extended family unified not only by hip-hop expression but also by a positive vision of African American community.[19]

The raps themselves began with the DJs calling out on microphones over the music to exhort the audience to dance harder, repeating phrases like "rock the house," "get down," or "you don't stop." But because DJ mixing is a demanding task requiring full concentration, soon they brought in friends to work the microphone full-time. Here again, DJ Kool Herc was an innovator, among the first to use an MC (microphone controller or master of ceremonies), his friend Coke La Rock.[20] The MCs not only gave the parties more of a live feel, but they also fulfilled the important task of crowd control, maintaining a positive feeling, and keeping potential violence at bay. Very quickly the MCs developed their own creative styles, using the latest slang and hippest rhymes to supplant the DJ as the focal point of the music.[21] The competitive aspect shifted over to the rappers as well, with the African American oral practices of boasting, toasting, woofing, and jiving taking root in the fertile ground of this new mode of expression, as MCs dueled on the microphone trying to show who was the best rhymer. Some of the early pioneers of hip-hop rapping were Grandmaster Flash and the Furious Five, Grand Wizard Theodore and the Fantastic Five, DJ Breakout and the Funky Four, the Treacherous Three, SoulSonic Force, and the Jazzy Five.

In these early days of rap, roughly 1974 to 1978, it was still primarily an underground party phenomenon. Crude bootleg tapes of DJ mixes and MC raps began to circulate and spread the music beyond the local neighborhoods. Toward the end of this period of time, rap began to penetrate into the clubs and become fashionable among a wider audience. Before long the first studio recordings of rap music were made and sowed the seeds for its breakthrough to commercial status and the mainstream. The first successful rap single was *Rapper's Delight* by the Sugar Hill Gang, a group put together by Sylvia Robinson of Sugar Hill Records in 1979. Lyrics like "With a hip, hop, the hipit, the hipidipit, hip, hop, hopit, you don't stop" (which popularized the term "hip-hop") were laid over what was essentially a reworking of Chic's disco hit *Good Times*. The song went on to sell over 2 million copies.[22]

This single had a huge impact, not only in demonstrating the commercial viability of rap, but also in influencing a new generation of African Americans who were hearing rap for the first time.[23] Three years later, another rap single released by Sugar Hill Records was to become even more influential. Grandmaster Flash and the Furious Five's *The Message,* featuring Melle Mel's rap on the harsh realities of urban street life, has been called "probably the one hit most responsible for creating what we now call hip-hop culture."[24] In 1983, this was followed by another important rap record, Afrika Bambaataa's innovative *Planet Rock,* which also became a hit. With the success of these three records, rap had quickly gone from an underground South Bronx phenomenon to a commercially viable musical one with the potential to cross over to the mainstream.

A new generation of rap artists capitalized on this crossover potential in the mid-1980s and brought rap music to national prominence. In particular, the rap group Run-DMC were instrumental in this process, as their incorporation of hard rock and heavy metal elements in their musical mix proved attractive to white teenagers. Their 1986 rap remake of 1970s iconic hard-rock group Aerosmith's song *Walk This Way* became the first number-one rap single and propelled their album *Raising Hell* to the top five, with more than 3 million copies sold.[25] The video for *Walk This Way,* featuring members of Aerosmith, was played frequently on MTV, breaking rap through to this important medium as well. Run-DMC toured nationally in large arenas, attracting huge integrated audiences. Articles on rap began to appear in bastions of mainstream journalism like the *New York Times* and *Time* magazine. Run-DMC's crossover paved the way for the commercial success of other rap artists like LL Cool J, Eric B. and Rahim, and Salt n' Pepa, one of the few prominent women rap groups.[26] At the same time, vibrant local rap subcultures emerged in other urban centers around the country like Miami, Boston, Houston, Oakland, and Los Angeles, each with their own distinctive sound and style.

This new generation of rap did not include the strong elements of break dancing and graffiti that had been such an important part of the original South Bronx subculture. It did, however, include many elements of style that have become hallmarks of hip-hop. Fashions that have endured include baseball caps, usually worn backward; expensive basketball shoes (Run-DMC started this trend with their untied Adidas); sweatshirts with hoods and other athletic clothes; and extremely baggy pants worn well below the waist. Hairstyles favored a close-cropped look with razor-cut sides and back, sometimes with messages or designs shaved in, and a variety of styles on top, as well as the shaved head. Language featured prominent use of the exclamation "yo!" stock phrases like "check it out" and "ya know what I'm saying," and buzzwords like "fresh," "fly," "dope," "phat," and "hype." There were also characteristic body postures and gestures, foremost of which was the rhythmic movement of the raised arm with two or three fingers and the hand bent down. Dancing at the shows consisted largely of bouncing up and down with the arms extended in this way, although club dancers added some more vigorous variations.

Like many other musical subcultures that crossed over to mainstream popularity, rap began to succumb to commercial appropriation, as white acts like the Beastie Boys and Vanilla Ice scored hit rap records. MTV, which had shut out African American videos in its early days, now catered to the rap market with its show *Yo! MTV Raps*. Corporate heavyweights like Coca Cola and McDonald's began to use sanitized rap music in their commercials. Boutiques and department stores now sold hip-hop style clothing to middle-class suburban white youth in malls across the country. Even the success of African American rappers like Oakland's MC Hammer, whose huge single *U Can't Touch This* propelled his album *Please Hammer Don't Hurt 'Em* to sales of six million, spawned a backlash among rap purists who took exception to its "pop" sensibility.

In contrast, a number of rap artists made a strong push in the opposite direction, toward a more hard-core musical sound and a more militant political message. Foremost among these was the New York rap group Public Enemy, whose 1988 album *It Takes a Nation of Millions to Hold Us Back* sold 1 million copies and whose 1990 album *Fear of a Black Planet* hit the top ten.[27] Public Enemy's angry social and political critique, nationalist message of black pride, and uncompromisingly black sound proved that rappers did not have to soften their stance to attain commercial success. KRS-One was another New York–based rapper who not only took a similar lyrical and musical approach in his work with Boogie Down Productions, but was also involved in community organizing with projects like the 1988 Stop the Violence and the 1991 H.E.A.L Yourself campaigns.[28] In combining an unflinching critique of contemporary black oppression with a visionary call to resistance and liberation, Public Enemy and KRS-One have continued and updated the musicoreligious legacy of the blues. As hip-hop scholar Angela Spence Nelson writes: "Public Enemy is *aware;* they clearly see the state of affairs in America and they tell the truth—the blues truth." She calls this truth-telling approach "combative spirituality," a uniquely African American religious sensibility that reflects the particularities and contradictions of their historical circumstances.[29]

The hard-core sound was to attain its greatest success, however, with the ascendancy of the Los Angeles area "gangsta" rap subculture in the late 1980s and early 1990s. The word "gangsta" is a reference to the centrality of gang activities among African American and Hispanic youth in Los Angeles, which includes some of the worst crime and violence in the country and an underground economy largely based on crack cocaine.[30] In areas like South Central Los Angeles, not only is gang violence like the drive-by shooting commonplace, but the panicked response of white authorities has resulted in the creation of a virtual police state with its own violent excesses. The brutal beating of Rodney King by Los Angeles police in March, 1991, the acquittal of the responsible officers, and the subsequent riots on the streets give an indication of the high level of hatred and tension in the area. It was out of this tableau of economic despair, gang violence, the crack epidemic, and police repression that gangsta rap emerged. The seminal gangsta group was N.W.A. (Niggaz with Attitude), whose 1988 album *Straight Outta Compton,* with its in-your-face attitude, funky West Coast sound, and gritty tales of violent gang life formed the template for the gangsta style. Originally released on the local independent label Ruthless Records, this album went on to sell over 2 million copies and thrust gangsta rap into national prominence.[31]

For many who had had no previous exposure to the harsh realities of places like South Central Los Angeles, this album was a shocking revelation. As LA hip-hop chronicler Brian Cross notes, "N.W.A. placed themselves on the hip hop map with authenticity, capturing the aggression and anger of the streets of south central in their intonation and timbre."[32] Such authenticity has a spiritual as well as a commercial function. Angela Spence Nelson writes:

> Contemporary rappers, like early bluespeople, are responding to the "burden of freedom," in part by relaying portrayals of reality to their audiences through their personal experiences. They also relay positive portrayals of themselves as a means of affirming their personhood (and vicariously the personhood of their people) in a world that is constantly telling them they are nobodies.[33]

Certainly, there are many African Americans who feel that a positive portrayal of the gangsta lifestyle sends the wrong message to young people. But the ongoing controversy over positive or negative images misses the larger spiritual and religious question of transcendence, an issue that Cornel West has articulated:

> Black rap music is . . . a class-specific form of the Afro-American spiritual-blues impulse which mutes, and often eliminates, the utopian dimension of this impulse. . . . Certain versions of this music radically call into question the roots of this impulse, the roots of transcendence and opposition. Without a utopian dimension—without transcendence from or opposition to evil—there can be no struggle, no hope, no meaning.[34]

Thus, some critics consider this debate over rap music a struggle for the heart and soul of the African American musicoreligious tradition:

> At its best, African American rap music can be a profound extension of the prophetic or blues tradition and the legacy of heroism within the Afro-American experience. At its worst, rap music can disregard its sources and be an expression of the worst type of norms enforced by contemporary culture. Rap music must consider what its intentions are, understand its larger musical tradition, and fulfill the liberating potential in its form.[35]

As I will show, my fieldwork in the Oakland underground indicates that the prophetic, utopian, transcendental element within contemporary rap is not only very strong but, according to the rappers I interviewed, constitutes the core of the hip-hop tradition.

For now, it is important to point out that the forms of rap show clear continuities with the African American musicoreligious tradition. This is true in structural elements such as the centrality of the groove, polyrhythmic texture, foregrounded orality, vocal styles, call and response, audience participation, and dance, and also in its essentially celebratory ritual form. As West notes, "The celebratory form of black rap music, especially its upbeat African rhythms, contains utopian aspirations. . . . The form has basically a ritualistic function: music for cathartic release at the black rituals of parties and dances."[36] This has been true of rap music since its origins as the sound for neighborhood parties in the South Bronx, and it continues today in parties, clubs, and arenas around the country where the hip-hop community gathers in musical celebration.

N.W.A.'s stylistic and commercial breakthrough opened the door for a number of other Los Angeles area gangsta rap artists to attain success, including Ice-T, Snoop Doggy Dogg, and the original N.W.A. members Ice Cube and Dr. Dre as solo artists. Gangsta rap has also penetrated the mainstream through other media, not only through a major presence on MTV, but with movies like *New Jack City, Boyz in the Hood, Juice,* and *Menace II Society* by African American filmmakers like John Singleton, Mario Van Peebles, and the Hughes Brothers. For better or for worse, controversy and violence have also thrust gangsta rap into the national consciousness, particularly with the shooting deaths of rappers Tupac Shakur and the Notorious B.I.G., also known as Christopher Wallace.[37] More recently, a large number of rap artists with a wide variety of styles and messages have attained mainstream success: Lauryn Hill, Puff Daddy, Wu-Tang Clan, DMX, Master P, Jay-Z, Mase, and Eminem, to mention only the most obvious.

Despite its dismissal by critics since its inception, rap music has showed remarkable staying power, enjoyed great popularity, and exerted a large cultural influence not only in the United States, but all around the world. For the young African Americans who comprise its core subculture, as well as its other devoted adherents, white suburbanites and dispossessed minorities alike, it is the primary means through which they orient themselves to the world. Like the Deadheads, the ravers, and the metalheads, the musical subculture of rap functions in the same way for rappers as a religion, providing a meaning system, a sense of community, a ritual form, and, in the heat of the music, a religious experience.

The Religious Experience

One of the first things that stands out when I look at the interviews I conducted with members of this subculture is that hip-hop became part of participants' lives at a relatively early age, especially compared to the experiences of members of the other music subcultures in this study. Most of the hip-hop aficionados mentioned junior high school or even earlier as the time of their first exposure to the music and culture: "I started listening to it and hearing it all the way back in junior high school."[38] "Since about the age of ten, I've been actually into the music, doing the music, and trying to achieve the music."[39] "I've always been into hip-hop ever since I can remember."[40] "Around the seventh, eighth grade is when I first embraced hip-hop, found out what that was all about. And I've been connected with it ever since."[41] "I really started going to hip-hop kind of stuff around eighth grade or ninth grade."[42]

Interestingly, even though they were very young at the time of their initial exposure, the experiences they had were profound and life-changing, often with a strong flavor of conversion. Here are two accounts:

> Somebody gave it to me. It was actually my cousin Paula. I'll never forget the day. One morning, she woke me up. She was all "Listen. Come here. This is rap." And she let me hear Electric Kingdom and, the minute I heard it, it was just like it took over my life. . . . I just knew, straight up. It changed my whole life. After that, I lived my life through it.[43]

"As soon as I heard my first rap song, I was really into it. . . . It really shook me. . . . I always carried that with me. I really got grabbed by the rap music."[44] These kinds of experiences were usually followed by a total immersion in rap music and the hip-hop subculture.

Often, there was a discernible progression to that immersion, one which involved moving sequentially through the different forms of expression of hip-hop culture. Several rappers mentioned break dancing as the first form they got involved with and learned to master. "I remember the first thing I was into was dancing, break dancing."[45] "Before I started rhyming, I started to dance first. . . . We would have these little dance groups we would make up. . . . On Fridays, we would all hook up, like five or six of us, like get in the living room and turn on the music and dance. Then, on Saturday, we'd go to the club. It was cool."[46] "My first introduction to the music was the dance. And I used to love to dance to the sound. It used to get me really excited. . . . We used to make it a point to go dance and start breakoffs. It was just the thing to do. It was beautiful because a lot of people were good at it. . . . Everywhere we went, we'd start breaking."[47]

Just as with the ravers, hip-hop dancing creates a deeper experience of the music and leads into intensified bodily states: "I was taking the energy of the beat and then just amplifying it through my movement. Like making the music almost seem like it was coming more intensely by seeing what I'm doing, or by me feeling what I'm doing, it seemed like the music became more intense."[48] These intensified states have spiritual implications, some of which strongly echo the possession experience.

> What I felt as a kid was strictly vibration, rhythm, and that music has a rhythm that just called my soul. It would make my soul jump out of my

body, literally, and I'd have to move to it. . . . It really calls me, it really does. . . . Sometimes my body does things I can't even control and it's like I'm not even here. . . . It's just a link. Something touches you one day, just sparks your whole consciousness, and shows your body you can. Time and space is all about the rhythm in your body. It's hard to understand when you're a kid. . . . I mean, now that I'm older, I can put in perspective what I felt as a young kid. . . . It's the ancients. It's definitely the ancients.[49]

This same rapper also talked about how this profound dance experience has now become integrated into his everyday life: "It's in my day-to-day every day. . . . It's not different from my life. It's what I do. It's just what's in life. Every day I'm hearing it. I'm always shaking like that."[50] This is a powerful testimonial not only to the music's bodily capacity to link people to their spiritual heritage but also to bring this connection into day-to-day life.

In this sequence of engagement with forms of hip-hop expression, the next step after break dancing is often to become involved with DJ mixing. Sometimes this begins almost as a calling. "I saw two turntables and I didn't even know what that was but right when I saw it, I knew I wanted to know what it was about."[51] While many DJs teach themselves the art of mixing through long hours alone in a room with their turntables and cross-fade mixer, one aficionado was fortunate enough to find someone who could teach him the skills involved and he went through an apprenticeship that became a kind of initiation rite.

> He had to teach me and I had to go through this whole ritual, and he would teach me the skills. Like, he would make a tape. I would sit there for hours and hours and he would work on it and, at the end, "All right, Malcolm, come in and do the last thing." Or we would do parties and I would carry a lot of the equipment. It was like an initiation. And then, at the end, I would work there. The party, four hours, one in the morning, sitting next to the equipment, waiting. And, at one, he'd be, "Okay, I'm going to adjourn now. Here." And my fifteen minutes in and then it would be over.[52]

One of the reasons this kind of intensive training is necessary is because the hip-hop DJ draws from a wide range of musics, yet must mix them together seamlessly into an integrated whole with a continuous beat. "You have orchestras at your command. . . . A DJ is a musician because he masters the sounds and rhythms that go together and holds a roomful of those things."[53]

In this regard, the DJ is not only the musician but the navigator as well, the one with the power to set the direction for the collective musical journey. "That's what it's all about to me, setting the vibe. I learned early on the power that I had. I could start a fight in five minutes if I wanted to. I could break one up. I could have people go home and have sex. I could do anything and I started to understand what that was all about. It's really powerful."[54] And just as with the rave DJs, there is a conscious recognition that this power is spiritual: "This is where I definitely feel like I have a power that is infinite. That's where I tap into something that is all time, been here before me and it'll be here after me."[55]

The third form of hip-hop expression that aficionados become involved with is rapping. As with mixing, often one feels called to start rapping: "I couldn't not rhyme. I couldn't not do it. So I just started rhyming, writing my rhymes every day."[56] Rappers use the word flow to describe the process of rapping and the experiential state one enters when the rhymes are just coming through: "Being able to speak nonstop, on rhythm, at a fast pace, cohesive, forgetting about everything and being able to drop back into just right here, and being able to let those words come out in a flow, make sense, and be heard."[57] When rappers are in this flow, there is some sense of being connected to *nommo*, the West African term for the spiritual power of words: "I listen to some MCs, like even Tupac, his flow and the way he does his words is so easy, it's real a long time ago to me. Some people I hear and it sounds like a long time ago. . . . I'm starting to see the effects of it, just barely, right now. These are words of power, like certain words, like positive suggestions of just certain frequencies of sounds."[58] And when one experiences the power of that flow, it has a transforming effect in one's day-to-day life. "When I was feeling that flow, I could say that it really gave me . . . a purpose. That was my flow, directly. . . . I always knew what I was here for."[59]

In addition to the flow aspect of rapping, there is also another central component, which is truth-telling. In this regard, flow can be understood as the form and truth-telling the content or, as some rappers put it, the message. "It's very important to speak about how you really feel about something. . . . This is one of the first times in music where you can really say what's going on. . . . It's very honest. There's a lot of references to whatever's happening right now."[60] Rapper Chuck D of Public Enemy called rap the CNN of black urban youth because it provides information for them about what's going on in their world.[61] Another rapper confirmed this function:

> Hip-hop music is always speaking to me, the lyrics. Especially in the late
> eighties, there were some real conscious things in hip-hop, and that was
> what was offsetting high school education, mainstream society, with all
> the information I was getting from KRS One and Public Enemy and X-
> Clan, all those groups. So I just needed it at the time. We all needed it.
> They were speaking to me and educating me. I know they were. And I felt
> it. I needed it. It came at the right time.[62]

There is a deeper spiritual aspect to this truth-telling which goes beyond simply educating and informing.

> One thing about rapping is always that you've got to come with your
> heart, who you are. And whatever that be, whether it be LA gangster
> music or New York quote unquote righteous music or antigovernment
> music, whatever. It's all about coming from your heart, saying what you
> believe in. Whether it was Ice Cube or Chuck D, it was just the spirit
> there. That's what was attractive, beyond the word itself, because you
> knew it was coming from the heart, for real.[63]

In coming from the heart and speaking their truth, rappers are also speaking for their larger community. As one aficionado put it: "There is a culture of people who feel the voices of [rappers] represent them.[64] Represent is a word widely used by rappers to describe their function. Some take the implications of this even further and make the connection to the role of the priest and the griot:

> MCs are like the priests or the pastors of the people right now because a
> lot of children don't listen to their parents any more. A lot of kids don't
> go to church any more. So MCs have been elevated to this recognizable
> status that's easily accessible. It's our duty as MCs to try to bring morals
> to the community, just like the griots in Africa brought morals and they
> try to pass down things that were basic . . . and that's like the role of
> MCs today.[65]

Certain threads emerge from this cursory examination of the experiential dimensions of what one rapper has called the "trinity" of dancing, mixing, and rapping.[66] One of these is the sense that these forms of expression are part of a whole culture. "Hip-hop is not the music; hip-hop is the culture. The music is rap music. . . . And those fuller aspects of hip-hop are graffiti, break dancing, MCing, and DJing."[67] "On a spiritual level, I think what now I know as hip-hop culture and respect as such [consists of] the graffiti, the dress, the language, the art, the people, the mind-set that's the commonality of thought."[68] So, immersing oneself in hip-hop culture creates connections and links to many different vital aspects of one's life: "It's just been my link to everything—my own spirituality, my self-knowledge, and music also. . . . Everywhere I go, everywhere I grow, starts with hip-hop."[69] "It linked me to everything—my future, my past, my family."[70]

"The past," in this context, is not one's personal past, but hip-hop culture's roots in African American and West African cultures and their religious traditions. This can be seen in the references to "the ancients," the "something that is all time" and has "been here before me," and the feeling of "a long time ago." This connection is consciously recognized and articulated by many in the hip-hop culture.

> We've been rapping forever. You know, there's nothing new under the sun. The griots were doing the same, the storytellers, oral tradition people. . . . And the drum's also the center of it. You can't have it without the drum. And now hip-hop is experimenting, trying new things, but really the beat is what's always [been there]. It's the drums, just like drums in any form. That's definitely African.[71]

> Always our people are going to find their culture. They're going to connect with our old culture no matter how much you try to take it from us. So, hip-hop is the first thing, the sign that we're here again. Our people are back and we're always going to be here and we don't forget. And everything we went through, all the slavery, all the conquering, and all that, we're still here. Our ancestors are still calling. And the breakbeats we used in the beginning are still from God, still ally your soul.[72]

One veteran who said that hip-hop was "obviously grounded and rooted in African traditions" talked about his early experiences at hip-hop block parties in New York: "In those block parties, you'd have drumming circles where you'd have the Latin guys playing congas and doing salsa chants that now I understand were Cuban religious [Santeria] chants."[73] So for him the African religious connection was there from the beginning, both implicitly and explicitly, and it continues through to today. "I have to be true to not just the music and the musics that I'm bringing in, but now there's this religious thing. Santeria is a religion, so I can't water that down. I'm not here to rip off Santeria and sell out and make a record. I'm not in it for that. I'm trying to reach another level of enlightenment."[74]

However, the African connection does not need to be present for aficionados to understand the spiritual dimensions of hip-hop culture and eloquently articulate them. "Hip-hop culture is a spirituality. And it's everything I can think of. Anything I am that I can do, that happens in this world, it's like that music, it's the culture. . . . It just gives you a purpose. It shows you why you're here. . . . It knows that I know God every day."[75] "I think of hip-hop culture as a big part of my spirituality."[76]

> Hip-hop's always been a spiritual culture. To me, it's just the mainstream doesn't let that show. . . . I went to something called the B-Boy Summit in San Diego . . . and that was just one of the most spiritual things I've ever been to as far as all young people, all different colors, connected by this culture, hip-hop. All peace and love, you know. I mean, the exact opposite of what they'd have you think. . . . To me, that's what hip-hop is all about. It always has been, that kind of thread, that spiritual thread running through the culture.[77]

This message of peace and love would seem to run counter to the mainstream media's portrayal of angry, destructive gangsta rappers, but it was a consistent theme that emerged in the interviews: "The part of hip-hop culture being that, one of the basic premises being based in peace and love for everyone, that also appealed to me. I just got absorbed into it. So, that's one of the messages that you got from hanging out in the scene."[78] It is important to understand that this is not simply a romanticization of rap music and hip-hop culture, but that this message of peace and love was there from the beginning, in the very midst of poverty and violence and drugs. In fact, it arose as a direct response to these things: "There was always fighting and there's obviously drugs in the community and wanting things that we didn't have. So, the music was an outlet. The art was an outlet. All these things."[79] "Hip-hop, originally, the dancers, the breaking groups were this alternative similar to the fighting groups. They were just redirecting that energy. That's what they're still doing right now.

You know, the energy's there. It's going to happen, it's going to get out one way or another. Hip-hop culture, to me, is one of the best alternatives that I've seen."[80] "What it does for me is it calms my soul and all the struggle. I have a lot of anger in me from my ancestors and expressing it through music really gives me a venue. It's like God gave me a gift and He said, 'I know that if I don't give you this gift, you're going to do a lot of crazy stuff.'"[81]

I should clarify, however, that most of the rappers I interviewed were part of the regional Bay Area "underground scene," which is distinct from other expressions and styles of rap music. So this sense of peace and love and unity largely refers to their experiences in this underground hip-hop subculture: "There is unity in the underground crew. . . . There's been no violence whatsoever."[82] "The underground is where it's at, as far as I've seen so far."[83] "There's so much underground stuff going on with people with real creative aspects of it that's beautiful. . . . I like the vibrant energy of the underground thing going on."[84]

One of the reasons I have included a lengthy discussion of hip-hop culture in this section about musical experience is because they are so closely tied into each other. In some sense, they are mutually self-generating. One rapper's description of his experience at a Pharcyde concert illustrates this point:

> Everybody in the place was going back and forth at the same time. I remember looking back and seeing a whole moving wave of people. And it occurred to me how music brings people together. White people, Asian, Latino, black, different ages. And there wasn't any difference in being noticed. Everybody was one. The music was pulling everyone together.[85]

And as I have shown, this oneness is felt not just with those in the room in the present time, but with the ancestral lineage stretching into the past. In discussing his unitive experience of the music, this same rapper made unmistakable reference to this continuity with the past. "That peak—it's like a whole. It's like a recollection almost. It's almost like I'm remembering how it feels. . . . It's almost like it's doing its own. It's almost like I'm meditating."[86]

Interestingly, although this musical peak contains a strong connection to the collective past, at the same time it is also a way of stepping out of the oppressive circumstances of one's immediate personal past into the present moment: "Forget about going to work and forget about any problems you had during the day. All of that is totally obliterated. It's more like just totally in the present, like right now and it's good. . . . It seems like all our insecurities are washed away. It's like chilling with the moment. It's that simple."[87] "People go to concerts or people go to hip-hop functions to get away from whatever ails them during the day and they get out to release themselves."[88]

This is not simple escapism, however, but a means of tapping into deeper parts of oneself and the spiritual world: "I've come to take my music more seriously and my music has actually been a process of self-knowing. It's been a vehicle for me to learn about myself."[89] "The music keeps me centered on what I'm here for. So it's really an expression. It's like praying. It's like being with God, literally like being with God. . . . I look around at everything, and everything I absorb is God and I can express that, literally."[90]

And using the music to connect with God then feeds back into the day-to-day world to effect positive change. I would like to conclude this section with a quotation that sums up this point of view:

> I've always taken the spiritual power seriously. . . . The people that I know, they're really trying to learn some things about themselves and tap into the rest of the spring that we don't use and these spiritual powers. . . . So the hope is there in the spirit again. People are putting their hope in spirit, you know, God. Not God as an abstract form but God in here and in there, you know, that's what we can use to get out of this mess. Hip-hop is just one of the manifestations. That's what we call it in the physical world, that's what some of us call it. . . . To me, music is the future religion of the world.[91]

The Ritual Dimension

Hip-hop and rap demonstrate the diversity of the different forms of ritual expression of the musical subcultures we are exploring, even within this one genre. In the world of hip-hop, there are several important kinds of live performance which coalesce into distinctive ritual forms. In its original nascent form in the South Bronx and other inner-city contexts, rap began on the street corners with small groups of young people gathered around a beatbox, rapping and break dancing. The larger ritual context is the neighborhood block party, where a PA system is set up, often also on the street or in a community center, and DJs mix, rappers rap, and the crowd dances. Sometimes these gatherings have a strong competitive aspect, with different DJs and rappers competing to see who is best. There are also special break dance gatherings where different crews of dancers compete in the same way.

As rap became a commercially viable genre marketed more widely, rap acts began to play the clubs and concert halls in a context that more closely resembled the live rock concert. All these forms evince the same kind of temporal sequencing, spatial structuring, somatic organization, and social bonding which I have shown to be distinguishing character-istics of the ritual process. The sheer number and diversity of these rit-ual forms within hip-hop necessitates that I limit my focus primarily to the block party and rap concert, mainly because these are the forms which are roughly comparable to the rock concerts and raves I have been examining.

I begin with the block party which, in many respects, is the quintessen-tial hip-hop gathering. In terms of temporal sequencing, these weekend parties can take place not only at night, but also in the daytime. Because the larger context is that of a party and not simply a musical perfor-mance, there are usually a variety of other activities that precede the dance floor jams or proceed concurrently with them. This includes the preparation and consumption of food and drinks, and socializing in a number of different configurations. At a certain point, DJs move to the turntables and begin mixing music for dancing, followed by dancers tak-ing to the dance floor to dance to the music. "Mixing was a big part of it because we always had block parties and DJs would come out and spin records."[92] MCs also take to the microphone to work the crowd and lay down their raps. In the course of a block party, there is usually a succes-sion of several DJs and MCs, each of whom take the party through their particular musical and poetic journey.

One important element often associated with the block party is that of organized competition. This can be competition between DJs showing off their mixing skills, particularly their ability to scratch. It can also be com-petition between MCs showing off their rhyming skills or engaging in verbal sparring with boasts and insults. The MCs might be rapping to the same DJ, or they can team with their own DJ. In fact, there might be com-petition between entire crews or posses, including not only the DJ and several MCs, but break dancing groups as well. Each competitor or group of competitors gets to be center stage for a period of time to display their skills and work the crowd, and then they give way to the next competitor or group. The competitions are usually decided by whoever gets the most enthusiastic audience response. The rewards for winning are primarily prestige, reputation, and bragging rights. As I mentioned earlier, these competitions are a nonviolent, constructive alternative to gang warfare. But while there is value attached to winning, the process of getting to a level where one is good enough to compete is also valued: "It was such a strong competition, not necessarily competition to be better [than someone else], but always being good, you're progressing, you get as good as you can. . . . The thing about hip-hop, it's always about showing improvement."[93] Just as with any other musical performance, the best or most popular DJs, MCs, break dancers, and crews are usually scheduled at the end of the night, so as to culminate in a high energy peak.

The same type of scheduling of acts also occurs with rap concerts in clubs or larger venues, although the headliners are more likely to be non-local and nationally known. Rap concerts tend to follow a pattern of temporal sequencing similar to rock concerts: promotional activities, anticipation, going with friends, waiting in line, socializing, finding one's place, opening acts, breaks between sets, bringing the lights down for the main act, the rush toward the front as they take the stage. Much has been made in the mainstream media of incidents of violence in audiences at rap concerts, but such incidents are extremely unusual. As one hip-hop veteran put it: "This year, I went to like eight or nine shows, and there's been no violence whatsoever. . . . I haven't seen the violence that the media tries to hype, tries to portray as the norm for hip-hop."[94] The sequencing within the musical set also tends to save the most popular or uptempo songs for the end, so as to build the energy to a crescendo. If they succeed in doing so, the group will come back for an encore.

In terms of spatial structuring, block parties can take place in a variety of locations, but obviously the traditional context is to cordon off a block and have the party out on the street. There is usually (but not always) a stage set up for the performers at one end or the other, with the dance floor in the street itself, as well as food and drink areas and, in many cases, vendor booths on the periphery. The placement of the DJ can vary—sometimes he or she is up onstage, behind the MC or on the side; but sometimes, like the raves, the DJ is off to the side of the dance floor. The PA system and sound person are likely to be local in origin. One interesting aspect of this type of location is that it serves as a kind of semipermeable membrane to the neighborhood, with easy access in and out of the proceedings, and a sense of integration into the community. Other locations for block parties can include local schools or schoolyards, community centers or auditoriums, and even skating rinks. Because they do not have the expansiveness and festive feel of the outdoors, the enclosed indoor locations have a different atmosphere, although this is usually not a serious impediment to having a good party. In general, the block party is characterized by a sense of family, neighborhood, and community, with a lot of close-knit connection and interaction occurring not only in the performances, but in the field as a whole.

This type of intimacy and cohesion is diluted somewhat when the performance context is transposed to a concert mode, but many local clubs manage to maintain a strong community feel. In a club context, the venue is often small and crowded and, although the performers are more widely separated from the audience than in the block party, they are still likely to be pressed right up against the crowd. Hip-hop clubs tend to book local rap artists and local audiences turn out for their shows, so there is still a high degree of personal interaction.

The community feel is substantially reduced when the concerts become bigger and the venue moves from the club to the concert hall. In this context, the main act is probably nonlocal and nationally known, attracting a much larger and more diverse audience beyond the core of African Americans and other minority ethnic groups, including a strong percentage of middle-class white youth. The demarcation between performer and audience is more pronounced, with the traditional raised stage for the performers and sometimes even assigned seating for the audience. The MC is center stage in the spotlight, surrounded by his or her crew, with the DJ usually to the back or off to the side, but definitely removed from the dance floor. The larger concerts tend to have a more developed light show and visual element, often including backdrops, projections, costumes, and choreographed dance routines. Sometimes a DAT (digital audio tape) machine is used to play some of the music. Overall, there is a continuum with these different performance contexts, moving from the local community, which has a high degree of personal interactivity, to the more anonymous crowd of the large concerts, with the traditional performer-audience separation.

Even in the concert context, however, this musical subculture exhibits a stronger interactive dynamic in rap performance between the rapper and the audience than any of the other subcultures we have studied so far, featuring the traditional African element of call and response. The MC can call for particular vocal or gestural responses from the audience, and skillfully use these techniques to build up the energy in particular ways. The classic example of this type of interaction is when the MC shouts "everybody say 'wo,'" and the audience shouts back "wo!" gradually building into a rhythmic vocal exchange that might culminate in a group scream. The classic gestural instruction is to "put your hands in the air and wave them like you just don't care," and the audience is usually happy to oblige. But these interactions do not consist simply of such stock phrases and gestures. "They'll throw changes in according to the mood of the crowd, and have everybody vibing off of that."[95]

These kinds of dynamic interactions often result in the peaks that I have already discussed at length. They also reflect the priestly role of the MC mentioned earlier in leading the group to such peaks, a role which demonstrates strong continuities with African African church traditions. I should reiterate here that the DJ plays a crucial role in this interactive process as well, "setting the vibe," in the words of one DJ.[96] Earlier, this same DJ described his training as a kind of initiation which culminated in the ultimate rite of passage for the DJ, spinning successfully for a live audience.

There are some specific spatial configurations and characteristic body movements in the audience that emerge out of this interactive dynamic. "Most of the concerts are, if the crew's getting off, then you got a lot of fools at the front of the stage waving their hands like this."[97] So, in a concert situation, both in the club and the concert hall, the audience is facing the performers onstage and the most fanatical members are close to the front, where the interaction with the performers is the strongest. Hand waving is one of the primary movements associated with hip-hop and there are numerous nuances in hand position which modulate the gesture. Typically, the arms are extended upward while the hands are bent down, with the thumb and first two fingers extended and pointing. Rappers use this gesture with one arm and hand moving in time to the rap, almost like a conductor, while the other hand holds the microphone. Audience members wave their arms in time to the beat, often in counterpoint to a rhythmic stepping motion with their legs which is also a primary hip-hop movement.

The rhythmic groove of the music is the key to these movements: "My main thing is what I call the head bop quotient. You know, if it's bad, if it's a great groove, then your head will start bopping, your toe will start tapping, and that really is the bottom line. . . . If hip-hop is done right, it'll get people dancing."[98] Because these dance movements are participatory extensions of the rhythmic groove, they tend to unify the audience as a bodily, kinaesthetic whole.

The part of the audience which is further back tends to direct their attention a bit less on the performers and more on each other. "There are a lot of situations in the concert where people will form a circle and there's still a lot of break dancers."[99] The break dancing movements have a distinctive style and gestural vocabulary of their own, involving a lot of spins and leaps, with the body low to the floor, usually featuring one dancer in the middle of the circle. One break dancer noted the similarities to the Afro-Brazilian musical movement practice and martial art, Capoeira: "I spent just hours in front of my mirror, practicing waves and shit, the stuff that I do now instinctively, for many many years. Back spins. Now I learned that when I see those moves, I see Capoeira . . . and I'm like 'damn, that's hip-hop.' But, at the time, I didn't know."[100] These similarities between characteristic hip hop movements and Afro-diasporic and African dance forms have also been noted by anthropologist and movement analyst Isabel Fine:

> The grounded feeling is shared in these cultures, with the supporting legs often bent and the pelvis strongly grounded. Isolations of the shoulder, ribs, hips, and head also figure prominently in hip hop and some African styles. . . . The spatially "up" emphasis on the down beat is something that I have seen quite a bit in Senegalese dance, the feet gliding under a suspended torso which is leaning slightly forward, and I have noticed this structure in some hip hop dance as well. Some of the fast and strong foot movements are almost identical to Makuta, which is a Congolese based Afro-Cuban secular dance form, and some moves are even identical in structure to African based Brazilian Samba.[101]

This external similarity in form is mirrored by the internal somatic experiential states, which strongly echo the possession experience. I repeat the following quotation from earlier in the chapter to emphasize this point:

> What I felt as a kid was strictly vibration, rhythm, and that music has a rhythm that just called my soul. It would make my soul jump out of my body, literally, and I'd have to move to it. . . . It really calls me, it really does. . . . Sometimes my body does things I can't even control and it's like I'm not

even here. . . . It's just a link. Something touches you one day, just sparks your whole consciousness, and shows your body you can. Time and space is all about the rhythm in your body. It's hard to understand when you're a kid. . . . I mean, now that I'm older, I can put in perspective what I felt as a young kid. . . . It's the ancients. It's definitely the ancients.[102]

So the unity experienced on the dance floor includes not only fellow members of the hip-hop community but also a connection to the spirit world and the ancestral lineage stretching back in time, which, as I showed earlier, has a strong African American and African component.

Such profound shared experiences at live rap performances create a powerful bond among the participants. "I recognized it as something that brought me closer to other people. . . . All of a sudden, we had something that brought us together and made us feel good."[103] This in turn leads to "the formation of crews, of families [with] a common goal, a common interest."[104] Particularly with the block parties or small club performance contexts, there is a strong sense of local style with which the community identifies. This style includes not only the music, but also "the graffiti, the dress, the language, the art, the people, the mind-set that's the commonality of thought."[105] In this regard, I reiterate the importance of the word "represent" to describe the close relationship of rap style to its local community. These styles tend to develop along regional lines, not only in a national sense, but also within a particular area.

There's the New York style hip-hop. There's the West Coast style hip-hop. There's the Midwest and there's also Southern. And even the West Coast is kind of factionalized where you have the Bay Area style of music and the LA style of music. . . . [In terms of Bay Area style], right now, I'm into the underground style of stuff. And right now, the Bay Area is becoming known as the Pimp Player style, like E40 and even Too Short to some degree and JT the Bigga Figga and so on and so forth. And a lot of the crews out of Vallejo have that Pimp Player style. A lot of people are into the underground style of music . . . but, generally, these two styles don't come together. . . . But there is unity in the underground crew.[106]

Thus there may be factionalizing between regional styles, but *within* a style, there is unity and a sense of community, and the local concert is the ritual in which these bonds are forged and expressed:

The underground, though, it's just a strong vibe, it's real. It's like, the shows, people are hungry in there. People onstage are hungry. There's passion, fire in their eyes. The audience has it. It's not a lot of people, so it's intimate. It's just beautiful. . . . There is so much underground talent in the Bay Area, it's ridiculous. In Oakland, by itself, the Oakland Renaissance is happening right now. But, Richmond, Vallejo, San Francisco, Daly City. . . .[107]

And, although there is factionalization between styles and regions, there is also an overarching sense of belonging to a larger hip-hop culture. As one rapper put it in describing his experience at the B-Boy Summit: "people of all different colors" from "all over the world . . . connected by this culture, hip-hop"—"to me, that's what hip-hop is all about."[108] Within this framework of a larger, more inclusive hip-hop culture, the different regional styles can be appreciated for their diverse articulations of the underlying hip-hop sensibility. Going to a large concert headlined by a nonlocal rap group can be an opportunity to see what's going on in other hip-hop communities and create connections beyond one's region. "If you wanted to find out what was going on in the Bronx or in East Oakland or now in Chicago or in Texas, this is maybe the only way you could find out about it."[109] As another rapper put it: "It just links and connects."[110] And this connection has now become international and global, as hip-hop has spread beyond the United States across the planet. "Hip-hop culture is worldwide now. It's big in Japan. I know it's big in Germany. And I hear from people all the time in places I would never expect."[111]

Worldviews, Philosophies, and Codes for Living

One element that the hip-hop subculture shares with heavy metal is an awareness of the dark, chaotic nature of the world. As one aficionado says: "A lot of it, philosophically, has to do with being in an apocalyptic age, being in the end of things. . . . It definitely comes out of chaos."[112] In hip-hop, however, this chaotic element is more specifically rooted in the political, economic, and racial dynamics of the African diaspora and its particular historical development in the United States. I have already discussed the bleak conditions facing African Americans and other minorities, especially the young males who comprise the core of the hip-hop subculture. These conditions, as one hip-hop veteran put it, are "pretty basic things—we're poor, we're in the ghetto. . . . There was always fighting."[113] Another rap fan summed it up succinctly in noting a homology between these tough conditions and the feeling tone of the music: "Mainly, I think it's just [that] life is hard and so the music's hard too."[114] So, once again, the template for the worldview is contained within the music itself.

First of all, the foundation of the music is the rhythm, the beats on top of which everything else is layered. These beats are much more polyrhythmic and interactive than any of the other musics we have been studying. "That is what, to me, makes hip-hop. It's got the rhythmic conversation of the drum and the rhythmic conversation of the bass."[115] I have already noted that interactive polyrhythms are a central feature of the West African complex of musicoreligious practices, and that many hip-hop aficionados are well aware of this continuity. The continuity in the beats also includes the tradition of a distinctively African American articulation of these polyrhythms. "The beat is accented on the weak beats, which are the two and the four, which is pretty much a constant in all African American music. It's pretty much the mark they put in music. That, and the concept of swing, and that feel."[116] Another, more contemporary term used for swing is groove: "I'm pretty much focusing on the groove."[117] So the foundation of hip-hop, the groove, links it to the entire tradition of African American musics and even further back, all the way to West Africa.

If the foundation is the connection to the past, the rest of the musical structure is more reflective of contemporary circumstances. Earlier, I referred to Tricia Rose's analysis of rap music's sonic architecture as consisting of three main elements: flow, layering, and rupture. Rose goes on to suggest that these principles provide a homologous model for the contemporary African American philosophy and worldview:

> These effects at the level of style and aesthetics suggest affirmative ways in which profound social dislocation and rupture can be managed and perhaps contested in the social arena. Let us imagine these hip hop principles as a blueprint for social resistance and affirmation: create sustaining narratives, accumulate them, layer, embellish, and transform them. However, be also prepared for rupture, find pleasure in it, in fact, *plan on* social rupture. When these ruptures occur, use them in creative ways that will prepare you for a future in which survival will demand a sudden shift in ground tactics.[118]

Thus the continuities with West African and previous African American traditions are carried forward and embellished through flow and layering, but the jarring disjunctions of the contemporary African American experience are also accounted for and built into the mix, forming the template for a hip-hop code for living.

The raps which are laid over the music also serve this function of reflecting the chaos and difficulties of contemporary urban life. Earlier, I quoted Chuck D of Public Enemy who said that rap is black urban youth's CNN. But this is more than simply reporting the news; as I noted previously, there is an important element of truth-telling in the raps. In other words, by saying what's really going on and speaking from the heart, rappers empower themselves and their listeners to momentarily transcend their historical circumstances. In this regard, rap continues a distinctively African American spiritual lineage which includes not only so-called secular musical forms like the blues, but also the black church and the role of the priest. To repeat one rapper's view: "MCs are the priests or pastors of the people right now."[119]

Sometimes the resonance with this priestly role is so strong that the message of the MCs can sound very much like a church sermon. This same rapper talked about an experience he had listening to KRS-One, demonstrating this resonance and expressing the spiritually uplifting side of the hip-hop philosophy and code for living:

> He said: "These are the practices we need to do. Act like the god that you know. Whatever god you know, act like him. If your god is loving and merciful, be loving and merciful. The things that you want to happen in your life, visualize them in your mind before you go to sleep." And he said something that was profound to me, because after all that attack, he came back with love, saying, "Here's something you can do for yourself regardless of what I'm saying or what you said." I talked to other people afterward, and they were saying they do something like that every day of their life, and it works.[120]

This sense of hip-hop as a source of spirituality, spiritual values, and living a spiritual life was a consistent theme that emerged throughout the interviews I conducted.

I return here to the flow, layering, rupture style of composition of the music to develop two more important points. First, I argue that this is a perfect expression of the postmodern sensibility, in which the traditional structures have broken down and new forms have been reconstituted from the deconstructed bits and pieces in what one hip-hop artist calls "the art of collage."[121] According to one DJ, this art "is all about recombinant potential. . . . Each and every source sample is fragmented and bereft of prior meaning . . . [and] given meaning only when re-presented in the assemblage of the mix. . . . A mix, for me, is a way of providing a rare and intimate glimpse into the process of cultural production in the late twentieth century."[122] In rap music, "there's a lot of breaking the form of what has traditionally been what you're supposed to do. Like, just leaving odd amounts of space, doing something and coming in on the backside."[123] Even the technology used in the creation of the music—drum machines, cross-fade mixers, samplers, sequencers, computers—reflects this postmodern sensibility. Originating in the elite, white, high-tech, corporate world, these technologies were taken by low-income African Americans, used in entirely different ways, and transformed into a new mode of expression.

Second, this postmodern cut-and-paste style of bricolage illustrates another positive element of the hip-hop worldview, namely, the universalistic inclusion of many different musics and cultures. "Every music made in our last millennium . . . leads up to hip-hop because it uses every aspect of every music completely. . . . It's a universal way of connecting all these different styles of music into one thing. . . . Mixing is like the universal language."[124] This musical practice of including many diverse sources in creating a new whole is mirrored in a hip-hop philosophy stressing inclusion and unity that cuts across race, class, nationality, and ethnicity.

Finally, hip-hop's power to be a source of political and spiritual awakening in people's lives and to bring them together in this way leads to a sense that it can be a vehicle for change in the larger world.

> I see it being one of the major forces in the world bringing about change . . . new ways, new types of lifestyles, because the old ones, we just can't use them any more. For young people, that'll be our political party, what everyone calls, we don't have it, it's the closest thing we have to that. It includes politics. It includes spirituality. It includes music. It includes having a good time. It's inclusive of so much. . . . So, the hope is there in the spirit again, people are putting their hope in spirit, you know, God. Not God as an abstract form, but God in here and in there, you know. That's what we can use to get out of this mess. Hip-hop is just one of the manifestations. That's what we call it in the physical world.[125]

Conclusion

There's More to the Picture than Meets the Eye

In the Grateful Dead's classic song *Truckin'*, the memorable line from the chorus reflects on "what a long strange trip it's been." The same can be said for the route this study has traced. It was indeed a long strange trip for the Yoruba and the Fon and other peoples from the coastal rain forests of West Africa through the Middle Passage across the Atlantic Ocean to slavery in the New World. In these foreign lands, in completely different contexts, their musicoreligious practices also went through a long strange trip from their traditional forms to strongly African hybrids like Vodun, Santeria, and Candomble to the more Christianized African American manifestations of the black church.

It was a long strange trip for some of the sensibilities and structural elements of these practices to make their way into secular entertainment musics and eventually evolve into distinctly African American styles like the blues. It was a long strange trip for African Americans from slavery on the plantations in the South to the difficulties of the postemancipation era to the migrations northward to the ghettos of large cities to contemporary forms of racism and the continuing struggle for equal opportunity and civil rights. It was a long strange trip for rhythm and blues to cross over from its historic African American community to a rebellious young white audience in the form of rock and roll to eventually become a major cultural force and a multibillion dollar industry. And finally, it was a long strange trip for distinctive musical subcultures to evolve with powerful religious dimensions that profoundly impact their adherents in ways that are strikingly similar to the original West African musicoreligious practices.

In doing research and fieldwork for this study, I have also journeyed on a long strange trip that has taken me from possession dances in the dirt courtyards of villages in Ghana to high-tech psychedelic raves in the postindustrial warehouses of San Francisco. In the course of these travels, I have

traversed great distances not only geographically but psychologically, culturally, intellectually, and spiritually as well. As I reflect on this journey,
what stands out most strongly for me is the depth and power of the religious
dimensions that the young people in these contemporary musical subcultures have experienced. Through my interviews with participants and
through my own participation in their events, I have come to understand
just how profound and significant a religious phenomenon is taking place
in these musical subcultures. In tying together various loose threads from
the theoretical, historical, and ethnographic sections, I would like to highlight several important themes that have emerged in the course of this
study. As I will show, I think these themes have far-reaching implications
both for scholars and for lay music fans everywhere.

The first and foremost point I wish to make is simply the power of
music to deeply affect people at every level. It is this power that makes
music one of the most universal conveyors of religious meaning known
to human beings. In chapter 1, I discussed how the musical experience is
a unique mode of being-in-the-world in which the dualities of subject-
object, body-mind, and spiritual-material are transcended in a unified
field. Music allows people to become part of this unified field in which
the spiritual dimension is directly experienced as a powerful state that is
integrated with all the other levels. This theoretical model has been
strongly confirmed not only by countless cultures around the world but
also by the striking testimonials of the members of the musical subcultures I interviewed. Time and again, participants spoke at length of how
the music brought them to profound experiential states imbued with
deep spiritual and religious implications, particularly through the triggering mechanism of the musical motto. In the modern secular Western
world where such experiences rarely occur even within the framework of
traditional religions, these testimonials point to a significant religious
phenomenon. For this reason alone, the spiritual and religious power of
music deserves serious study by numerous scholarly disciplines that have
largely overlooked its importance. Moreover, my research has convinced
me that there are millions of people who are probably having similar experiences through music but who may not fully understand their religious implications, and such studies could provide many laypeople with
information critical to their spiritual and religious self-understanding.

The second major theme flows out of the first, namely, the central importance of these powerful experiential states in the newly emerging
forms of popular religiosity. Here I repeat historian of religion Charles H.

Long's crucial formulation of how the "locus and meaning of religion in contemporary industrialized societies" has shifted significantly:

> Because of the intensity of transmission, the content of what is transmitted tends to be ephemeral; thus, the notion of religion as establishing powerful, pervasive, and long-lasting moods and motivations is shifted away from content and substance to *modes of experience*. Popular religion is thus no longer defined in terms of sustaining traditions, but in the *qualitative meaning of the nature of experience.*[1]

When this shift from content and substance to modes of experience is applied to popular music, one is led to the same conclusion as sociologist William C. Shepherd: "We are witnessing the birth of a new religious life style in which religious experience *is* precisely analogous to the aesthetic experience of music."[2] The remarkable testimonials of the members of the musical subcultures I interviewed strongly support this conclusion. As I conducted my interviews, I was deeply struck by the accounts of the extraordinary experiences that took place at musical events and by how widespread such experiences were and are. It is clear that the experiences were intense, profound, and life-changing. At the same time, they were not of a uniform nature but covered an enormous spectrum of vastly divergent states. Not only does each subculture have its own distinct flavor and texture of experience, but each person *within* each subculture has his or her own distinct flavor and texture of experience, as well as his or her own attendant meaning system. Thus, as I argued in the semiological and virtual sections in chapter 1, a myriad of experiential worlds and meaning systems are contained within each subculture's musical events. That is why I have attached central importance to "the qualitative meaning of the nature of experience" in these musical subcultures and studied these experiential states very closely. I think this kind of emphasis will be increasingly important for scholars of religion as we try to make sense of the diverse forms of popular religiosity that continue to proliferate at an ever-accelerating pace.

There is another key issue related to the central importance of modes of experience, namely, the crucial role of the body as the locus of integration of these modes. In chapter 1, I quoted musicologist Susan McClary who wrote that "music is foremost among cultural 'technologies of the body,' that it [the body] is a site where we learn how to experience socially mediated patterns of kinetic energy, being in time, emotions, desire, pleasure and much more."[3] Ethnomusicologist Steven M. Friedson, in describing the musical experience of the Tumbuka healers of Malawi, went even further in arguing that "there the body has an ontological status different from its status in Western conceptions of the individual."[4] In chapter 2, I showed how this unique ontological status of the body is critical in the West African musicoreligious practices of possession dances and the transformed expressions of these practices in the Americas. This unique ontological status of the body then made its way into the blues, rhythm and blues, rock and roll, and most subsequent popular musics since the 1950s. Here again the material that emerged from my fieldwork with members of contemporary musical subcultures confirms this crucial role of the body not only in modes of experience but also in external form. Interviewees in these subcultures made extensive references to powerful states experienced through the body, many of which strongly echoed the bodily experiences of traditional West African possession religion. The rave subculture in particular explicitly acknowledged the central importance of the body. Indeed, the attainment of such bodily experiential states is a primary goal of the rave.

Both West African possession religion and contemporary musical subcultures are very different from most liturgical Western religious traditions in that they are *danced* religions and the body is obviously central in the activity of dancing. One of the interesting structural aspects that emerged from my fieldwork was the fact that each musical subculture has its own distinctive style of dance, with vocabularies of characteristic gestures and movements. Moreover, these distinctive dance styles correlate to the specific experiential states they produce. For example, the vigorous headbanging and slamdancing of heavy metal produces a very different experiential state from the flowing circular movements and spinning of the Deadheads.

It is these visceral movement forms of the body, rather than verbal discourse, that constitute the central ritual activity of these musical subcultures. Anthropologist David Parkin, in arguing for a bodily understanding of the meaning of ritual, articulates this critical difference in emphasis. Rather than "privileging words," he writes: "ritual is held to privilege physical action; but it is an action that can only be understood as bodily movement towards or positioning with respect to other bodily movements and positions. If such movements are a principal feature of ritual, then it must be through them rather than through verbal assertions that people make their main statements."[5] Elsewhere, historian William H.

McNeill has advanced the hypothesis that moving together rhythmically in time is one of the primary human means of creating group solidarity. In discussing this "visceral" phenomenon, he coined the term "muscular bonding" to describe "the euphoric fellow feeling that prolonged and rhythmic muscular movements arouse among nearly all participants."[6] Muscular bonding is a good description of what happens on the dance floor in contemporary musical subcultures and provides another interesting way of articulating the ritual efficacy of bodily movements.

The power of music to deeply affect people, the central importance of experiential states, and the crucial role of the body are all features that West African possession religion and contemporary Western musical subcultures have in common, and they demonstrate significant continuities. I would be remiss, however, if I did not point out the substantial ways in which these subcultures *differ* from West African possession religion, particularly because such differences illustrate the complexities of emergent forms of popular religiosity in the contemporary postmodern West. To continue the preceding discussion of ritual activity, one of the obvious differences is the context within which the ritual activity takes place. In West African possession dances, it takes place within the formal structure of sacred religious traditions. In contrast, the ritual activity of popular music subcultures takes place within the secular framework of performative genres and commercial entertainment.

While scholars like anthropologist Victor Turner and performance theorist Richard Schechner have done important work in establishing the continuities and connections between religious ritual and secular performance, there is nevertheless an enormous gulf of difference between the two.[7] In West African possession dances, not only are the possessing spirits known and identified and the correct protocols for relating to them established, but the explicit intent of the ritual activity is to summon these spirits for the purposes of healing, counseling, divination, and the restoration of harmony. In popular music concerts or dances, spiritual energies, if acknowledged at all at a conscious level, are usually vague and amorphous, and there is little knowledge of how to relate to them or what to do with them once they appear. This is because the historic framework of these performative genres is primarily aesthetic, the contemporary intent is to have fun and be entertained, and the spiritual energies seem to be an unexpected by-product.

However, the increasing consciousness of the spiritual energies latent in these activities articulated so powerfully by my interviewees is a strong indication that performance is becoming an important contemporary form of ritual expression that is rapidly transcending its secular framework. In the course of my fieldwork, particularly with the rave subculture, I was struck by how many musical events now begin with some sort of rudimentary ritual invocation and setting of sacred intention. There is no question that these are baby steps compared to the highly developed knowledge and precise ritual practices of musicoreligious traditions like the West African possession dances. Nevertheless, it is clear that an awareness of spirituality is making its way into many musical performance contexts and that this awareness is manifesting itself in explicitly sacred ritual activities. Given that it took hundreds of years and complex historical processes for this awareness to be forced underground and hidden from view, I consider its reemergence, even in these nascent forms, to be an extremely significant development.

Moreover, based on the trends indicated by my research, I expect that this reemergence of spiritual awareness in the performative genres will continue to grow and to manifest increasingly explicit sacred ritual forms in these contexts. What these forms will look like is difficult to predict, not only because they are in the early stages of development but also because of their highly ephemeral and changeable nature. However, I believe these sacred ritual forms in performance contexts already constitute an important religious phenomenon in our contemporary cultural landscape and it is clear that their importance will only increase.

Finally, I wish to emphasize the hybridized, cut-and-paste, postmodern nature of this emergent religious phenomenon. In contrast to the crisp formal elegance of the sacred ritual practices of traditional religions, the contemporary musical subcultures have a crass superficial flavor bordering on vulgarity. There are a number of reasons for this. First of all, they are embedded within the capitalistic market dynamics of a multibillion dollar popular music industry built on commercialization and commodification. In chapter 1, I discussed the dynamics of how the popular music industry routinely appropriates the styles of underground musical subcultures for market purposes, commercializing and commodifying these styles to the point where they become superficial caricatures of their former selves. These dynamics are also an important feature of the religious phenomenon in question and illustrate the complexities of its hybridized nature. My research in the four musical subcultures examined in this book revealed an ongoing negotiation of the tension between purity of expression and the forces of commercialization. Each subculture had its own particular discourse and history of coming to terms with its contradictions.

There is a second aspect to the seemingly superficial nature of these subcultures as religious phenomena, namely, the notion of the "popular." Popular music subcultures are certainly "popular" in the market sense that significant numbers of people buy their recordings and attend the musical events. But they are also popular in the deeper sense that they are phenomena created and sustained by ordinary people rather than by religious, musical, or cultural elites. As such, they reflect the complications and contradictions of the postmodern Western world that most ordinary people live in. This is a world that includes distinctions and varied admixtures of race, nationality, ethnicity, class, gender, sexual orientation, and religion, as well as advanced digital technology, global mass media communications, and multinational politicoeconomic entities. This world is a hodge-podge in which all these variables are stitched together in endlessly creative permutations by ordinary people in the course of their day-to-day lives, not necessarily as a creative or spiritual expression but as a matter of basic survival. It is only natural, therefore, that hybridized forms of popular religiosity have emerged from this cut-and-paste postmodern ethos. Moreover, because these forms incorporate the enormous range and diversity of several variables, it is only natural that depth of "content and substance" tends to be sacrificed in favor of breadth and "intensity of transmission," which is another important aspect of their "popular" nature.

Compared to some religious traditions, these new forms may indeed seem superficial and vulgar, but this makes them no less legitimate or serious as religious expressions. On the contrary, it is clear that powerful religious phenomena are occurring within these musical subcultures and that these phenomena are having a life-changing impact on many young people. And as I have already noted, my research indicates that the new forms are developing a greater depth and a more explicit consciousness of the sacred as they continue to evolve at a rapid pace. I believe that close examination of such forms will be at the cutting edge of twenty-first century religious studies scholarship. In a cultural landscape strewn with increasingly strange combinations of the sacred, secular, and profane, we as scholars need to develop theoretical and methodological tools that allow us to see traces of the spirit in these hybrid forms and bring them into sharp relief and focus. My examination of the hidden religious dimensions of popular music subcultures has been a small contribution toward that end.

Just as I began my study with the voices of members of these four musical subcultures, I would now like to conclude in the same way.

I believe that a great spiritual movement is now passing and that in fact something really beautiful happened and it maintained itself for thirty years. . . . There was a serious, profound, religious revival around the Grateful Dead. It happened, it blossomed, it manifested [itself], and now it's going away and dispersing.[8]

It was what I always thought that religion was supposed to be, the community lightening of yourself, and to come out of a party and just be so filled with pure love and leaving the frustration of the week behind at the rave. It showed me true spirituality, from within flowing out of myself and joining it with other people. Undoubtedly the most spiritual feeling I've ever had.[9]

There's that one connection where you feel the whole thing come together. You feel the whole experience come together and there's nothing that can top it. It is like a religious experience. I imagine it's just like some people say that they're finding God. . . . It's a way for us to interpret our lives. Music, to me, is an interpretation of what we're all about.[10]

So, the hope is there in the spirit again, people are putting their hope in spirit, you know, God. Not God as an abstract form, but God in here and in there, you know. That's what we can use to get out of this mess. Hip-hop is just one of the manifestations. . . . To me, music is the future religion of the world.[11]

Appendix

Interview Methodology

Selection Process

I did not attempt to systematically create a representative sample, except insofar as I wanted to include several people from each subculture. I simply pursued any and all means available to me to find knowledgeable and willing participants. This included putting ads in local publications, Internet networking, contacts from concerts, dances, record stores, and personal friends, as well as academic connections. Some of the best contacts came from interviewees who suggested people they thought would be helpful. I did not specifically try to get detailed personal information from each person, preferring to keep the proceedings informal and the focus on our shared interest in music. However, I can say that the interviewees turned out to be relatively diverse in terms of age, gender, ethnicity, class, and location. As one might expect, the hip-hop interviewees had a higher concentration of African Americans and Latinos, while interviewees from the other three subcultures were more affluent and white.

Interview Process

All the interviews were conducted in a face-to-face, one-on-one context, either in my home, the interviewee's home, or a neutral public setting like a coffeehouse. Two were actually conducted in a bar and two in outdoor locations. I used a small, unobtrusive tape recorder with a lapel microphone to record the interviews so that I could transcribe them later. The interviews typically lasted around an hour, with some variations. Prior to each interview, I spoke with the interviewee briefly about my dissertation work as well as my musical background, so he or she had a basic understanding of my orientation and focus. I worked from a prepared list of questions but was also sensitive to the direction the conversation was taking. Thus I pursued good material that arose outside the prepared questions, and likewise dropped a particular line of questioning that was clearly unproductive. Each interview was unique and produced an interactive dynamic which often led to unexpected discoveries and insights for both of us.

Interview Questions

1. Let's begin with a little about your background. Where were you born and raised? What was your family like? Tell me about your religious upbringing. Your musical background.

2. How did you first begin to get involved with this music scene?

3. Was there a particular moment or experience which confirmed your sense of yourself as a hard-core fan?

4. How much music do you listen to per day, week? Where and in what context (home, concert, club, car, etc.)?

5. Let's talk about your experience at live shows, jams, raves. How is it different from your normal day-to-day experience?

6. What is your sense of self within this experience?

7. How do you experience your body—in-body, out-of-body? Are there characteristic dance movements or body postures you associate with the music?

8. Describe your relationship to other people in this experiential state—are you aware of them, connected to them? In what way? Is your experience totally private, or shared, or somewhere in between?

9. Do you have any sense of the sacred during this experience?

10. Do you ever feel the presence of something beyond yourself? Does this presence have a specific character or identity, or is it an energy form, like a wave? How would you characterize this energy or presence—loving, angry, humorous, etc.? What is your connection with it?

11. What drugs, if any, do you do at these events?

12. Is there a particular time in the music (the concert, jam, rave) when you are more likely to have certain types of experiences?

13. Have these experiences had any impact on your normal day-to-day life, changed it in any way?

14. What do you pay attention to when you listen to the music—the rhythm, the instruments, the composition, the lyrics, the visuals, social interactions, etc.?

15. What is the vibe you tend to associate with the music?

16. Is there some sort of way of looking at the world or living your life that you associate with this music scene? Can you spell this out?

17. To what degree is your identity tied up in this music scene?

18. How would you characterize your relationship with other people involved in the scene? How important are they in your life as compared to people in other sectors? What kind of bond do you share?

19. What is the significance/importance of going to the shows/raves/jams regularly? What do you get from it?

20. Do they ever feel like a religious gathering or a ritual? In what way?

21. Is there a set structure—sequence of events and music, spatial arrangement, etc.—that you can count on? What is the significance or meaning of that structure for you?

22. Is there anything significant for you about the music or the scene that we haven't covered? Any closing thoughts?

The Interviewees

Bahar Badizadegan was born and raised in Iran, spent her adolescence in Los Angeles, lived in the Bay Area for a number of years, and currently resides in New York City. She is in her twenties and works for a record store. She has been involved with various electronic music genres for several years. The interview was conducted at a coffeehouse in San Francisco.

Joel Dinolt, born and raised in Detroit, Michigan, lives in San Francisco. He is in his twenties and is a guitarist in a band. He has been involved with the rave subculture for eleven years. The interview was conducted at a coffeehouse in San Francisco.

Jim Dunn was born and raised in a small town in Indiana and lives in San Francisco. Unique among interviewees, he has been involved with all four of the musical subcultures, beginning with hip-hop and heavy metal as a teenager, and going on tour as a Deadhead in his early twenties. He has been involved with the rave subculture for nine years and is a DJ himself for many of these events. He was born in 1970. The interview was conducted in Golden Gate Park in San Francisco.

Steve Gaines was born and raised in Philadelphia, Pennsylvania, and lives in Richmond, California. He is in his twenties and has been involved with hip-hop since he was a teenager. He is a rapper who works under the name Zion I. The interview was conducted at a coffeehouse in Berkeley.

Jorge Guerrero was born in Nicaragua, raised in the San Francisco Bay Area, and lives in Concord, California. Now in his twenties, he has been involved with hip-hop since he was ten and is a rapper himself. The interview was conducted at a coffeehouse in Berkeley.

Kathleen Harrison was born in 1948 on Santa Catalina Island in southern California, spent her early adult years in the San Francisco Bay area, and currently lives in Occidental, California. She is an ethnobotanist who co-founded Botanical Dimensions, a nonprofit educational and preservation group. She has been a Deadhead since 1972. The interview was conducted at her home.

Charlotte Kaufman, born and raised in Chicago, lives in San Francisco. She was exposed to house music as a teenager and has been involved with the electronic dance music world ever since. Now in her thirties, she is a respected DJ known as the Baroness who spins at numerous raves and clubs and has released two CDs. The interview was conducted at a coffeehouse in San Francisco.

Paris King was born and raised in Oakland, California, and continues to reside there. Born in 1974, he has been a hip-hop aficionado for over a decade. He is a bass player involved with various projects in the Oakland underground. The interview was conducted in his home.

Galen Klein was born and raised in various locations in California and currently resides in Rohnert Park, California. Now in his twenties, he has been a fan of heavy metal music since he was ten and a guitarist in his own band for over ten years. The interview was conducted in his home.

Gus Lanzas was born and raised in Nicaragua, moved to the San Francisco Bay area in 1982, and currently lives in San Francisco. He is in his twenties and has been involved with the rave subculture for twelve years. He works in multimedia technology and composes electronic dance music himself. The interview was conducted at a coffeehouse in San Francisco.

Chris Lum grew up in southern California and moved to San Francisco in 1993. He is twenty-nine years old and works at a record store. He went to his first rave in 1990 and has been involved in the rave subculture since then, including being a DJ himself. The interview was conducted at a restaurant in San Francisco.

Bill Lyman was born and raised in the San Francisco Bay area and currently lives in Berkeley. Now in his forties, he saw his first Grateful Dead show in 1970 and has been a regular Deadhead since 1978. The interview was conducted at my home.

Malcolm (no last name given) was born in San Francisco, raised in Concord, California, and now resides in Oakland. He is in his twenties and has been involved with hip-hop since he was in junior high school. He is a DJ working in the Oakland underground. The interview was conducted in his home.

Carlos Mena was born and raised in Brooklyn, New York, and lives in San Jose, California, where he works in the computer industry. Now in his thirties, he has been a hip-hop aficionado since 1979, and is a key member of the rap group 10 Bass T. The interview was conducted in a bar in San Jose.

Lisa Mishke was born and raised in New York and now lives in Berkeley. She is forty-one years old and works as a teacher. She has been a Deadhead since she was twenty. The interview was conducted at my home.

Alaura O'Dell was born and raised in London, England, and, as a member of the band Psychic TV, was strongly involved with the original British acid house and rave scenes in the mid-1980s. Now in her thirties, she resides in Occidental, California, and has her own business conducting travel tours with a spiritual and geomantic orientation. The interview took place in her home.

Lance Ozanix was born and raised in Healdsberg, California, and lives in Rohnert Park, California. Now thirty-six years old, he has been a metalhead for over twenty years and makes his living as the lead singer and guitarist for the metal band Skitzo. The interview was conducted at an arcade in Rohnert Park.

Sabrina Page was born and raised in New Jersey and lives in Fairfax, California. Born in 1948, she has been involved with various dance communities for over ten years and is a DJ herself who spins twice a week in San Rafael, California. The interview was conducted at her home.

Steve Rice was born and raised in the San Jose area and lives in Belmont, California. Now in his thirties, he has been a fan of heavy metal since he was ten years old. He has also played guitar since he was a teenager and has been in a metal band for many years. The interview was conducted at a bar in Belmont.

James Romero was born and raised in various locations in California and has lived in the Bay Area for eight years. Now in his forties, he was a Deadhead for a number of years from the mid-1980s through Jerry Garcia's death. He subsequently became involved with the rave subculture since living in San Francisco and is now a DJ himself. The interview was conducted in his home.

Tiffany Scott was born and raised in Los Angeles and has lived in San Francisco since 1994. Now in her twenties, she was involved with the rave scene in Los Angeles since its early days in the late 1980s and has continued her involvement in San Francisco. She is a graduate student who also works for XLR8R, an electronic dance music magazine. The interview took place in a coffeehouse in San Francisco.

Steve Silberman was born and raised in New Jersey and has lived in San Francisco for almost twenty years. Now in his forties, he has been a Deadhead since high school and is coauthor of *Skeleton Key: A Dictionary for Deadheads* and author of numerous articles on the Grateful Dead. The interview took place on the Berkeley campus of the University of California.

Jeff Taylor was born and raised in the San Francisco Bay area and lives in San Francisco. Now in his twenties, he has been involved with the rave subculture since the early 1990s. He works in the computer industry and composes his own electronic dance music. The interview was conducted in his home.

Vince Thomas lives in San Francisco and works for the computer industry. Now in his thirties, he has been involved with the rave subculture since the late 1980s, including organizing large raves and ongoing weekly events in clubs. He is also a key figure in the local electronic dance music label Zoe Magik. The interview took place in his home.

Keith Williams was born and raised in Pittsburgh, Pennsylvania, and has lived in San Jose, California, for many years. Now in his twenties or thirties, he has been a hip-hop aficionado since he was a teenager. He is a bass player as well as a music engineer and producer who goes by the name of K Double. He is the founder of the Urban Underground, and his ongoing project is to discover, record, and promote local hip-hop talent. The interview took place at his studio in San Jose.

Notes

NOTES TO THE INTRODUCTION

1. Bill Lyman, interview by author, tape recording, Berkeley, Calif., 3 July 1997. See Appendix for more information.

2. Jeff Taylor, interview by author, tape recording, San Francisco, Calif., 24 July 1997. See Appendix for more information.

3. Lance Ozanix, interview by author, tape recording, Rohnert Park, Calif., 30 July 1997. See Appendix for more information.

4. Jorge Guerrero, interview by author, tape recording, Berkeley, Calif., 6 August 1997. See Appendix for more information.

5. The notion of subculture is sociological; it began as a term used to describe juvenile delinquents in the 1950s and evolved from there. For a good overview of the sociological definitions of subculture, see Michael Clarke, "On the concept of 'Sub-Culture,'" *British Journal of Sociology* 25:4 (December 1975): 428–41; and David Arnold, ed., *The Sociology of Subcultures* (Berkeley: Glendessary Press, 1970). In the 1970s, sociologists working out of the Birmingham school in England with a quasi-Marxist orientation began applying the term to social groups constellating around particular youth musical genres. See Stuart Hall and Tony Jefferson, eds., *Resistance through Rituals: Youth Subcultures in Postwar Britain* (London: HarperCollins Academic, 1976); and Dick Hebdige, *Subculture: The Meaning of Style* (New York: Methuen, 1979). More recently, scholars have begun to use the term in a more sophisticated and nuanced way. See, for example, Holly Kruse, "Subcultural Identity in Alternative Music Culture," *Popular Music* 12:1 (1993): 33–41; and Will Straw, "Systems of Articulation, Logics of Change: Communities and Scenes in Popular Music," *Cultural Studies* 5:3 (October 1991): 368–88. I use the term here and throughout this work in the same sense as Hall, Jefferson, Hebdige, Kruse, and Straw—to refer to the social groups constellated around particular popular musical genres and the cultural forms they produce.

6. I am drawing here on Ninian Smart's model of the seven dimensions of religion: (1) the ritual or practical (2) the experiential or emotional (3) the narrative or mythic (4) the doctrinal or philosophical (5) the ethical or legal (6) the social or institutional, and (7) the material or artistic. See Ninian Smart, *Dimensions of the Sacred: An Anatomy of the World's Beliefs* (Berkeley: University of

California Press, 1996). I think a convincing case can be made that these musical subcultures function at all seven levels, but I am choosing to focus on the ritual, experiential, philosophical, and social dimensions because they provide the strongest evidence for my argument. I should make clear, however, that I am not conflating these musical subcultures with traditional religions, which integrate all these dimensions into a whole system that pervades all aspects of life.

7. There is an enormous amount of scholarship on the subject of postmodernism, too much to adequately cite here. For a succinct summary of some of the main tenets of postmodern theory, particularly in relation to popular musics, see Peter Manuel, "Music as Symbol, Music as Simulacrum: Postmodern, Pre-Modern, and Modern Aesthetics in Subcultural Popular Musics," *Popular Music* 14:2 (1995): 227–39.

8. Rudolf Otto, *The Idea of the Holy* (New York: Oxford University Press, 1958).

9. Charles H. Long, "Popular Religion," in Mircea Eliade, ed., *The Encyclopedia of Religion,* vol. 18 (New York: Macmillan, 1987), 444.

10. Gerardus Van der Leeuw, *Religion in Essence and Manifestation* (New York: Harper and Row, 1963), vol. 2, 679.

11. Catherine L. Albanese, *America: Religions and Religion,* 2d ed. (Belmont, Calif.: Wadsworth, 1992), 463–500.

12. On the nearly universal connection between music and religion, see Philip P. Bohlman, "Is All Music Religious?" *Criterion* 28:2 (Spring 1989): 19–24. For voluminous examples of this connection, see Charles L. Boiles, *Man, Magic, and Musical Occasions* (Columbus: Collegiate Publishing, 1978).

13. By "West African," I am referring primarily to the Ibo, Yoruba, Fon, Ewe, Ga, and Ashanti peoples of modern Nigeria, Benin, Togo, and Ghana, peoples who inhabit a contiguous geographical region and share striking cultural similarities, particularly in terms of the religious practice of possession dances which we are examining. There is far too much literature on the subject of possession dances to cite here, but for a brief introduction, see John Beattie and John Middleton, eds., *Spirit Mediumship and Society in Africa* (New York: Africana Publishing, 1969), particularly the West African chapters by Margaret Field, "Spirit Possession in Ghana," and Pierre Verger, "Trance and Convention in Nago-Yoruba Spirit Mediumship."

14. For an excellent survey of African American diasporic possession religions, see Joseph Murphy, *Working the Spirit: Ceremonies of the African Diaspora* (Boston: Beacon Press, 1994). And for a structural comparison of West African and African American possession religions, see Sheila S. Walker, *Ceremonial Spirit Possession in Africa and Afro-America: Forms, Meanings, and Functional Significance for Individuals and Social Groups* (Leiden: E. J. Brill, 1972).

15. For more on the continuity between West African musicoreligious practices and sensibilities in African American musics, see Samuel A. Floyd, *The*

Power of Black Music: Interpreting Its History from Africa to the United States (New York: Oxford University Press, 1995); Charles Keil, *Urban Blues* (Chicago: University of Chicago Press, 1966); Portia Maultsby, "West African Influences and Retentions in U.S. Black Music: A Sociocultural Study," in Irene V. Jackson, ed., *More than Dancing* (Westport, Conn.: Greenwood Press, 1985); Paul Oliver, *Savannah Syncopators: African Retentions in the Blues* (New York: Stein and Day, 1970); John Storm Roberts, *Black Music of Two Worlds* (New York: Praeger, 1972); Eileen Southern, *The Music of Black Americans* (New York: Norton, 1983); Michael Ventura, "Hear That Long Snake Moan," *Whole Earth Review,* Spring and Summer 1987, 28–43 and 82–93; Richard Waterman, "African Influences on Music of the Americas," in Sol Tax, ed., *Acculturation in the Americas* (Chicago: University of Chicago Press, 1952); and Olly Wilson, "The Significance of the Relationship between Afro-American Music and West African Music," *The Black Perspective in Music* 2:1 (Spring 1974): 3–22.

16. For more on rock and roll as music for youth rebellion, see Jonathon S. Epstein, ed., *Adolescents and Their Music: If It's Too Loud, You're Too Old* (New York: Garland, 1994), particularly his introduction, the articles by Deena Weinstein, "Rock: Youth and Its Music" and "Expendable Youth: The Rise and Fall of Youth Culture," and Lawrence Grossberg, "The Political Status of Youth and Youth Culture." For more on the appropriation of black styles and musics by rebellious white youth, see Iain Chambers, "A Strategy for Living: Black Music and White Subcultures," in Hall and Jefferson, *Resistance through Rituals.*

17. For the classic formulation of rites of passage, see Arnold Van Gennep, *The Rites of Passage* (London: University of Chicago Press, 1960). For more contemporary work on adolescents and rites of passage, see Louise Carus Mahdi, Steven Foster, and Meredith Little, eds., *Betwixt and Between: Patterns of Masculine and Feminine Initiation* (La Salle: Open Court, 1987).

18. Turner developed these notions of liminality, communitas, and antistructure in his classic *The Ritual Process: Structure and Anti-Structure* (Chicago: Aldine, 1969), thus creating the foundation for the subfield of ritual studies.

19. For interesting scholarship exploring Turnerian notions of liminality, communitas, antistructure, and the ritual aspects of the rock concert, see J. Patrick Gray, "Rock as a Chaos Model Ritual," *Popular Music and Society* 2:7 (1980): 75–83.

20. For the best current overview of contemporary religious studies scholarship on religion and popular culture, see Catherine L. Albanese, "Religion and Popular American Culture: An Introductory Essay," *Journal of the American Academy of Religion* 519:4 (Fall 1996): 733–42, as well as the following set of articles on the same theme. An excellent overall work is Charles H. Lippy, *Being Religious, American Style: A History of Popular Religiosity in the United States* (Westport, Conn.: Praeger, 1994). For an excellent article on the religious dimensions of rock and roll which makes the connection with West African spirituality, see

Ventura, "Hear That Long Snake Moan." Jon Michael Spencer has done a great deal of work on this topic, to which he gives the awkward name of theomusicology, although I find his approach overemphasizes discursive elements at the expense of the musical and experiential. He edits *Black Sacred Music: A Journal of Theomusicology,* and has written several books on the subject, including *Theological Music: An Introduction to Theomusicology* (Westport, Conn.: Greenwood Press, 1991).

21. For an exposition on the Romantic thematic elements in rock and roll, see Robert Pattison, *The Triumph of Vulgarity: Rock Music in the Mirror of Romanticism* (New York: Oxford University Press, 1987).

22. Taylor Rogan has explored the shamanistic roots of rock and roll in his *The Death and Resurrection Show: From Shaman to Superstar* (London: A. Blond, 1985).

23. Charles Long, class lectures, and personal communication, Santa Barbara, 1990–94. Long argues that the notion of "fetish" was the mistaken result of Portuguese misunderstanding of West African sacred objects. The product of this mistake was the creation of a "religious" phenomenon in which spiritual value is given to material commodities and their accumulation. This latent spiritual component in the materialistic drive is a peculiar innovation underlying the European conquest and colonization of the New World and can still be seen in the "religion" of economic growth that dominates American corporate and political discourse.

24. See Gray, "Rock as a Chaos Model Ritual."

25. For good work in the subfield of ritual studies in developing specific categories for structural comparison and analysis, see Ronald Grimes, *Beginnings in Ritual Studies* (Lanham: University Press of America, 1982). For similar categories in the more inclusive subfield of performance studies, as well as a sophisticated theoretical framework, see Richard Schechner, *Performance Theory* (New York: Routledge, 1988).

26. For a first-rate overview of the oppositional, alternative stance of various musical youth subcultures, see Andrew Ross and Tricia Rose, eds., *Microphone Fiends: Youth Music and Youth Culture* (New York: Routledge, 1994). For the liminal qualities of youth subcultures, see Bernice Martin, *A Sociology of Contemporary Cultural Change* (New York: St. Martin's Press, 1981).

27. Susan McClary has done an excellent job of articulating the centrality of the body and its various modalities in organizing meanings of popular musics in "Same as It Ever Was: Youth Culture and Youth Music," in Ross and Rose, *Microphone Fiends.*

28. For a good discussion of the crossroads, see Ventura, "Hear That Long Snake Moan."

29. This is certainly the case with three of the four subcultures in this study: the Deadheads, rave, and hip-hop. The postmortem cult of Elvis and the Church

of John Coltrane are two further examples of the increasingly conscious recognition of the religious dimensions of popular music and the innovative forms emerging as vehicles for their expression.

NOTES TO PART ONE

1. Samuel A. Floyd, Jr., *The Power of Black Music: Interpreting Its History from Africa to the United States* (New York: Oxford University Press, 1995), 33–34.

2. Portia Maultsby, "West African Influences and Retentions in U.S. Black Music: A Sociocultural Study," in Irene V. Jackson, ed., *More than Dancing* (Westport, Conn.: Greenwood Press, 1985), 51.

3. Cornel West, "On Afro-American Music: From Bebop to Rap," *Black Sacred Music* 6:1 (Spring 1992): 283.

4. Michael Ventura, "Hear That Long Snake Moan," *Whole Earth Review*, Spring and Summer 1987, 91.

NOTES TO CHAPTER 1

1. David McAllester, "Some Thoughts on 'Universals' in World Music," *Ethnomusicology* 15:3 (1971): 380.

2. See Andrew Neher, "A Physiological Explanation of Unusual Behavior in Ceremonies Involving Drums," *Human Biology* 34 (1962): 151–60. Neher's work has been attacked for a number of methodological reasons, particularly the lack of causality in explaining the results. See, for example, Gilbert Rouget, *Music and Trance: A Theory of the Relations between Music and Possession* (Chicago: University of Chicago Press, 1985). Rouget's attack, however, never disputes the actual results of the experiment that establishes the physiological impact of the drums. Rouget himself writes of "the sound of the drums, which does incontestably have, at least in certain cases, a genuine physical impact on the listener" and is "capable of producing certain perturbations of the physiological nervous state" (1985: 175).

3. See Barbara Lex, "The Neurobiology of Ritual Trance," in Eugene d'Aquili, Charles D. Laughlin, Jr., and John McManus, eds., *The Spectrum of Ritual: A Biogenetic Structural Analysis* (New York: Columbia University Press, 1979).

4. See Eliot Chapple, *Culture and Biological Man: Explorations in Behavioral Anthropology* (New York: Holt, Rinehart and Winston, 1970), 38.

5. Rouget, *Music and Trance*, 84.

6. Quoted in Leonard Meyer, *Emotion and Meaning in Music* (Chicago: University of Chicago Press, 1956), 10–11.

7. Olly Wilson, "The Association of Movement and Music as a Manifestation of a Black Conceptual Approach to Music-Making," in Irene V. Jackson, ed., *More than Dancing* (Westport, Conn.: Greenwood Press, 1985).

8. Frances Mischel and Walter Mischel, "Psychological Aspects of Spirit Possession," *American Anthropologist* 60 (1958): 250.

9. The phenomenon of spirit possession is complex and multifaceted and I am not suggesting that it is reducible to its physiological component or the physical impact of music. I will discuss this phenomenon in more detail in the next chapter.

10. Susan McClary, "Same as It Ever Was: Youth Culture and Youth Music," in Andrew Ross and Tricia Rose, eds., *Microphone Fiends: Youth Music and Youth Culture* (New York: Routledge, 1994), 33.

11. Rouget, *Music and Trance,* 316.

12. Arnold Ludwig, "Altered States of Consciousness," in Raymond Prince, ed., *Trance and Possession States* (Montreal: University of Montreal Press, 1968), 69–70.

13. McAllester, "'Universals' in World Music," 380.

14. John Blacking, *"A Commonsense View of All Music": Reflections on Percy Grainger's Contribution to Ethnomusicology and Music Education* (Cambridge: Cambridge University Press, 1987), 29.

15. McAllester, "'Universals' in World Music," 380.

16. Blacking, *A Commonsense View,* 67.

17. John Blacking, *How Musical Is Man?* (Seattle: University of Washington Press, 1973), 10. Emphasis added.

18. Blacking, *A Commonsense View,* 21.

19. I should note that the linguistic-semiological model is in no way a definitive or universally accepted or even an agreed-upon framework for understanding music. For a useful survey and critique of linguistic approaches to music, see Steven Feld, "Linguistic Models in Ethnomusicology," *Ethnomusicology* 18:2 (May 1974): 197–217. I am choosing to use semiological terminology here because it offers the best set of conceptual tools to discuss the points I wish to make.

20. Here I am following the work of Jean-Jacques Nattiez in his excellent book, *Music and Discourse: Toward a Semiology of Music* (Princeton: Princeton University Press, 1990).

21. Ibid., 118.

22. Rouget, *Music and Trance,* 101.

23. J. Gonda, *Visnuism and Sivaism: A Comparison* (London: The Athlone Press, 1970), 67.

24. Gerardus Van der Leeuw, *Sacred and Profane Beauty: The Holy in Art* (New York: Holt, Rinehart and Winston, 1963), 253.

25. William Gibson, *Neuromancer* (New York: Ace Books, 1984). This book created an entire genre of science fiction referred to as "cyber-punk," spawning a myriad of imitators not only in novels, but in cinema as well.

26. For a good introduction to some of the basic concepts and technologies, see Howard Rheingold, *Virtual Reality* (New York: Summit Books, 1991).

27. Van der Leeuw, *Sacred and Profane Beauty*, 253.

28. Blacking, *A Commonsense View*, 27.

29. I am well aware that this is a particularly Western understanding of music and that there are other equally valid non-Western understandings. But for the time being I am using these concepts as metaphors to make a specific point.

30. Jonathan Z. Smith, *Imagining Religion: From Babylon to Jonestown* (Chicago: University of Chicago Press, 1982), 63. Emphasis in original.

31. Jonathan Z. Smith, *To Take Place: Toward Theory in Ritual* (Chicago: University of Chicago Press, 1987), 85. Smith uses the term "semiotic."

32. See Victor Turner, *The Ritual Process: Structure and Anti-Structure* (Chicago: Aldine, 1969), for a good discussion of the multivocality of symbols in a ritual context.

33. See Henry Geerts, "An Inquiry into the Meaning of Ritual Symbolism: Turner and Peirce," in H. Barbara Boudewijnse and Hans-Gunter Heimbrock, eds., *Current Studies on Rituals: Perspectives for the Psychology of Religion* (Atlanta: Rodopi, 1990).

34. Ronald Grimes, *Beginnings in Ritual Studies* (Lanham: University Press of America, 1982), 14.

35. Ibid., 207.

36. Ann Dhu Shapiro and Ines Talamantez, "The Mescalero Apache Girl's Puberty Ceremony: The Role of Music in Structuring Ritual Time," in *Yearbook for Traditional Music* 18 (1986): 82.

37. Ibid., 85.

38. Ibid.

39. Ibid., 78. Emphasis in original.

40. Mircea Eliade, *The Myth of the Eternal Return* (London: Routledge and Kegan Paul, 1955), 85.

41. Here, Otto is following the philosophical work of Immanual Kant.

42. Rudolf Otto, *The Idea of the Holy* (New York: Oxford University Press, 1958), 6.

43. Ibid., 48–49.

44. Ibid., 49.

45. Ibid.

46. Van der Leeuw, *Sacred and Profane Beauty*, 231.

47. Ibid., 248.

48. Ibid., 253.

49. Ibid., 261.

50. W. Komla Amoaku, "Toward a Definition of Traditional African Music: A Look at the Ewe of Ghana," in Irene V. Jackson, ed., *More than Drumming: Essays on African and Afro-Latin Music and Musicians* (Westport, Conn.: Greenwood Press, 1985), 34–35.

51. Ibid., 37.

52. Ravi Shankar, *My Music, My Life* (New York: Simon and Schuster, 1968), 16.

53. Quoted in Arun Bhattacharya, *A Treatise on Ancient Hindu Music* (Calcutta: K. P. Bagchi and Company, 1978), 103.

54. Steven M. Friedson, *Dancing Prophets: Musical Experience in Tumbuka Healing* (Chicago: University of Chicago Press, 1996), 5, 168. Emphasis in original.

55. McAllester, "'Universals' in World Music," 380.

NOTES TO CHAPTER 2

1. Although it is their possession groups which are of interest here, I should make clear that they were (and are) part of a larger constellation of religious groups and practices which permeated all sectors of society and all human activities. Some other aspects of this larger constellation included divine kingship and court activities, ancestor worship, divination, male and female societies, medicine and healing, rites of passage such as birth and marriage, mythology and storytelling, and work and agricultural ceremonials.

2. The descriptions and summations in this survey are based on two sets of sources. The first is fieldwork that I conducted in the villages of Kisame, Nungua, and Konkonuru in Ghana, and the greater metropolitan area of Accra, the capital city, in July 1995. The second is gleaned from scholarly sources on the subject. There is too huge a body of material to cite completely, but some of the more important sources I used include John Beattie and John Middleton, eds., *Spirit Mediumship and Society in Africa* (New York: Africana Publishing, 1969); and Michel Huet, *The Dance, Art, and Ritual of Africa* (New York: Pantheon Books, 1978).

3. There are other ways of selecting for initiation or being called, such as family inheritance, but spontaneous possession is the most common.

4. Botchway (no last name given), personal communication, Accra, Ghana, July 1995.

5. For an excellent description of the rigorous training a drummer must go through, see John Miller Chernoff, *African Rhythm and African Sensibility: Aesthetics and Social Action in African Musical Idioms* (Chicago: University of Chicago Press, 1979).

6. There are both female *and* male initiates and priestly officiants. I am using the feminine gender terms here for grammatical simplicity, and because the participants in the ceremonies I witnessed were primarily women. I will use the masculine gender terms for the drummers because they were exclusively men.

7. Robert Farris Thompson, *Flash of the Spirit: African and Afro-American Art and Philosophy* (New York: Random House, 1983), 9.

8. Ibid.

9. Richard Waterman was the first ethnomusicologist to develop this notion

of metronome sense with regard to the polyrhythmic nature of African music. See Richard Waterman, "African Influences on Music of the Americas," in Sol Tax, ed., *Acculturation in the Americas* (Chicago: University of Chicago Press, 1952), 211. More recently, Chernoff has explicated this principle in greater detail based on his own drum apprenticeship to Ibrahim Abdulai, a Dagomba master drummer from northern Ghana. See Chernoff, *African Rhythm and African Sensibility*, 50–60. Many scholars and musicians consider this book to be the definitive work on the rhythmic principles of African music, an opinion with which I concur.

10. Chernoff, *African Rhythm and African Sensibility*, 51.

11. See J. H. Kwabena Nketia, *The Music of Africa* (New York: Norton, 1974) and John Storm Roberts, *Black Music of Two Worlds* (New York: Praeger, 1972).

12. See Cedric J. Robinson, *Black Marxism: The Making of the Black Radical Tradition* (Totowa, N.J.: Biblio Distribution Center, 1983). For more in-depth statistics on the trans-Atlantic slave trade, see Philip D. Curtin, *The Atlantic Slave Trade: A Census* (Madison: University of Wisconsin Press, 1969); Robert William Fogel and Stanley L. Engerman, *Time on the Cross: The Economics of American Slavery* (Boston: Little, Brown and Co., 1974); George Eaton Simpson, *Black Religions in the New World* (New York: Columbia University Press, 1978), 3–12; and Mechal Sobel, *Trabelin' On: The Slave Journey to an Afro-Baptist Faith* (Westport, Conn.: Greenwood Press, 1979).

13. Simpson, *Black Religions in the New World*, 7.

14. Ibid., 4–5.

15. Ibid., 12.

16. See Albert Raboteau, *Slave Religion: The "Invisible Institution" in the Antebellum South* (New York, Oxford University Press, 1978), 16–42, for an historical overview of the many African American diasporic possession religions. For an excellent survey of contemporary forms, see Joseph Murphy, *Working the Spirit: Ceremonies of the African Diaspora* (Boston: Beacon Press, 1994). And for a structural comparison of West African and African American possession religions, see Sheila S. Walker, *Ceremonial Spirit Possession in Africa and Afro-America: Forms, Meanings, and Functional Significance for Individuals and Social Groups* (Leiden: E. J. Brill, 1972).

17. Simpson reports, for example, that "At the end of the eighteenth century, the average sugar plantation in Jamaica was staffed with about 180 slaves; in Virginia and Maryland the average plantation had less than 13 slaves." Simpson, *Black Religions in the New World*, 18.

18. Ibid., 19. This is in contrast to the slave populations of the Caribbean, which had a majority of African-born.

19. This statement is a generalization and is correct in characterizing the overall restrictions on religious and musical practice in the United States during slavery, especially in comparison with the Caribbean and South America. However, in more

specific circumstances, slave systems varied greatly throughout the United States, and there is evidence of some retentions of African practices such as festivals like 'Lection Day and Pinkster Day, rain ceremonials, and African songs and stories. See Portia Maultsby, "Africanisms in African-American Music," in Joseph E. Holloway, ed., *Africanisms in American Culture* (Bloomington: Indiana University Press, 1990), 196–97.

20. Harriet Ware, quoted in Murphy, *Working the Spirit,* 148. For more on the ring shout, see Raboteau, *Slave Religion,* 68–75.

21. Charles H. Long, personal communication, May 21, 1998.

22. This is not to imply that there weren't important differences in liturgies, worship styles, church membership, and other elements. Obviously, there were. But I am choosing here to note their overall similarities in order to highlight the striking differences between the *musical* practices of these African American churches and those of their white counterparts.

23. Clifton Furness, quoted in Murphy, *Working the Spirit,* 149.

24. See Maultsby, "Africanisms in African-American Music," 197–98.

25. The awakenings took the form of large religious revival gatherings in tent encampments in fields and forests throughout the country. In these liminal contexts, African Americans and European Americans would intermingle in ways that were not possible in normal contexts at that time, joining together in Christian liturgy, prayer, song, and dance. The religious fervor of these gatherings was intense and contagious, and swept across the country in three distinct waves. For an excellent exposition on the awakenings, see William McLoughlin, *Revivals, Awakenings, and Reform: An Essay on Religion and Social Change in America, 1607–1977* (Chicago: University of Chicago Press, 1978).

26. See Maultsby, "Africanisms in African-American Music," 186.

27. Ibid., 200.

28. Michael Ventura, "Hear That Long Snake Moan," *Whole Earth Review,* Spring and Summer 1987, 36–37.

29. Henry Edward Durell, 1853, quoted in Ventura, "Hear That Long Snake Moan," 37–38.

30. Ventura, "Hear That Long Snake Moan," 38. Emphasis in original.

31. For an excellent chronology and genealogy of blues styles, see Charles Keil, *Urban Blues* (Chicago: University of Chicago Press, 1966), 217–20.

32. A typical blues structure would consist of a basic 4/4 twelve-bar pattern divided into three stanzas, each with a call and response. The harmonic structure usually falls into a I—IV—I—V—I chord progression. The distinctive "blues" feeling comes from the flatting of the third, fifth, and seventh notes of the scale. For a more detailed description of typical blues structures, see Keil, *Urban Blues,* 51–53.

33. John Storm Roberts, *Black Music of Two Worlds* (New York: Praeger, 1972), 180–94.

34. Keil, *Urban Blues,* 143

35. Ibid., 164.

36. The classic exposition of this theme is James Cone, *The Spirituals and the Blues: An Interpretation* (New York: Seabury Press, 1972).

37. Lawrence Levine has traced the development of these African American sacred musical traditions in great detail, from the spirituals of slave times, to the postemancipation rise of gospel song in the 1930s. These sacred song forms have become part and parcel of African American culture, and still exert an enormous influence today on contemporary African American religion and music. Lawrence Levine, *Black Culture and Black Consciousness: Afro-American Folk Thought from Slavery to Freedom* (New York: Oxford University Press, 1977).

38. For a detailed discussion of these theological issues, see Cone, *The Spirituals and the Blues.*

39. James Cone, "Blues: A Secular Spiritual," in Jon Michael Spencer, ed., *Sacred Music of the Secular City: From Blues to Rap* (Durham: Duke University Press, 1992), 96–97. Emphasis in original.

40. This is not to say that there were not any number of white aficionados in the audience, or even accomplished white musicians in any given African American musical genre. There were, particularly in jazz. It is simply that the core constituency of these musics remained primarily African American.

41. For an excellent analysis of these affinities from a class-oriented perspective, see Iain Chambers, "A Strategy for Living," in Stuart Hall and Tony Jefferson, eds., *Resistance through Rituals: Youth Subcultures in Postwar Britain* (London: HarperCollins Academic, 1976), 157–66. For more on the important role black radio stations played in exposing white listeners to rhythm and blues, see Nelson George, *The Death of Rhythm and Blues* (New York: Pantheon Books, 1988).

42. Ventura, "Hear That Long Snake Moan," 89.

43. One example of this is the popularization of minstrelsy in the nineteenth century by white performers. The popularity of early jazz musicians like Bix Beiderbecke and Benny Goodman among mainstream white audiences is another good example of this phenomenon. For a more detailed discussion of the dynamics of white appropriation of African American musics, see LeRoi Jones, *Blues People: Negro Music in White America* (New York: William Morrow, 1963). For more on appropriation with respect to rock and roll, see Chambers, "A Strategy for Living," and Joe Ferrandino, "Rock Culture and the Development of Social Consciousness," in George Lewis, ed., *Side-Saddle on the Golden Calf: Social Structure and Popular Culture in America* (Pacific Palisades: Goodyear Publishing, 1972).

44. See David Szatmary, *Rockin' in Time: A Social History of Rock-and-Roll,* 3d ed. (Uppersaddle River, N.J.: Prentice Hall, 1996), 46.

45. Quoted in Ventura, "Hear That Long Snake Moan," 91.

46. Ventura, "Hear That Long Snake Moan," 90.

47. Country and western was, and continues to be, another popular genre of music with a predominantly white audience. Country and western grew out of British acoustic guitar–based folk idioms as they evolved in the rural and hillbilly cultures of the Appalachians and the southern United States. It features primarily I—IV—V chord progressions, simple four rhythms, the pedal steel guitar, and "twangy"-style vocals.

48. See, for example, James S. Coleman, *The Adolescent Society* (New York: Free Press, 1961).

49. For more on white appropriations of jazz, see Neil Leonard, *Jazz and the White Americans: The Acceptance of a New Art Form* (Chicago: University of Chicago Press, 1962), and Kathy J. Ogren, *The Jazz Revolution: Twenties America and the Meaning of Jazz* (New York: Oxford University Press, 1989).

50. For more on the emergence of youth culture in the 1950s, its oppositional stance, and its appropriation of African American musics like rhythm and blues to rock and roll, see Jonathon S. Epstein, ed., *Adolescents and Their Music: If It's Too Loud, You're Too Old* (New York: Garland, 1994), particularly his introduction, "Introduction: Misplaced Youth: An Introduction to the Sociology of Youth and Their Music." In the same volume, also see Deena Weinstein, "Rock: Youth and Its Music" and "Expendable Youth: The Rise and Fall of Youth Culture"; Lawrence Grossberg, "The Political Status of Youth and Youth Culture"; and Daniel Dotter, "Rock and Roll Is Here to Stay: Youth Subculture, Deviance, and Social Typing in Rock's Early Years."

51. Ventura, "Hear That Long Snake Moan," 90.

52. Ibid., 91.

53. One of the best is Robert Palmer, *Rock and Roll: An Unruly History* (New York: Harmony Books, 1995).

54. McLoughlin, *Revivals, Awakenings, and Reform*, 1–23.

55. I will go into the history of these musics in more detail in the section on hip-hop and rap.

56. See Szatmary, *Rockin' in Time*, 104–12.

57. For more on the splintering of youth culture and rock audiences at the end of the 1960s, see Deena Weinstein, *Heavy Metal: A Cultural Sociology* (New York: Lexington Books, 1991), 12–13.

58. In 1976, for example, disco music, which had begun in gay African American clubs in New York and other large American cities, crossed over to the mainstream with the movie *Saturday Night Fever* and its best-selling sound track by the white British group, the Bee Gees. At the same time, punk rock was attracting a completely different subcultural audience in London and New York. Also at the same time, classical rock groups like Yes were enjoying huge success among a different audience, while heavy metal bands were doing the same with their own distinctive audience. Likewise with glam rock stars like David Bowie, funk stars like George Clinton, and so forth.

59. For an excellent overview of the punk phenomenon, as well as insightful analysis pertaining to the symbolic uses of style and the dynamics of appropriation, see Dick Hebdige, *Subculture: The Meaning of Style* (New York: Methuen, 1979). Punk provides another example of the importance of England in rock music history and the trans-Atlantic musical exchange between England and the United States.

60. Ventura, "Hear That Long Snake Moan," 90.

NOTES TO PART TWO

1. For more information on interview methodology, including the selection process, the interview process, the questions, and the interviewees, see the Appendix.

2. See Andrew Greeley, *God in Popular Culture* (Chicago: Thomas More Press, 1988).

3. See Jon Wiley Nelson, *Your God Is Alive and Well and Appearing in Popular Culture* (Philadelphia: Westminster Press, 1976).

4. Jon Michael Spencer, "Preface: Sacred Music of the Secular City," *Black Sacred Music: A Journal of Theomusicology* 6:1 (Spring 1992): v–vi.

5. Charles H. Long, "Popular Religion," in Mircea Eliade, ed., *The Encyclopedia of Religion* (New York: Macmillan, 1987), vol. 18, 447.

6. Ibid. Emphasis added.

7. William C. Shepherd, "Religion and the Counter Culture—A New Religiosity," *Sociological Inquiry* 42:1 (1972): 3–9. Emphasis in original.

8. Ninian Smart has proposed what I believe is one of the best working models to broadly categorize these forms, outlining seven dimensions of religion: (1) the ritual or practical, (2) the experiential or emotional, (3) the narrative or mythic, (4) the doctrinal or philosophical, (5) the ethical or legal, (6) the social or institutional, and (7) the material or artistic. Ninian Smart, *Dimensions of the Sacred: An Anatomy of the World's Beliefs* (Berkeley: University of California Press, 1996). Using this model, I think that a convincing case can be made for each one of these dimensions with respect to popular music subcultures. However, I will focus primarily on the ones mentioned above because they are the most important, because they provide the strongest evidence, and also because spatial constraints necessitate limiting the scope of this study.

9. William James, *The Varieties of Religious Experience: A Study in Human Nature* (London: Collins, 1968).

10. Joachim Wach, *The Comparative Study of Religions* (New York: Columbia University Press, 1958), 18.

11. Van der Leeuw, quoted in Eric J. Sharpe, *Comparative Religion: A History* (La Salle, Ill.: Open Court, 1986), 231.

1. David Shenk and Steve Silberman, *Skeleton Key: A Dictionary for Deadheads* (New York: Doubleday, 1994), 4–5.

2. For more on the Haight-Ashbury scene, see Hank Harrison, *The Dead: A Social History of the Haight-Ashbury Experience* (San Francisco: Archives Press, 1990), 123–46; Rock Scully, with David Dalton, *Living with the Dead: Twenty Years on the Bus with Garcia and the Grateful Dead* (Boston: Little, Brown and Company, 1996), 51–134; Shenk and Silberman, *Skeleton Key,* 130–35; and Sandy Troy, *One More Saturday Night: Reflections with the Grateful Dead, Dead Family, and Dead Heads* (New York: St. Martin's Press, 1991), 5–16.

3. Interestingly, Garcia himself was always uncomfortable being viewed in this way, calling the Captain Trips title "bullshit" (Shenk and Silberman, *Skeleton Key,* 32), and making a conscious attempt to not be seen as a religious figure (ibid., 165). As a whole, the rest of the Grateful Dead mirror this reticence with regard to being viewed as religious or spiritual leaders. I will return to this subject in more detail later.

4. Although this is a subject of some debate, it is generally acknowledged that the live Grateful Dead concert experience has never been effectively captured in studio recordings. Interestingly, in its thirty-year history, while becoming one of the largest-grossing concert acts of all time, the band has never had a hit record, perhaps mirroring the untranslatability of the concert experience.

5. For more on the San Francisco sound and acid rock, see Paul Friedlander, *Rock and Roll: A Social History* (Boulder: Westview Press, 1996), 190–208; and David Szatmary, *Rockin' in Time: A Social History of Rock-and-Roll,* 3d ed. (Uppersaddle River, N.J.: Prentice Hall, 1996), 139–60.

6. Szatmary, *Rockin' in Time,* 188.

7. Troy, *One More Saturday Night,* 19.

8. These were the last albums with founding member and keyboardist Pigpen (Ron McKernan), who began to suffer from alcohol-related illness and died in 1973. He was replaced by keyboardist Keith Godchaux.

9. The Grateful Dead released two records on their label: *Wake of the Flood* (1973) and *From the Mars Hotel* (1974).

10. Troy, *One More Saturday Night,* 25–27.

11. Shenk and Silberman, *Skeleton Key,* 61.

12. Ibid., 290–91.

13. Toura Williams, quoted in ibid., 291.

14. "A 1988 *Relix* magazine survey states that 91 percent of Deadheads regularly travel away from their home base to attend shows, and most Heads who responded to a survey in *DeadBase* see an average of seven or so consecutive shows at a time. According to Steve Marcus of Grateful Dead Ticket Sales, there are approximately two thousand Heads who order tickets for every show, and another

five hundred who go to every show, but don't necessarily try to get in." Ibid., 292–93.

15. Robert Sardiello, "Secular Rituals in Popular Culture: A Case for Grateful Dead Concerts and Dead Head Identity," in Jonathon S. Epstein, ed., *Adolescents and Their Music: If It's Too Loud, You're Too Old* (New York: Garland, 1994), 122. This is an interesting paper that argues for Dead concerts as rituals, drawing heavily on anthropologist Victor Turner's concepts.

16. Quoted in Sardiello, "Secular Rituals in Popular Culture," 122.

17. Quoted in ibid., 123–24.

18. Tie-dyes tend to be brightly colored, swirling patterns that bear some resemblance to hallucinogenic visions. The word "tie-dye" refers to the technical process of fabric dyeing, in which sections of the cloth are tied off.

19. Sardiello discusses Deadhead iconography and totemic symbolization in his article, "Secular Rituals in Popular Culture," 124–27.

20. I attended several Grateful Dead shows in the late 1970s and early 1980s in Seattle, Washington, and Portland and Eugene, Oregon.

21. Steve Silberman, "The Only Song of God," in *Garcia: A Grateful Celebration* (New York: Dupree's Diamond News, 1995), 87.

22. Paul Hoffman, quoted in Shenk and Silberman, *Skeleton Key,* 136.

23. Ibid., 269.

24. Quoted in ibid., 270.

25. Ibid., 252.

26. Silberman, "The Only Song of God," 89. Emphasis in original.

27. Helen Rossi, Gary Greenberg, and Gary Burnett, quoted in Shenk and Silberman, *Skeleton Key,* 336.

28. Shan C. Sutton, "The Deadhead Community: A Popular Religion in Contemporary American Culture," Master's Thesis, Wright State University, 1993, quoted in Shenk and Silberman, *Skeleton Key,* 65.

29. Sutton, quoted in Shenk and Silberman, *Skeleton Key,* 127.

30. Sardiello, "Secular Rituals in Popular Culture," 128.

31. Bob Bralove, from the liner notes for *Infrared Roses,* Grateful Dead, BMG 14014.

32. Garcia, quoted in Shenk and Silberman, *Skeleton Key,* 256.

33. Quoted in Shenk and Silberman, *Skeleton Key,* 290.

34. David Gans, "Introduction: I'll Show You Snow and Rain," in David Gans, ed., *Not Fade Away: The On-Line World Remembers Jerry Garcia* (New York: Thunder's Mouth Press, 1995), 16–17.

35. Ibid., 22.

36. Bill Lyman, interview by author, tape recording, Berkeley, Calif., 3 July 1997.

37. Lisa Mishke, interview by author, tape recording, Berkeley, Calif., 9 August 1997.

38. Ibid.

39. Steve Silberman, interview by author, tape recording, Berkeley, Calif., 17 February 1996.

40. Bill Lyman, interview by author, tape recording, Berkeley, Calif., 3 July 1997.

41. Steve Silberman, interview by author, tape recording, Berkeley, Calif., 17 February 1996.

42. James Romero, interview by author, tape recording, San Francisco, Calif., 7 July 1997.

43. Bill Lyman, interview by author, tape recording, Berkeley, Calif., 3 July 1997.

44. Steve Silberman, interview by author, tape recording, Berkeley, Calif., 17 February 1996.

45. Kathleen Harrison, interview by author, tape recording, Occidental, Calif., 13 July 1997.

46. Steve Silberman, interview by author, tape recording, Berkeley, Calif., 17 February 1996.

47. Kathleen Harrison, interview by author, tape recording, Occidental, Calif., 13 July 1997.

48. Steve Silberman, interview by author, tape recording, Berkeley, Calif., 17 February 1996.

49. Ibid.

50. Ibid.

51. James Romero, interview by author, tape recording, San Francisco, Calif., 7 July 1997.

52. Kathleen Harrison, interview by author, tape recording, Occidental, Calif., 13 July 1997.

53. Steve Silberman, interview by author, tape recording, Berkeley, Calif., 17 February 1996.

54. Bill Lyman, interview by author, tape recording, Berkeley, Calif., 3 July 1997.

55. Steve Silberman, interview by author, tape recording, Berkeley, Calif., 17 February 1996.

56. See, for example, Peter Furst, "The Roots and Continuities of Shamanism," in Anne Trueblood Brodzky, Rose Danesewich, and Nick Johnson, eds., *Stones, Bones and Skin: Ritual and Shamanic Art* (Toronto: Society for Art Publications, 1977), 8–28.

57. Victor Turner, *The Ritual Process: Structure and Anti-Structure* (Chicago: Aldine, 1969).

58. Bill Lyman, interview by author, tape recording, Berkeley, Calif., 3 July 1997.

59. James Romero, interview by author, tape recording, San Francisco, Calif., 7 July 1997.

60. Steve Silberman, interview by author, tape recording, Berkeley, Calif., 17 February 1996.

61. James Romero, interview by author, tape recording, San Francisco, Calif., 7 July 1997.

62. Quoted in Steve Silberman, interview by author, tape recording, Berkeley, Calif., 17 February 1996.

63. Ibid. Emphasis added.

64. Kathleen Harrison, interview by author, tape recording, Occidental, Calif., 13 July 1997.

65. Ibid.

66. Steve Silberman, interview by author, tape recording, Berkeley, Calif., 17 February 1996, and Kathleen Harrison, interview by author, tape recording, Occidental, Calif., 13 July 1997.

67. Kathleen Harrison, interview by author, tape recording, Occidental, Calif., 13 July 1997.

68. Ibid.

69. Bill Lyman, interview by author, tape recording, Berkeley, Calif., 3 July 1997.

70. Steve Silberman, interview by author, tape recording, Berkeley, Calif., 17 February 1996.

71. Ibid.

72. Ibid.

73. Ibid.

74. Ibid.

75. Lisa Mishke, interview by author, tape recording, Berkeley, Calif., 9 August 1997.

76. Steve Silberman, interview by author, tape recording, Berkeley, Calif., 17 February 1996.

77. Lisa Mishke, interview by author, tape recording, Berkeley, Calif., 9 August 1997.

78. Steve Silberman, interview by author, tape recording, Berkeley, Calif., 17 February 1996.

79. Bill Lyman, interview by author, tape recording, Berkeley, Calif., 3 July 1997.

80. Ibid.

81. Steve Silberman, interview by author, tape recording, Berkeley, Calif., 17 February 1996.

82. Kathleen Harrison, interview by author, tape recording, Occidental, Calif., 13 July 1997.

83. Steve Silberman, interview by author, tape recording, Berkeley, Calif., 17 February 1996.

84. Ibid.

85. Bill Lyman, interview by author, tape recording, Berkeley, Calif., 3 July 1997.

86. Gilbert Rouget, *Music and Trance: A Theory of the Relations between Music and Possession* (Chicago: University of Chicago Press, 1985), 101.

87. Bill Lyman, interview by author, tape recording, Berkeley, Calif., 3 July 1997.

88. Steve Silberman, interview by author, tape recording, Berkeley, Calif., 17 February 1996.

89. Bill Lyman, interview by author, tape recording, Berkeley, Calif., 3 July 1997.

90. Lisa Mishke, interview by author, tape recording, Berkeley, Calif., 9 August 1997.

91. Steve Silberman, interview by author, tape recording, Berkeley, Calif., 17 February 1996.

92. Bill Lyman, interview by author, tape recording, Berkeley, Calif., 3 July 1997.

93. Kathleen Harrison, interview by author, tape recording, Occidental, Calif., 13 July 1997.

94. Ibid.

95. Steve Silberman, interview by author, tape recording, Berkeley, Calif., 17 February 1996.

96. Lisa Mishke, interview by author, tape recording, Berkeley, Calif., 9 August 1997.

97. Bill Lyman, interview by author, tape recording, Berkeley, Calif., 3 July 1997.

98. Steve Silberman, interview by author, tape recording, Berkeley, Calif., 17 February 1996.

99. Kathleen Harrison, interview by author, tape recording, Occidental, Calif., 13 July 1997.

100. Steve Silberman, interview by author, tape recording, Berkeley, Calif., 17 February 1996.

101. Kathleen Harrison, interview by author, tape recording, Occidental, Calif., 13 July 1997.

102. Steve Silberman, interview by author, tape recording, Berkeley, Calif., 17 February 1996.

103. Lisa Mishke, interview by author, tape recording, Berkeley, Calif., 9 August 1997.

104. Kathleen Harrison, interview by author, tape recording, Occidental, Calif., 13 July 1997.

105. Steve Silberman, interview by author, tape recording, Berkeley, Calif., 17 February 1996.

106. Bill Lyman, interview by author, tape recording, Berkeley, Calif., 3 July 1997.

107. Kathleen Harrison, interview by author, tape recording, Occidental, Calif., 13 July 1997.

108. Lisa Mishke, interview by author, tape recording, Berkeley, Calif., 9 August 1997.

109. Bill Lyman, interview by author, tape recording, Berkeley, Calif., 3 July 1997.

110. Ibid.

111. Oren Baruch Stier, "Virtual Torah, Digital Mourning: Communal Experiences in Cyberspace," paper presented at the annual meeting of the American Academy of Religion, New Orleans, Louisiana, 24 November 1996, unpublished draft. This paper contains a survey of numerous Grateful Dead and Deadhead locations and resources on the Internet as well as interesting theoretical formulations as to the implications of Internet communities. See also Shenk and Silberman, *Skeleton Key,* for a compendium of Grateful Dead and Deadhead locations and resources on the Internet.

112. Steve Silberman, interview by author, tape recording, Berkeley, Calif., 17 February 1996.

113. For an excellent document of this spontaneous virtual gathering, see Gans, *Not Fade Away.*

114. Bill Lyman, interview by author, tape recording, Berkeley, Calif., 3 July 1997.

115. Steve Silberman, interview by author, tape recording, Berkeley, Calif., 17 February 1996.

116. Gary Greenberg, quoted in Gans, *Not Fade Away,* 42–44.

117. Kathleen Harrison, interview by author, tape recording, Occidental, Calif., 13 July 1997.

118. Steve Silberman, interview by author, tape recording, Berkeley, Calif., 17 February 1996.

119. Ibid.

120. Lisa Mishke, interview by author, tape recording, Berkeley, Calif., 9 August 1997.

121. Bill Lyman, interview by author, tape recording, Berkeley, Calif., 3 July 1997.

122. Ibid.

123. James Romero, interview by author, tape recording, San Francisco, Calif., 7 July 1997.

124. Bill Lyman, interview by author, tape recording, Berkeley, Calif., 3 July 1997.

125. Steve Silberman, interview by author, tape recording, Berkeley, Calif., 17 February 1996.

126. Kathleen Harrison, interview by author, tape recording, Occidental, Calif., 13 July 1997.

127. Ibid.

128. Robert Hunter, *The Wheel*, in *The Annotated Grateful Dead Lyrics: A Web Site* [database on-line] (Santa Cruz, Calif.: January 1995, accessed 26 March 1998); available from http://arts.ucsc.edu/GDead/AGDL/wheel.html; Internet.

129. Robert Hunter, *Stella Blue*, in *The Annotated Grateful Dead Lyrics: A Web Site* [database on-line] (Santa Cruz, Calif.: January 1995, accessed 5 June 1998); available from http://arts.ucsc.edu/GDead/AGDL/stella.html; Internet.

130. Steve Silberman, interview by author, tape recording, Berkeley, Calif., 17 February 1996.

131. Kathleen Harrison, interview by author, tape recording, Occidental, Calif., 13 July 1997.

132. Robert Hunter, *Eyes of the World*, in *The Annotated Grateful Dead Lyrics: A Web Site* [database on-line] (Santa Cruz, Calif.: January 1995, accessed 26 March 1998); available from http://arts.ucsc.edu/GDead/AGDL/eyes.html; Internet.

133. Robert Hunter, *Scarlet Begonias*, in *The Annotated Grateful Dead Lyrics: A Web Site* [database on-line] (Santa Cruz, Calif.: January 1995, accessed 5 June 1998); available from http://arts.ucsc.edu/GDead/AGDL/scarlet.html; Internet.

134. Robert Hunter, *Dark Star*, in *The Annotated Grateful Dead Lyrics: A Web Site* [database on-line] (Santa Cruz, Calif.: January 1995, accessed 26 March 1998); available from http://arts.ucsc.edu/GDead/AGDL/darkstar.html; Internet.

NOTES TO CHAPTER 4

1. The *Saturday Night Fever* sound track sold more than 30 million copies worldwide. David Szatmary, *Rockin' in Time: A Social History of Rock-and-Roll* (Uppersaddle River, N.J.: Prentice Hall, 1996), 218.

2. "Throughout the country in 1978, more than 36 million Americans danced on the floors of 20,000 discos. . . . By 1979, disco . . . was a $5-billion industry." Ibid.

3. Established stars like Rod Stewart and the Rolling Stones recorded disco-influenced songs which became hits (*Do Ya Think I'm Sexy* and *Miss You*, respectively), and even the Grateful Dead showed a disco influence in their 1978 song *Shakedown Street*.

4. Harvey Tyler, *History of Rave* [article on-line] (April 1995, accessed 14 December 1996); available from http://www.breaks.com/Journey/intro.html; Internet.

5. Chris Torella, Dino & Terry, and 2 Hillbillies, "Explorer's Guide to House, 2nd Edition," *Streetsound*, August 1993, 16.

6. Kai Fikentscher, "Feel the Groove: An Examination of the Interaction be-

tween House Music DJs and Dancers," paper presented at the annual meeting of the Society for Ethnomusicology, Los Angeles, California, 19 October 1995, un-published draft, 4.

7. Mike Lasmanis, "High on Raving," in *The Spirit of Raving: Archives* [database on-line] (San Francisco: Hyperreal, 28 June 1995, accessed 24 January 1997); avail-able from http://www.hyperreal.com/raves/spirit//testimonials/High_on_Raving .html; Internet.

8. Vita Miezitis, *Night Dancin'* (New York: Ballantine, 1980), xx.

9. Steven Harvey, quoted in Fikentscher, "Feel the Groove," 7.

10. See Fikentscher, "Feel the Groove," 6–7.

11. Ibid., 6.

12. Frankie Knuckles, quoted in Fikentscher, "Feel the Groove," 6.

13. Some examples of this kind of success were: Madonna's 1989 hit single *Vogue,* which was not only strongly house-influenced musically but featured dance moves lifted directly from house clubs in New York; Deee-Lite's 1989 single *Groove Is in the Heart*; and Technotronic's 1990 hit *Pump Up the Jam.*

14. Sarah Thornton, *Club Cultures: Music, Media, and Subcultural Capital* (Hanover: Wesleyan University Press, 1996), 14–25.

15. A sampler allows one to record any sound, "take a sample," so to speak, and store it digitally. One can then reproduce this sound in any pitch by simply pressing a button or the appropriate key on a keyboard, or the samples can be looped to repeat themselves over and over. Samples have been used in a variety of ways, forming the rhythm tracks of songs with grooves sampled from James Brown, for example, or as a novelty, such as sampling the theme from old televi-sion shows. A sequencer allows one to write musical sequences for keyboards, bass, drum machine, or any other synthesized sound, and play them with the press of a button. This relieves a musician of the need to play difficult parts live, or having accompanying musicians, or playing certain parts over and over, or playing at a humanly impossible speed.

16. This is where the subgenre of "ambient" music got its start, at least in rela-tion to the acid house and rave subcultures.

17. See, for example, Sarah Thornton, "Moral Panic, the Media and British Rave Culture," in Andrew Ross and Tricia Rose, eds., *Microphone Fiends: Youth Music and Youth Culture* (New York: Routledge, 1994), 176–92.

18. Tyler, *History of Rave.*

19. Alaura O'Dell, interview by author, tape recording, Occidental, Calif., 13 July 1997.

20. Bob (no last name), "Rave Mass," in *The Spirit of Raving: Archives* [data-base on-line] (San Francisco: Hyperreal, 28 November 1995, accessed 24 January 1997); available from http://www.hyperreal.com/raves/spirit/culture/Rave_Mass .html; Internet.

21. Lee (no last name), "Rave Mass." This caught the attention of Oakland-

based American priest, theologian, and author Matthew Fox. Inspired by his experience, Fox organized his own "Techno Cosmic Mass" under the auspices of his Center for Creation Spirituality (now the University of Creation Spirituality) and held it in the basement of Grace Cathedral in 1994. This gathering proved to be quite popular and generated enough interest for subsequent Techno Cosmic Masses to be held at irregular intervals up to the present day.

22. See *The Spirit of Raving: Archives* section on PLUR for more information concerning its origins, further articulations of its ideology, and ramifications for daily life.

23. Tyler, *History of Rave.*

24. Guy Garcia, "Tripping the Night Fantastic," *Time,* 17 August 1992, 60–61.

25. Charlotte Kaufman, interview by author, tape recording, San Francisco, Calif., 23 July 1997.

26. Gus Lanzas, interview by author, tape recording, San Francisco, Calif., 16 July 1997.

27. Jeff Taylor, interview by author, tape recording, San Francisco, Calif., 24 July 1997.

28. Tiffany Scott, interview by author, tape recording, San Francisco, Calif., 24 July 1997.

29. James Romero, interview by author, tape recording, San Francisco, Calif., 7 July 1997.

30. Joel Dinolt, interview by author, tape recording, San Francisco, Calif., 16 July 1997.

31. Sabrina Page, interview by author, tape recording, Fairfax, Calif., 14 July 1997.

32. Charlotte Kaufman, interview by author, tape recording, San Francisco, Calif., 23 July 1997.

33. Vince Thomas, interview by author, tape recording, San Francisco, Calif., 2 February 1996.

34. Ibid.

35. Jim Dunn, interview by author, tape recording, San Francisco, Calif., 25 July 1997.

36. Bahar Badizadegan, interview by author, tape recording, San Francisco, Calif., 2 August 1997.

37. James Romero, interview by author, tape recording, San Francisco, Calif., 7 July 1997.

38. Tiffany Scott, interview by author, tape recording, San Francisco, Calif., 24 July 1997.

39. Chris Lum, interview by author, tape recording, San Francisco, Calif., 10 July 1997.

40. James Romero, interview by author, tape recording, San Francisco, Calif., 7 July 1997.

41. Ibid.

42. Vince Thomas, interview by author, tape recording, San Francisco, Calif., 2 February 1996.

43. Charlotte Kaufman, interview by author, tape recording, San Francisco, Calif., 23 July 1997.

44. Ibid.

45. Sabrina Page, interview by author, tape recording, Fairfax, Calif., 14 July 1997.

46. James Romero, interview by author, tape recording, San Francisco, Calif., 7 July 1997.

47. Sabrina Page, interview by author, tape recording, Fairfax, Calif., 14 July 1997.

48. Ibid.

49. Ibid.

50. Jeff Taylor, interview by author, tape recording, San Francisco, Calif., 24 July 1997.

51. Ibid.

52. Joel Dinolt, interview by author, tape recording, San Francisco, Calif., 16 July 1997.

53. Gus Lanzas, interview by author, tape recording, San Francisco, Calif., 16 July 1997.

54. Jeff Taylor, interview by author, tape recording, San Francisco, Calif., 24 July 1997.

55. Sabrina Page, interview by author, tape recording, Fairfax, Calif., 14 July 1997.

56. James Romero, interview by author, tape recording, San Francisco, Calif., 7 July 1997.

57. Sabrina Page, interview by author, tape recording, Fairfax, Calif., 14 July 1997.

58. I think this theoretical model is too simplistic and mechanistic, especially in light of the complex multidimensionality of music laid out in chapter 1. Nevertheless, it raises some interesting and potentially fruitful directions for further theorizing and research on the relationship between the type of music, its effect on areas of the body, and the production of characteristic experiential states.

59. Chris Lum, interview by author, tape recording, San Francisco, Calif., 10 July 1997.

60. Tiffany Scott, interview by author, tape recording, San Francisco, Calif., 24 July 1997.

61. Jeff Taylor, interview by author, tape recording, San Francisco, Calif., 24 July 1997.

62. James Romero, interview by author, tape recording, San Francisco, Calif., 7 July 1997.

63. Gus Lanzas, interview by author, tape recording, San Francisco, Calif., 16 July 1997.

64. Vince Thomas, interview by author, tape recording, San Francisco, Calif., 2 February 1996.

65. Joel Dinolt, interview by author, tape recording, San Francisco, Calif., 16 July 1997.

66. Gus Lanzas, interview by author, tape recording, San Francisco, Calif., 16 July 1997.

67. Joel Dinolt, interview by author, tape recording, San Francisco, Calif., 16 July 1997.

68. Alaura O'Dell, interview by author, tape recording, Occidental, Calif., 13 July 1997.

69. Vince Thomas, interview by author, tape recording, San Francisco, Calif., 2 February 1996.

70. Charlotte Kaufman, interview by author, tape recording, San Francisco, Calif., 23 July 1997.

71. Chris Lum, interview by author, tape recording, San Francisco, Calif., 10 July 1997.

72. Jeff Taylor, interview by author, tape recording, San Francisco, Calif., 24 July 1997.

73. Tiffany Scott, interview by author, tape recording, San Francisco, Calif., 24 July 1997.

74. James Romero, interview by author, tape recording, San Francisco, Calif., 7 July 1997.

75. Jim Dunn, interview by author, tape recording, San Francisco, Calif., 25 July 1997.

76. Vince Thomas, interview by author, tape recording, San Francisco, Calif., 2 February 1996.

77. Alaura O'Dell, interview by author, tape recording, Occidental, Calif., 13 July 1997.

78. James Romero, interview by author, tape recording, San Francisco, Calif., 7 July 1997.

79. Ibid.

80. Vince Thomas, interview by author, tape recording, San Francisco, Calif., 2 February 1996.

81. Jim Dunn, interview by author, tape recording, San Francisco, Calif., 25 July 1997. Interestingly, there is, in fact, a group called St. John's Divine Rhythm Society which puts on raves in a church in San Francisco.

82. Vince Thomas, interview by author, tape recording, San Francisco, Calif., 2 February 1996.

83. Gus Lanzas, interview by author, tape recording, San Francisco, Calif., 16 July 1997.

84. Charlotte Kaufman, interview by author, tape recording, San Francisco, Calif., 23 July 1997.

85. Gus Lanzas, interview by author, tape recording, San Francisco, Calif., 16 July 1997.

86. James Romero, interview by author, tape recording, San Francisco, Calif., 7 July 1997.

87. Tiffany Scott, interview by author, tape recording, San Francisco, Calif., 24 July 1997.

88. Ibid.

89. Ibid.

90. James Romero, interview by author, tape recording, San Francisco, Calif., 7 July 1997.

91. Tiffany Scott, interview by author, tape recording, San Francisco, Calif., 24 July 1997.

92. Sabrina Page, interview by author, tape recording, Fairfax, Calif., 14 July 1997.

93. Ibid.

94. Bahar Badizadegan, interview by author, tape recording, San Francisco, Calif., 2 August 1997.

95. Gus Lanzas, interview by author, tape recording, San Francisco, Calif., 16 July 1997.

96. Charlotte Kaufman, interview by author, tape recording, San Francisco, Calif., 23 July 1997.

97. Vince Thomas, interview by author, tape recording, San Francisco, Calif., 2 February 1996.

98. Joel Dinolt, interview by author, tape recording, San Francisco, Calif., 16 July 1997.

99. Gus Lanzas, interview by author, tape recording, San Francisco, Calif., 16 July 1997.

100. Joel Dinolt, interview by author, tape recording, San Francisco, Calif., 16 July 1997.

101. James Romero, interview by author, tape recording, San Francisco, Calif., 7 July 1997.

102. Jim Dunn, interview by author, tape recording, San Francisco, Calif., 25 July 1997.

103. Alaura O'Dell, interview by author, tape recording, Occidental, Calif., 13 July 1997.

104. Jeff Taylor, interview by author, tape recording, San Francisco, Calif., 24 July 1997.

105. James Romero, interview by author, tape recording, San Francisco, Calif., 7 July 1997.

106. Jim Dunn, interview by author, tape recording, San Francisco, Calif., 25 July 1997.

107. See Victor Turner, *The Ritual Process: Structure and Anti-Structure* (Chicago: Aldine, 1969).

108. Sabrina Page, interview by author, tape recording, Fairfax, Calif., 14 July 1997.

109. I should also point out that, not unexpectedly, there is often a considerable gap between the ideal of this alternative model and its actual execution in real-life situations. My exposure to the rave subculture showed it to be rife with the same kinds of personal conflicts and ideological divisions that are found in mainstream culture.

110. Tiffany Scott, interview by author, tape recording, San Francisco, Calif., 24 July 1997.

111. Bahar Badizadegan, interview by author, tape recording, San Francisco, Calif., 2 August 1997.

112. Lee Fogel, "FMM—The Legend Continues," in *The Spirit of Raving: Archives* [database on-line] (San Francisco: Hyperreal, 28 March 1994, accessed 24 January 1997); available from http://www.hyperreal.com/raves/spirit//testimonials/FMR_Santa_Cruz_CA.html; Internet.

113. James Romero, interview by author, tape recording, San Francisco, Calif., 7 July 1997.

114. Charlotte Kaufman, interview by author, tape recording, San Francisco, Calif., 23 July 1997.

115. Bahar Badizadegan, interview by author, tape recording, San Francisco, Calif., 2 August 1997.

116. Ibid.

117. Sabrina Page, interview by author, tape recording, Fairfax, Calif., 14 July 1997.

118. Jim Dunn, interview by author, tape recording, San Francisco, Calif., 25 July 1997.

119. Jeff Taylor, interview by author, tape recording, San Francisco, Calif., 24 July 1997.

120. Tiffany Scott, interview by author, tape recording, San Francisco, Calif., 24 July 1997.

121. Joel Dinolt, interview by author, tape recording, San Francisco, Calif., 16 July 1997.

122. Gus Lanzas, interview by author, tape recording, San Francisco, Calif., 16 July 1997.

123. Joel Dinolt, interview by author, tape recording, San Francisco, Calif., 16 July 1997.

124. Jim Dunn, interview by author, tape recording, San Francisco, Calif., 25 July 1997.

125. Tiffany Scott, interview by author, tape recording, San Francisco, Calif., 24 July 1997.

126. James Romero, interview by author, tape recording, San Francisco, Calif., 7 July 1997.

127. Jeff Taylor, interview by author, tape recording, San Francisco, Calif., 24 July 1997.

128. Bahar Badizadegan, interview by author, tape recording, San Francisco, Calif., 2 August 1997.

129. Ibid.

NOTES TO CHAPTER 5

1. Robert Walser, *Running with the Devil: Power, Gender, and Madness in Heavy Metal Music* (Hanover: Wesleyan University Press, 1993), x.

2. Deena Weinstein, *Heavy Metal: A Cultural Sociology* (New York: Lexington Books, 1991), 11–57.

3. See Jeffrey Jensen Arnett, *Metalheads: Heavy Metal Music and Adolescent Alienation* (Boulder: Westview Press, 1996), 43; Walser, *Running with the Devil*, 8; and Weinstein, *Heavy Metal*, 19–20.

4. Walser, *Running with the Devil*, 8.

5. Ibid, 9.

6. Ibid.

7. "Power chords result from distortion of the chord voicing most often used in metal and hard rock, an open fifth or fourth played on the lower strings. Power chords are manifestly more than these two notes, however, because they produce resultant tones. An effect of both distortion and volume, resultant tones are created by the acoustic combination of two notes. They are most audible at high volume levels, and they are intensified by the type of harmonic distortion used in metal guitar playing." Ibid., 43.

8. Weinstein, *Heavy Metal*, 18.

9. Ibid., 100.

10. Ibid., 101.

11. Ibid.

12. The Yardbirds had a history of being the proving ground for a lineage of influential and talented blues-rock guitarists, beginning with Eric Clapton, continuing with Jeff Beck, and followed by Jimmy Page.

13. Plant himself said of the band: "Although we were all steeped in blues and R & B, we found out . . . that we had our own identity." David Szatmary, *Rockin' in Time: A Social History of Rock-and-Roll*, 3d ed. (Uppersaddle River, N.J.: Prentice Hall, 1996), 184.

14. Walser, *Running with the Devil*, 10.

15. For more details and accounts of the heavy metal rock star lifestyle practiced by Led Zeppelin, see Stephen Davis, *The Hammer of the Gods* (New York: William Morrow, 1985).

16. See Walser, *Running with the Devil,* 158–59, for an excellent musical and lyrical analysis of this song, which he refers to as a "founding document" of heavy metal.

17. Ibid., 10.

18. Weinstein, *Heavy Metal,* 32–33.

19. Quoted in Szatmary, *Rockin' in Time,* 185.

20. There is some disagreement as to which bands are really "heavy metal," as opposed to merely "hard rock." Walser, for example, has listed Kiss, Aerosmith, Ted Nugent, Rush, and Blue Oyster Cult as heavy metal bands from this period (Walser, *Running with the Devil,* 10). Some would take issue with this appellation, preferring to designate them as hard rock. In this regard, Jeffrey Arnett has challenged the status of Deep Purple as a heavy metal band, relegating them to the hard rock category (Arnett, *Metalheads,* 175). Others, like Def Leppard lead vocalist Joe Elliot, place Deep Purple in the same rarified heavy metal status as Led Zeppelin and Black Sabbath (Walser, *Running with the Devil,* 10). This disagreement continues through to such bands as Van Halen, Guns N' Roses, and Bon Jovi, whom Arnett dismisses as hard rock, while Walser devotes considerable space to analyzing their music as typical heavy metal.

21. Again, there is some debate as to the origins of this term as an appellation for the musical genre. However, it is clear that by 1971 and 1972 this term was being used by a number of rock music critics in this way. Lester Bangs's name is most often mentioned in this context. See Weinstein, *Heavy Metal,* 18–20, and Walser, *Running with the Devil,* 8.

22. Arnett, *Metalheads,* 63.

23. Weinstein, *Heavy Metal,* 35–43.

24. Arnett, *Metalheads,* 63.

25. For example, Walser has devoted an entire chapter of his book to exploring the connection between heavy metal and classical music, providing detailed musicological analyses of the guitar solos and compositions of heavy metal guitarists Ritchie Blackmore, Eddie Van Halen, Randy Rhoads, and Yngwie Malmsteen. Walser, *Running with the Devil,* 57–107.

26. Weinstein, *Heavy Metal,* 99.

27. Arnett, *Metalheads,* 97–98.

28. Weinstein, *Heavy Metal,* 127–29.

29. Ibid., 27–29.

30. Slamdancing originated in the punk musical subculture and is generally rare in heavy metal except in the subgenres mentioned. The mosh pit is the area near the front of the stage where the slamdancing takes place. I will discuss the splintering of heavy metal into subgenres shortly.

31. Arnett, *Metalheads,* 65–66. Emphasis in original.

32. Ben, quoted in Arnett, *Metalheads,* 81–82.

33. Jack, quoted in Arnett, *Metalheads,* 3.
34. Steve, quoted in Arnett, *Metalheads,* 83.
35. Weinstein, *Heavy Metal,* 231.
36. See Weinstein, *Heavy Metal,* 44; and Szatmary, *Rockin' in Time,* 280–84.
37. Szatmary, *Rockin' in Time,* 256.
38. Walser, *Running with the Devil,* 12.
39. Szatmary, *Rockin' in Time,* 257.
40. See Walser, *Running with the Devil,* 12–13; and Weinstein, *Heavy Metal,* 281.
41. See Weinstein, *Heavy Metal,* 281.
42. Beginning with the 1988 album . . . *And Justice for All,* Metallica released four straight albums in the top ten. See Szatmary, *Rockin' in Time,* 283.
43. See Weinstein, *Heavy Metal,* 53–55; and Walser, *Running with the Devil,* 13.
44. Arnett, *Metalheads,* 25. Emphasis in original.
45. Steve Rice, interview by author, tape recording, Belmont, Calif., 20 July 1997.
46. Galen Klein, interview by author, tape recording, Rohnert Park, Calif., 30 July 1997.
47. Lance Ozanix, interview by author, tape recording, Rohnert Park, Calif., 30 July 1997.
48. Galen Klein, interview by author, tape recording, Rohnert Park, Calif., 30 July 1997.
49. Ibid.
50. Ibid.
51. Steve Rice, interview by author, tape recording, Belmont, Calif., 20 July 1997.
52. Lance Ozanix, interview by author, tape recording, Rohnert Park, Calif., 30 July 1997.
53. Galen Klein, interview by author, tape recording, Rohnert Park, Calif., 30 July 1997.
54. Lance Ozanix, interview by author, tape recording, Rohnert Park, Calif., 30 July 1997.
55. Ibid.
56. Ibid.
57. Galen Klein, interview by author, tape recording, Rohnert Park, Calif., 30 July 1997.
58. Steve Rice, interview by author, tape recording, Belmont, Calif., 20 July 1997.
59. Lance Ozanix, interview by author, tape recording, Rohnert Park, Calif., 30 July 1997.

60. Galen Klein, interview by author, tape recording, Rohnert Park, Calif., 30 July 1997.

61. Steve Rice, interview by author, tape recording, Belmont, Calif., 20 July 1997.

62. Lance Ozanix, interview by author, tape recording, Rohnert Park, Calif., 30 July 1997.

63. Steve Rice, interview by author, tape recording, Belmont, Calif., 20 July 1997.

64. Lance Ozanix, interview by author, tape recording, Rohnert Park, Calif., 30 July 1997.

65. Galen Klein, interview by author, tape recording, Rohnert Park, Calif., 30 July 1997.

66. Ibid.

67. Lance Ozanix, interview by author, tape recording, Rohnert Park, Calif., 30 July 1997.

68. Steve Rice, interview by author, tape recording, Belmont, Calif., 20 July 1997.

69. Weinstein, *Heavy Metal,* 231–32.

70. Arnett, *Metalheads,* 16–17.

71. Lance Ozanix, interview by author, tape recording, Rohnert Park, Calif., 30 July 1997.

72. Galen Klein, interview by author, tape recording, Rohnert Park, Calif., 30 July 1997.

73. Steve Rice, interview by author, tape recording, Belmont, Calif., 20 July 1997.

74. Ibid.

75. Walser, *Running with the Devil,* 2.

76. Ibid., 53.

77. Lance Ozanix, interview by author, tape recording, Rohnert Park, Calif., 30 July 1997.

78. Galen Klein, interview by author, tape recording, Rohnert Park, Calif., 30 July 1997.

79. Ibid.

80. Steve Rice, interview by author, tape recording, Belmont, Calif., 20 July 1997.

81. Ibid.

82. Lance Ozanix, interview by author, tape recording, Rohnert Park, Calif., 30 July 1997.

83. Ibid.

84. Ibid.

85. Galen Klein, interview by author, tape recording, Rohnert Park, Calif., 30 July 1997.

86. Lance Ozanix, interview by author, tape recording, Rohnert Park, Calif., 30 July 1997.

87. Steve Rice, interview by author, tape recording, Belmont, Calif., 20 July 1997.

88. Galen Klein, interview by author, tape recording, Rohnert Park, Calif., 30 July 1997.

89. Weinstein, *Heavy Metal*, 131.

90. Lance Ozanix, interview by author, tape recording, Rohnert Park, Calif., 30 July 1997.

91. Steve Rice, interview by author, tape recording, Belmont, Calif., 20 July 1997.

92. Galen Klein, interview by author, tape recording, Rohnert Park, Calif., 30 July 1997.

93. Lance Ozanix, interview by author, tape recording, Rohnert Park, Calif., 30 July 1997.

94. Steve Rice, interview by author, tape recording, Belmont, Calif., 20 July 1997.

95. Galen Klein, interview by author, tape recording, Rohnert Park, Calif., 30 July 1997.

96. Lance Ozanix, interview by author, tape recording, Rohnert Park, Calif., 30 July 1997.

97. Steve Rice, interview by author, tape recording, Belmont, Calif., 20 July 1997.

98. Ibid.

99. Lance Ozanix, interview by author, tape recording, Rohnert Park, Calif., 30 July 1997.

100. Steve Rice, interview by author, tape recording, Belmont, Calif., 20 July 1997.

101. Ibid. For the original source, see Anton Szandor LaVey, *The Satanic Bible* (New York: Avon, 1969). For more on LaVey and his life, see Susan Sward, "Satanist's Daughter to Keep the 'Faith,'" *San Francisco Chronicle*, 8 November 1997, sec. 1, p. 22.

102. See, for example, Arnett, *Metalheads*, 51–53 and 127; and Weinstein, *Heavy Metal*, 258–63.

103. See Davis, *The Hammer of the Gods*.

104. Lew (no last name given), quoted in Arnett, *Metalheads*, 93.

105. Steve Rice, interview by author, tape recording, Belmont, Calif., 20 July 1997.

106. Ibid.

107. Robert G. Pielke, *You Say You Want a Revolution: Rock Music in American Culture* (Chicago: Nelson-Hall, 1986), 202.

108. Weinstein, *Heavy Metal*, 38.

109. Walser, *Running with the Devil,* 42.

110. Lance Ozanix, interview by author, tape recording, Rohnert Park, Calif., 30 July 1997.

111. Steve Rice, interview by author, tape recording, Belmont, Calif., 20 July 1997.

112. Lance Ozanix, interview by author, tape recording, Rohnert Park, Calif., 30 July 1997.

113. Weinstein, *Heavy Metal,* 38 and 42.

NOTES TO CHAPTER 6

1. The other great African American secular music, jazz, has a somewhat different history in this regard, as white artists and audiences had a big impact, but it is beyond the scope of this study to go into that history. For more on the segregation of popular music markets, see Reebee Garofalo, "Crossing Over: 1939–1989," in William Barlow and Janette L. Dates, eds., *Split Image: African Americans in the Mass Media* (Washington, D.C.: Howard University Press, 1990), 57–121; and the chapter entitled "Black Roots, White Fruits: Racism in the Music Industry," in Reebee Garofalo and Steve Chapple, *Rock 'n' Roll Is Here to Pay: The History and Politics of the Music Industry* (Chicago: Nelson-Hall, 1977), 231–68.

2. See Tricia Rose, *Black Noise: Rap Music and Black Culture in Contemporary America* (Hanover: Wesleyan University Press, 1994), 47–50, for more on break dancing.

3. For more on the *jali*/griot tradition, see Thomas A. Hale, *Griots and Griottes: Masters of Words and Music* (Bloomington: Indiana University Press, 1998). For an interesting exposition on the continuities between the *jalis* and the blues, see Paul Oliver, *Savannah Syncopators: African Retentions in the Blues* (New York: Stein and Day, 1970).

4. See Ronald Jemal Stephens, "The Three Waves of Contemporary Rap Music," *Black Sacred Music* 5:1 (Spring 1991): 25–26.

5. See Albert Raboteau, *Slave Religion: The "Invisible Institution" in the Antebellum South* (New York: Oxford University Press, 1978), and Lawrence Levine, *Black Culture and Black Consciousness: Afro-American Folk Thought from Slavery to Freedom* (New York: Oxford University Press, 1977).

6. See Stephens, "Three Waves," 27. For more on the Harlem Renaissance, see Samuel A. Floyd, *The Power of Black Music: Interpreting Its History from Africa to the United States* (New York: Oxford University Press, 1995), 100–35.

7. William Eric Perkins, "Nation of Islam Ideology in the Rap of Public Enemy," *Black Sacred Music* 5:1 (Spring 1991): 42.

8. For an overview of soul music, see Michael Haralambos, *Soul Music: The Birth of a Sound in Black America* (New York: Da Capo Press, 1985); and Gerri Hirshey, *Nowhere to Run: The Story of Soul Music* (New York: Times Books, 1984).

9. The list of outstanding artists includes, among others, the Supremes, Smokey Robinson and the Miracles, Stevie Wonder, the Temptations, the Four Tops, Marvin Gaye, and the Jackson Five. "From 1964 through 1967, Motown placed 14 number-one pop singles, 20 number-one singles on the R & B charts, 46 more Top 15 pop singles, and 75 other Top 15 R & B records." David Szatmary, *Rockin' In Time: A Social History of Rock-and-Roll*, 3d ed. (Uppersaddle River, N.J.: Prentice Hall, 1996), 138.

10. Quoted in Szatmary, *Rockin' in Time*, 168.

11. Some classic songs in this regard include the Temptations' *Ball of Confusion*, the Chi-Lites' *Give More Power to the People*, James Brown's *Funky President (People, It's Bad)*, and the Isley Brothers' *Fight the Power*. Perhaps the greatest musical achievement centered on social themes was Marvin Gaye's 1971 album *What's Going On*, generally considered to be a masterpiece.

12. For an excellent history and overview of funk, see Rickey Vincent, *Funk: The Music, the People, and the Rhythm of the One* (New York: St. Martin's Griffin, 1996).

13. For more on disco, see the section in chapter 4.

14. Rose, *Black Noise*, 78.

15. Andre Craddock-Willis, "Rap Music and the Black Musical Tradition: A Critical Assessment," *Radical America* 23:4 (October–December 1989): 29–37.

16. S. H. Fernando, Jr., *The New Beats: Exploring the Music, Culture, and Attitudes of Hip-Hop* (New York: Anchor Books Doubleday, 1994), 2–3.

17. Herc, also known as Clive Campbell, was born in Jamaica and spent the first twelve years of his life living there before moving to New York. The Jamaican musical influence on Herc and, through him, on early rap was very strong. Some of the key elements were the huge bass-heavy "sound systems" (extremely loud amplification systems with enormous speakers), the DJ practices of "dub" (breaking a song down to its constituent components and reconstructing it with effects and new vocals) and "toasting" (DJs speaking, singing, rhyming, and rapping over the mix), and the competition between sound systems called "sound clashes." Jamaican popular music, both in Jamaica and in its diaspora, has developed its own distinctive genres parallel to rap—dancehall and ragga. For more on the Jamaican connection to rap, see Fernando, *The New Beats*, 30–57.

18. Rose, *Black Noise*, 39.

19. Fernando, *The New Beats*, 7.

20. Ibid., 10 and 44.

21. Ibid., 10–11.

22. Ibid., 12–13.

23. Rose, *Black Noise*, 56.

24. Stephens, "Three Waves," 30.

25. Szatmary, *Rockin' in Time*, 292. Run-DMC's chart success allowed their small, independent label Def Jam to flourish and paved the way for other rap-based independents like Tommy Boy and Profile to do the same.

26. The issue of women's role in rap is an enormous one that spatial limitations prevent me from addressing in any detail. For an excellent examination of this subject, see Rose's chapter in *Black Noise*, 146–82, entitled "Bad Sistas: Black Women Rappers and Sexual Politics in Rap Music."

27. Szatmary, *Rockin' in Time*, 294–95.

28. Rose, *Black Noise*, 142–44.

29. Angela Spence Nelson, "Theology in the Hip-Hop of Public Enemy and Kool Moe Dee," *Black Sacred Music* 5:1 (Spring 1991): 59. Emphasis in original.

30. The primary Hispanic neighborhoods are in East Los Angeles, while the primary African American neighborhoods are in South Central Los Angeles. As of May 1992, the best estimates put the number of gangs at one thousand, with a total membership of one hundred and fifty thousand. Gang-related homicides increased by 200 percent between 1984 and 1991. See Fernando, *The New Beats*, 92.

31. Ibid., 95.

32. Brian Cross, *It's Not about a Salary: Rap, Race, and Resistance in Los Angeles* (London: Verso, 1993), 37.

33. Nelson, "Theology in Hip-Hop," 56.

34. Cornel West, "On Afro-American Music: From Bebop to Rap," *Black Sacred Music* 6:1 (Spring 1992): 293.

35. Craddock-Willis, "Rap Music," 37.

36. West, "On Afro-American Music," 293.

37. Interestingly, both these rappers were killed just prior to the release of new albums which seemingly foreshadowed their deaths, and both albums went on to become huge sellers.

38. Paris King, interview by author, tape recording, Oakland, Calif., 3 July 1997.

39. Jorge Guerrero, interview by author, tape recording, Berkeley, Calif., 6 August 1997.

40. Keith Williams, interview by author, tape recording, San Jose, Calif., 4 July 1997.

41. Malcolm [no last name given], interview by author, tape recording, Oakland, Calif., 12 July 1997.

42. Steve Gaines, interview with author, tape recording, Berkeley, Calif., 20 July 1997.

43. Jorge Guerrero, interview by author, tape recording, Berkeley, Calif., 6 August 1997.

44. Carlos Mena, interview by author, tape recording, San Jose, Calif., 17 July 1997.

45. Malcolm, interview by author, tape recording, Oakland, Calif., 12 July 1997.

46. Steve Gaines, interview with author, tape recording, Berkeley, Calif., 20 July 1997.

47. Jorge Guerrero, interview by author, tape recording, Berkeley, Calif., 6 August 1997.

48. Steve Gaines, interview with author, tape recording, Berkeley, Calif., 20 July 1997.

49. Jorge Guerrero, interview by author, tape recording, Berkeley, Calif., 6 August 1997.

50. Ibid.

51. Malcolm, interview by author, tape recording, Oakland, Calif., 12 July 1997.

52. Ibid.

53. Jorge Guerrero, interview by author, tape recording, Berkeley, Calif., 6 August 1997.

54. Malcolm, interview by author, tape recording, Oakland, Calif., 12 July 1997.

55. Ibid.

56. Jorge Guerrero, interview by author, tape recording, Berkeley, Calif., 6 August 1997.

57. Malcolm, interview by author, tape recording, Oakland, Calif., 12 July 1997.

58. Steve Gaines, interview with author, tape recording, Berkeley, Calif., 20 July 1997.

59. Jorge Guerrero, interview by author, tape recording, Berkeley, Calif., 6 August 1997.

60. Paris King, interview by author, tape recording, Oakland, Calif., 3 July 1997.

61. Quoted in Malcolm, interview by author, tape recording, Oakland, Calif., 12 July 1997.

62. Ibid.

63. Ibid.

64. Paris King, interview by author, tape recording, Oakland, Calif., 3 July 1997.

65. Steve Gaines, interview with author, tape recording, Berkeley, Calif., 20 July 1997.

66. Jorge Guerrero, interview by author, tape recording, Berkeley, Calif., 6 August 1997.

67. Paris King, interview by author, tape recording, Oakland, Calif., 3 July 1997.

68. Carlos Mena, interview by author, tape recording, San Jose, Calif., 17 July 1997.

69. Malcolm, interview by author, tape recording, Oakland, Calif., 12 July 1997.

70. Jorge Guerrero, interview by author, tape recording, Berkeley, Calif., 6 August 1997.

71. Malcolm, interview by author, tape recording, Oakland, Calif., 12 July 1997.

72. Jorge Guerrero, interview by author, tape recording, Berkeley, Calif., 6 August 1997.

73. Carlos Mena, interview by author, tape recording, San Jose, Calif., 17 July 1997.

74. Ibid.

75. Jorge Guerrero, interview by author, tape recording, Berkeley, Calif., 6 August 1997.

76. Carlos Mena, interview by author, tape recording, San Jose, Calif., 17 July 1997.

77. Malcolm, interview by author, tape recording, Oakland, Calif., 12 July 1997.

78. Carlos Mena, interview by author, tape recording, San Jose, Calif., 17 July 1997.

79. Ibid.

80. Malcolm, interview by author, tape recording, Oakland, Calif., 12 July 1997.

81. Jorge Guerrero, interview by author, tape recording, Berkeley, Calif., 6 August 1997.

82. Keith Williams, interview by author, tape recording, San Jose, Calif., 4 July 1997.

83. Malcolm, interview by author, tape recording, Oakland, Calif., 12 July 1997.

84. Steve Gaines, interview with author, tape recording, Berkeley, Calif., 20 July 1997.

85. Ibid.

86. Ibid.

87. Ibid.

88. Keith Williams, interview by author, tape recording, San Jose, Calif., 4 July 1997.

89. Steve Gaines, interview with author, tape recording, Berkeley, Calif., 20 July 1997.

90. Jorge Guerrero, interview by author, tape recording, Berkeley, Calif., 6 August 1997.

91. Malcolm, interview by author, tape recording, Oakland, Calif., 12 July 1997.

92. Ibid.

93. Ibid.

94. Keith Williams, interview by author, tape recording, San Jose, Calif., 4 July 1997.

95. Ibid.

96. Malcolm, interview by author, tape recording, Oakland, Calif., 12 July 1997.

97. Keith Williams, interview by author, tape recording, San Jose, Calif., 4 July 1997.

98. Ibid.

99. Ibid. It is interesting to note how often this circular formation will spontaneously emerge on the dance floor in the musical performances of the subcultures we are studying.

100. Malcolm, interview by author, tape recording, Oakland, Calif., 12 July 1997.

101. Isabel Fine, "West African and Afro-Caribbean Music and Dance—Some Roots of Hip Hop?" Unpublished paper, University of California Los Angeles, 22 February 1994, 3.

102. Jorge Guerrero, interview by author, tape recording, Berkeley, Calif., 6 August 1997.

103. Carlos Mena, interview by author, tape recording, San Jose, Calif., 17 July 1997.

104. Malcolm, interview by author, tape recording, Oakland, Calif., 12 July 1997.

105. Carlos Mena, interview by author, tape recording, San Jose, Calif., 17 July 1997. Interestingly, with regard to the fashion aspect, although there are utterly characteristic hip-hop styles such as the backward-facing baseball cap, sweats and other athletic clothing, extremely baggy pants, basketball shoes, shaved heads, and so on, no one I interviewed mentioned this as a factor of any importance.

106. Keith Williams, interview by author, tape recording, San Jose, Calif., 4 July 1997.

107. Malcolm, interview by author, tape recording, Oakland, Calif., 12 July 1997.

108. Ibid.

109. Ibid.

110. Jorge Guerrero, interview by author, tape recording, Berkeley, Calif., 6 August 1997.

111. Malcolm, interview by author, tape recording, Oakland, Calif., 12 July 1997.

112. Paris King, interview by author, tape recording, Oakland, Calif., 3 July 1997.

113. Carlos Mena, interview by author, tape recording, San Jose, Calif., 17 July 1997.

114. Jim Dunn, interview by author, tape recording, San Francisco, Calif., 25 July 1997.

115. Paris King, interview by author, tape recording, Oakland, Calif., 3 July 1997.

116. Ibid.

117. Keith Williams, interview by author, tape recording, San Jose, Calif., 4 July 1997.

118. Rose, *Black Noise,* 39. Emphasis in original.

119. Steve Gaines, interview with author, tape recording, Berkeley, Calif., 20 July 1997.

120. Ibid.

121. Paris King, interview by author, tape recording, Oakland, Calif., 3 July 1997.

122. DJ Spooky (a.k.a. Paul D. Miller), brochure notes for the compact disc *Songs of a Dead Dreamer* (New York: Asphodel 0961, 1996), 7–8.

123. Paris King, interview by author, tape recording, Oakland, Calif., 3 July 1997.

124. Jorge Guerrero, interview by author, tape recording, Berkeley, Calif., 6 August 1997.

125. Malcolm, interview by author, tape recording, Oakland, Calif., 12 July 1997.

NOTES TO THE CONCLUSION

1. Charles H. Long, "Popular Religion," in Mircea Eliade, ed., *The Encyclopedia of Religion* (New York: Macmillan, 1987), vol. 18, 447. Emphasis added.

2. William C. Shepherd, "Religion and the Counter Culture—A New Religiosity," *Sociological Inquiry* 42:1 (1972): 6. Emphasis in original.

3. Susan McClary, "Same as It Ever Was: Youth Culture and Youth Music," in Andrew Ross and Tricia Rose, eds., *Microphone Fiends: Youth Music and Youth Culture* (New York: Routledge, 1994), 33.

4. Steven M. Friedson, *Dancing Prophets: Musical Experience in Tumbuka Healing* (Chicago: University of Chicago Press, 1996), 5.

5. David Parkin, "Ritual as Spatial Direction and Bodily Division," in Daniel de Coppet, ed., *Understanding Rituals* (London: Routledge, 1992), 12.

6. William H. McNeill, *Keeping Together in Time: Dance and Drill in Human History* (Cambridge: Harvard University Press, 1995), 2–3.

7. For example, see John J. MacAloon, ed., *Rite, Drama, Festival, Spectacle: Rehearsals toward a Theory of Cultural Performance* (Philadelphia: Institute for the Study of Human Issues, 1984); Richard Schechner, *Performance Theory* (New York: Routledge, 1988); Richard Schechner, *The Future of Ritual: Writings on Culture and Performance* (London: Routledge, 1993); and Victor Turner, *The Anthropology of Performance* (New York: PAJ Publications, 1986).

8. Steve Silberman, interview by author, tape recording, Berkeley, Calif., 17 February 1996.

9. Jim Dunn, interview by author, tape recording, San Francisco, Calif., 25 July 1997.

10. Steve Rice, interview by author, tape recording, Belmont, Calif., 20 July 1997.

11. Malcolm, interview by author, tape recording, Oakland, Calif., 12 July 1997.

Bibliography

Albanese, Catherine L. "Religion and Popular American Culture: An Introductory Essay." *Journal of the American Academy of Religion* 59:4 (Fall 1996): 733–42.

———. *America: Religions and Religion,* 3d ed. Belmont: Wadsworth, 1998.

Amoaku, W. Komla. "Toward a Definition of Traditional African Music: A Look at the Ewe of Ghana." In *More than Drumming: Essays on African and Afro-Latin American Music and Musicians,* ed. Irene V. Jackson, 31–40. Westport, Conn.: Greenwood Press, 1985.

Arnett, Jeffrey Jensen. *Metalheads: Heavy Metal Music and Adolescent Alienation.* Boulder: Westview Press, 1996.

Arnold, David, ed. *The Sociology of Subcultures.* Berkeley: Glendessary Press, 1970.

Beattie, John, and John Middleton, eds. *Spirit Mediumship and Society in Africa.* New York: Africana Publishing, 1969.

Bebey, Francis. *African Music: A People's Art.* New York: Lawrence Hill, 1975.

Behague, Gerard. "Patterns of Candomble Music Performance: An Afro-Brazilian Religious Setting." In *Performance Practice: Ethnomusicological Perspectives,* ed. Gerard Behague, 223–54. Westport, Conn.: Greenwood Press, 1984.

Bell, Catherine. *Ritual: Perspectives and Dimensions.* New York: Oxford University Press, 1997.

Bender, Wolfgang. *Sweet Mother: Modern African Music.* Chicago: University of Chicago Press, 1991.

Bhattacharya, Arun. *A Treatise on Ancient Hindu Music.* Calcutta: K. P. Bagchi and Company, 1978.

Blacking, John. *How Musical Is Man?* Seattle: University of Washington Press, 1973.

———. *"A Commonsense View of All Music": Reflections on Percy Grainger's Contribution to Ethnomusicology and Music Education.* Cambridge: Cambridge University Press, 1987.

Bohlman, Philip P. "Is All Music Religious?" *Criterion* 28:2 (Spring 1989): 19–24.

Boiles, Charles Lafayette. *Man, Magic, and Musical Occasions.* Columbus: Collegiate Publishing, 1978.

Brodzky, Anne Trueblood, Rose Daneseswich, and Nick Johnson, eds. *Stones, Bones and Skin: Ritual and Shamanic Art.* Toronto: Society for Art Publications, 1977.

Bourguignon, Erika, ed. *Religion, Altered States of Consciousness, and Social Change.* Columbus: Ohio State University Press, 1973.

Boyd, Jenny. *Musicians in Tune: Seventy-Five Contemporary Musicians Discuss the Creative Process.* New York: Simon and Schuster, 1992.

Braun, D. Duane. *Toward a Theory of Popular Culture: The Sociology and History of American Music and Dance, 1920–1968.* Ann Arbor: Ann Arbor Publishers, 1969.

Brewster, Bill, and Frank Broughton. *Last Night a DJ Saved My Life: The History of the Disc Jockey.* New York: Grove Press, 2000.

Broughton, Simon, Mark Ellingham, David Muddyman, and Richard Trillo, eds. *World Music: The Rough Guide.* London: Rough Guides, 1994.

Brown, Karen McCarthy. *Mama Lola: A Vodou Priestess in Brooklyn.* Berkeley: University of California Press, 1991.

Chambers, Iain. "A Strategy for Living." In *Resistance through Ritual: Youth Subcultures in Postwar Britain,* eds. Stuart Hull and Tory Jefferson, 157–66. London: HarperCollins Academic, 1976.

Chapple, Eliot. *Culture and Biological Man: Explorations in Behavioral Anthropology.* New York: Holt, Rinehart and Winston, 1970.

Chernoff, John Miller. *African Rhythm and African Sensibility: Aesthetics and Social Action in African Musical Idioms.* Chicago: University of Chicago Press, 1979.

Clarke, Michael. "On the Concept of 'Sub-Culture.'" *British Journal of Sociology* 25:4 (December 1975): 428–41.

Clifton, Thomas. *Music as Heard: A Study in Applied Phenomenology.* New Haven: Yale University Press, 1983.

Coakley, Sarah, ed. *Religion and the Body.* Cambridge: Cambridge University Press, 1997.

Coleman, James S. *The Adolescent Society.* New York: Free Press, 1961.

Collin, Matthew. *Altered State: The Story of Ecstacy Culture and Acid House.* London: Serpent's Tail, 1997.

Cone, James. *The Spirituals and the Blues: An Interpretation.* New York: Seabury Press, 1972.

———. "Blues: A Secular Spiritual." *Sacred Music of the Secular City: From Blues to Rap,* ed. John Michael Spencer, 96–97. Durham: Duke University Press, 1992.

Craddock-Willis, Andre. "Rap Music and the Black Musical Tradition: A Critical Assessment." *Radical America* 23:4 (October–December 1989): 29–37.

Crafts, Susan D., Daniel Cavicchi, Charles Keil, and the Music in Daily Life Project. *My Music.* Hanover: Wesleyan University Press, 1993.

Cross, Brian. *It's Not about a Salary: Rap, Race, and Resistance in Los Angeles.* London: Verso, 1993.

Curtin, Philip D. *The Atlantic Slave Trade: A Census.* Madison: University of Wisconsin Press, 1969.

d'Aquili, Eugene G., and Charles D. Laughlin Jr. "The Neurobiology of Myth and Ritual." In *The Spectrum of Ritual: A Biogenetic Structural Analysis,* eds. Eugene G. d'Aquili, Charles D. Laughlin Jr., and John McManus, 152–82. New York: Columbia University Press, 1979.

Davis, Stephen. *The Hammer of the Gods.* New York: William Morrow, 1985.

Deren, Maya. *Divine Horsemen: Voodoo Gods of Haiti.* New York: Chelsea House Publishers, 1970.

Eliade, Mircea. *The Myth of the Eternal Return.* London: Routledge and Kegan Paul, 1955.

———. *Patterns in Comparative Religion.* New York: Sheed and Ward, 1958.

———. *The Sacred and the Profane: The Nature of Religion.* New York: Harcourt, Brace and Company, 1959.

———. *Shamanism: Archaic Techniques of Ecstasy.* New York: Bollingen Foundation, 1964.

Epstein, Jonathon S., ed. *Adolescents and Their Music: If It's Too Loud, You're Too Old.* New York: Garland, 1994.

Ewens, Graeme. *Africa O-Ye! A Celebration of African Music.* New York: Da Capo Press, 1991.

Feld, Steven. "Linguistic Models in Ethnomusicology." *Ethnomusicology* 18:2 (May 1974): 197–217.

Fernando, S. H., Jr. *The New Beats: Exploring the Music, Culture, and Attitudes of Hip-Hop.* New York: Anchor Books Doubleday, 1994.

Ferrandino, Joe. "Rock Culture and the Development of Social Consciousness." In *Side-Saddle on the Golden Calf: Social Structure and Popular Culture in America,* ed. George Lewis, 263–90. Pacific Palisades: Goodyear Publishing, 1972.

Fikentscher, Kai. *"You Better Work!" Underground Dance Music in New York City.* Hanover: Wesleyan University Press, 2000.

———. "Feel the Groove: An Examination of the Interaction between House Music DJs and Dancers." Paper delivered at the Annual Meeting of the Society for Ethnomusicology, Los Angeles, California, 19 October 1995.

Fine, Isabel. "West African and Afro-Caribbean Music and Dance— Some Roots of Hip Hop?" Unpublished paper, University of California Los Angeles, 22 February 1994.

Floyd, Samuel A. *The Power of Black Music: Interpreting Its History from Africa to the United States.* New York: Oxford University Press, 1995.

Fogel, Robert William, and Stanley L. Engerman, *Time on the Cross: The Economics of American Slavery.* Boston: Little, Brown, 1974.

Friedlander, Paul. *Rock and Roll: A Social History.* Boulder: Westview Press, 1996.

Friedson, Steven M. *Dancing Prophets: Musical Experience in Tumbuka Healing*. Chicago: University of Chicago Press, 1996.

Frith, Simon. *Sound Effects: Youth, Leisure and the Politics of Rock 'n' Roll*. New York: Pantheon Books, 1981.

———. *Performing Rites: On the Value of Popular Music*. Cambridge: Harvard University Press, 1996.

Fritz, Jimi. *Rave Culture: An Insider's View*. Canada: SmallFry Press, 1999.

Furst, Peter. "The Roots and Continuities of Shamanism." In *Stones, Bones and Skin: Ritual and Shamanic Art*, eds. Anne Trueblood Brodzky, Rose Danesewich, and Nick Johnson, 8–28. Toronto: Society for Art Publications, 1977.

Gans, David, and Peter Simons. *Playing in the Band*. New York: St. Martin's Press, 1985.

———, ed. *Not Fade Away: The On-Line World Remembers Jerry Garcia*. New York: Thunder's Mouth Press, 1995.

Garcia, Guy. "Tripping the Night Fantastic." *Time*, 17 August 1992.

Garofalo, Reebee, and Steve Chapple. *Rock 'n' Roll Is Here to Pay: The History and Politics of the Music Industry*. Chicago: Nelson-Hall, 1977.

———. "Crossing Over: 1939–1989." In *Split Image: African Americans in the Mass Media*, eds. William Barlow and Janette L. Dates, 57–121. Washington, D.C.: Howard University Press, 1990.

Geerts, Henry. "An Inquiry into the Meaning of Ritual Symbolism: Turner and Pierce." In *Current Studies on Rituals: Perspectives for the Psychology of Religion*, eds. H. Barbara Boudewijnse and Hans-Gunter Heimbrock. Atlanta: Rodopi, 1990.

George, Nelson. *The Death of Rhythm and Blues*. New York: Pantheon Books, 1988.

Gibson, William. *Neuromancer*. New York: Ace Books, 1984.

Gilbert, Jeremy, and Ewan Pearson. *Discographies: Dance Music, Culture and the Politics of Sound*. London: Routledge, 1999.

Gonda, J. *Visnuism and Sivaism: A Comparison*. London: Athlone Press, 1970.

Gray, J. Patrick. "Rock as a Chaos Model Ritual." *Popular Music and Society* 2:7 (1980): 75–83.

Greeley, Andrew. *God in Popular Culture*. Chicago: Thomas More Press, 1988.

Grimes, Ronald. *Beginnings in Ritual Studies*. Lanham: University Press of America, 1982.

Hale, Thomas A. *Griots and Griottes: Masters of Words and Music*. Bloomington: Indiana University Press, 1998.

Hall, Stuart, and Tony Jefferson, eds. *Resistance through Rituals: Youth Subcultures in Postwar Britain*. London: HarperCollins Academic, 1976.

Haralambos, Michael. *Soul Music: The Birth of a Sound in Black America*. New York: Da Capo Press, 1985.

Harrison, Hank. *The Dead: A Social History of the Haight-Ashbury Experience*. San Francisco: Archives Press, 1990.

Hebdige, Dick. *Subculture: The Meaning of Style.* New York: Methuen, 1979.

Hirshey, Gerri. *Nowhere to Run: The Story of Soul Music.* New York: Times Books, 1984.

Huet, Michel. *The Dance, Art, and Ritual of Africa.* New York: Pantheon Books, 1978.

James, William. *The Varieties of Religious Experience: A Study in Human Nature.* London: Collins, 1968.

Japenga, Ann. "Grunge R Us: Exploiting, Co-Opting and Neutralizing the Counterculture." *Los Angeles Times Magazine* (4 November 1993): 26–28 and 44–461.

Jones, A. M. *Studies in African Music.* London: Oxford University Press, 1959.

Jones, LeRoi. *Blues People: Negro Music in White America.* New York: William Morrow, 1963.

Keil, Charles. *Urban Blues.* Chicago: University of Chicago Press, 1966.

Kempster, Chris, ed. *History of House.* London: Sanctuary Publishing, 1996.

King, Noel Q. *African Cosmos: An Introduction to Religion in Africa.* Belmont: Wadsworth Publishing, 1986.

Kruse, Holly. "Subcultural Identity in Alternative Music Culture." *Popular Music* 12:1 (1993): 33–41.

Lakoff, George, and Mark Johnson. *Metaphors We Live By.* Chicago: University of Chicago Press, 1980.

LaVey, Anton Szandor. *The Satanic Bible.* New York: Avon, 1969.

Leonard, Neil. *Jazz and the White Americans: The Acceptance of a New Art Form* (Chicago: University of Chicago Press, 1962).

Leppert, Richard. *The Sight of Sound: Music, Representation, and the History of the Body.* Berkeley: University of California Press, 1993.

Levine, Lawrence. *Black Culture and Black Consciousness: Afro-American Folk Thought from Slavery to Freedom.* New York: Oxford University Press, 1977.

Lewis, George, ed. *Side-Saddle on the Golden Calf: Social Structure and Popular Culture in America.* Pacific Palisades: Goodyear Publishing, 1972.

Lex, Barbara. "The Neurobiology of Ritual Trance." In *The Spectrum of Ritual: A Biogenetic Structural Analysis,* eds. Eugene G. d'Aquili, Charles D. Laughlin, Jr., and John McManus, 117–51. New York: Columbia University Press, 1979.

Lidov, David. "Mind and Body in Music." *Semiotica* 66:1/3 (1987): 69–97.

Lippy, Charles H. *Being Religious, American Style: A History of Popular Religiosity in the United States.* Westport, Conn.: Praeger, 1994.

Lipsitz, George. *Time Passages: Collective Memory and American Popular Culture.* Minneapolis: University of Minnesota Press, 1990.

———. *Dangerous Crossroads: Popular Music, Postmodernism and the Poetics of Place.* London: Verso, 1994.

Long, Charles H. "The History of the History of Religions." In *A Reader's Guide to the Great Religions,* ed. Charles J. Adams, 467–75. New York: Free Press, 1977.

Long, Charles H. "A Look at the Chicago Tradition in the History of Religions: Retrospect and Future." In *The History of Religions: Retrospect and Prospect,* ed. Joseph M. Kitagawa, 87–104. New York: Macmillan, 1985.

———. "Popular Religion." In *The Encyclopedia of Religion,* v. 18, ed. Mircea Eliade, 442–52. New York: Macmillan, 1987.

Lovell, John. *Black Song: The Forge and the Flame: The Story of How the Afro-American Spiritual Was Hammered Out.* New York: Macmillan, 1972.

Ludwig, Arnold. "Altered States of Consciousness." In *Trance and Possession States,* ed. Raymond Prince, 69–95. Montreal: University of Montreal Press, 1968.

McAllester, David P. *Peyote Music.* New York: Viking Fund, 1949.

———. "Some Thoughts on 'Universals' in World Music." *Ethnomusicology* 15:3 (1971): 379–80.

McClary, Susan. "Same as It Ever Was: Youth Culture and Youth Music." In *Microphone Fiends: Youth Music and Youth Culture,* eds. Andrew Ross and Tricia Rose, 29–40. New York: Routledge, 1994.

McLeod, Norma, and Marcia Herndon. *Music as Culture.* Darby, Pennsylvania: Norwood Editions, 1982.

McLoughlin, William. *Revivals, Awakenings, and Reform: An Essay on Religion and Social Change in America, 1607–1977.* Chicago: University of Chicago Press, 1978.

McNeill, William H. *Keeping Together in Time: Dance and Drill in Human History.* Cambridge: Harvard University Press, 1995.

MacAloon, John J., ed. *Rite, Drama, Festival, Spectacle: Rehearsals toward a Theory of Cultural Performance.* Philadelphia: Institute for the Study of Human Issues, 1984.

Mahdi, Louise Carus, Steven Foster, and Meredith Little, eds. *Betwixt and Between: Patterns of Masculine and Feminine Initiation.* La Salle: Open Court, 1987.

Manuel, Peter. "Music as Symbol, Music as Simulacrum: Postmodern, Pre-Modern, and Modern Aesthetics in Subcultural Popular Musics." *Popular Music* 14:2 (1995): 227–39.

Martin, Bernice. *A Sociology of Contemporary Cultural Change.* New York: St. Martin's Press, 1981.

Maultsby, Portia. "Africanisms in African-American Music." In *Africanisms in American Culture,* ed. James Holloway, 185–210. Bloomington: Indiana University Press, 1990.

———. "West African Influences and Retentions in U.S. Black Music: A Sociocultural Study." In *More than Dancing,* ed. Irene V. Jackson, 25–57. Westport, Conn.: Greenwood Press, 1985.

Mbiti, John S. *African Religions and Philosophy.* Portsmouth, N.H.: Heinemann, 1990.

Metraux, Alfred. *Voodoo in Haiti*. New York: Oxford University Press, 1959.

Meyer, Leonard. *Emotion and Meaning in Music*. Chicago: University of Chicago Press, 1956.

Middleton, Richard. *Studying Popular Music*. Milton Keynes: Open University Press, 1990.

Miezitis, Vita. *Night Dancin'*. New York: Ballantine, 1980.

Mischel, Frances, and Walter Mischel. "Psychological Aspects of Spirit Possession." *American Anthropologist* 60 (1958): 249–60.

Murphy, Joseph. *Working the Spirit: Ceremonies of the African Diaspora*. Boston: Beacon Press, 1994.

Nattiez, Jean-Jacques. *Music and Discourse: Toward a Semiology of Music*. Princeton: Princeton University Press, 1990.

Needham, Rodney. "Percussion and Transition." *Man* 2 (1967): 606–14.

Neher, Andrew. "A Physiological Explanation of Unusual Behavior in Ceremonies Involving Drums." *Human Biology* 34 (1962): 151–60.

Nelson, Angela Spence. "Theology in the Hip-Hop of Public Enemy and Cool Moe Dee." *Black Sacred Music* 5:1 (Spring 1991): 51–59.

Nelson, John Wiley. *Your God Is Alive and Well and Appearing in Popular Culture*. Philadelphia: Westminster Press, 1976.

Nketia, J. H. Kwabena. *Drumming in Akan Communities of Ghana*. London: Thomas Nelson and Sons, 1963.

———. *The Music of Africa*. New York: Norton, 1974.

Ogren, Kathy J. *The Jazz Revolution: Twenties America and the Meaning of Jazz*. New York: Oxford University Press, 1989.

Oliver, Paul. *Savannah Syncopators: African Retentions in the Blues*. New York: Stein and Day, 1970.

Otto, Rudolf. *The Idea of the Holy*. New York: Oxford University Press, 1958.

Palmer, Robert. *Rock and Roll: An Unruly History*. New York: Harmony Books, 1995.

Parkin, David. "Ritual as Spatial Direction and Bodily Division." In *Understanding Rituals*, ed. Daniel de Coppet, 11–25. London: Routledge, 1992.

Parrinder, Geoffrey. *West African Religion: A Study of the Beliefs and Practices of Akan, Ewe, Yoruba, Ibo, and Kindred Peoples*. London: Epworth Press, 1961.

Pattison, Robert. *The Triumph of Vulgarity: Rock Music in the Mirror of Romanticism*. New York: Oxford University Press, 1987.

Perkins, William Eric. "Nation of Islam Ideology in the Rap of Public Enemy." *Black Sacred Music* 5:1 (Spring 1991): 41–50.

Pielke, Robert G. *You Say You Want a Revolution: Rock Music in American Culture*. Chicago: Nelson-Hall, 1986.

Poschardt, Ulf. *DJ Culture*. London: Quartet Books Limited, 1998.

Raboteau, Albert. *Slave Religion: The "Invisible Institution" in the Antebellum South*. New York: Oxford University Press, 1978.

Reynolds, Simon. *Generation Ecstasy: Into the World of Techno and Rave Culture.* New York: Little, Brown and Company, 1998.

Rheingold, Howard. *Virtual Reality.* New York: Summit Books, 1991.

Roberts, John Storm. *Black Music of Two Worlds.* New York: Praeger, 1972.

Robinson, Cedric J. *Black Marxism: The Making of the Black Radical Tradition.* Totowa, N.J.: Biblio Distribution Center, 1983.

Rogan, Taylor. *The Death and Resurrection Show: From Shaman to Superstar.* London: A. Blond, 1985.

Rose, Tricia. *Black Noise: Rap Music and Black Culture in Contemporary America.* Hanover: Wesleyan University Press, 1994.

Ross, Andrew, and Tricia Rose, eds. *Microphone Fiends: Youth Music and Youth Culture.* New York: Routledge, 1994.

Rouget, Gilbert. *Music and Trance: A Theory of the Relations between Music and Possession.* Chicago: University of Chicago Press, 1985.

Sardiello, Robert. "Secular Rituals in Popular Culture: A Case for Grateful Dead Concerts and Dead Identity." In *Adolescents and Their Music: If It's Too Loud, You're Too Old,* ed. Jonathan S. Epstein, 122. New York: Garland, 1994.

Schechner, Richard. *Performance Theory.* New York: Routledge, 1988.

———. *The Future of Ritual: Writings on Culture and Performance.* London: Routledge, 1993.

Scully, Rock, with David Dalton. *Living with the Dead: Twenty Years on the Bus with Garcia and the Grateful Dead.* Boston: Little, Brown and Company, 1996.

Shankar, Ravi. *My Music, My Life.* New York: Simon and Schuster, 1968.

Shapiro, Ann Dhu, and Ines Talamantez. "The Mescalero Apache Girl's Puberty Ceremony: The Role of Music in Structuring Ritual Time." *Yearbook for Traditional Music* 18 (1986): 77–90.

Sharpe, Eric J. *Comparative Religion: A History.* La Salle, Ill.: Open Court, 1986.

Shenk, David, and Steve Silberman. *Skeleton Key: A Dictionary for Deadheads.* New York: Doubleday, 1994.

Shepherd, William C. "Religion and the Counter Culture—A New Religiosity." *Sociological Inquiry* 42:1 (1972): 3–9.

Silberman, Steve. "The Only Song of God." In *Garcia: A Grateful Celebration,* 86–93. New York: Dupree's Diamond News, 1995.

Silcott, Mireille. *Rave America: New School Dancescapes.* Toronto: ECW Press, 1999.

Simpson, George Eaton. *Black Religions in the New World.* New York: Columbia University Press, 1978.

Smart, Ninian. *Dimensions of the Sacred: An Anatomy of the World's Beliefs.* Berkeley: University Of California Press, 1996.

Smith, Jonathan Z. *Imagining Religion: From Babylon to Jonestown.* Chicago: University of Chicago Press, 1982.

———. *To Take Place: Toward Theory in Ritual.* Chicago: University of Chicago Press, 1987.

Sobel, Mechal. *Trabelin' On: The Slave Journey to an Afro-Baptist Faith.* Westport, Conn.: Greenwood Press, 1979.

Southern, Eileen. *The Music of Black Americans.* New York: Norton, 1983.

Spencer, Jon Michael. *Theological Music: An Introduction to Theomusicology.* Westport, Conn.: Greenwood Press, 1991.

———, ed. *Black Sacred Music: A Journal of Theomusicology* 3:2 (Fall 1989).

———, ed. *Black Sacred Music: A Journal of Theomusicology* 5:1 (Spring 1991).

———, ed. *Black Sacred Music: A Journal of Theomusicology* 6:1 (Spring 1992).

Stephens, Ronald Jemal. "The Three Waves of Contemporary Rap Music." *Black Sacred Music* 5:1 (Spring 1991): 25–40.

Stier, Oren Baruch. "Virtual Torah, Digital Mourning: Communal Experiences in Cyberspace." Paper presented at the annual meeting of the American Academy of Religion, New Orleans, Louisiana, 24 November 1996, unpublished draft.

Strasbaugh, John. *E: Reflections on the Birth of the Elvis Faith.* New York: Blast Books, 1995.

Straw, Will. "Systems of Articulation, Logics of Change: Communities and Scenes in Popular Music." *Cultural Studies* 5:3 (October 1991): 368–88.

Sward, Susan. "Satanist's Daughter to Keep the 'Faith.'" *San Francisco Chronicle,* 8 November 1997.

Szatmary, David. *Rockin' in Time: A Social History of Rock-and-Roll,* 3d ed. Uppersaddle River, N.J.: Prentice Hall, 1996.

Taves, Ann. "Knowing through the Body: Dissociative Religious Experience in the African- and British-American Methodist Traditions." *Journal of Religion* 73:2 (April 1993): 201–22.

Thompson, Robert Farris. *Flash of the Spirit: African and Afro-American Art and Philosophy.* New York: Random House, 1983.

Thornton, Sarah. *Club Cultures: Music, Media, and Subcultural Capital.* Hanover: Wesleyan University Press, 1996.

———. "Moral Panic, the Media, and British Rave Culture." In *Microphone Fiends: Youth Music and Youth Culture,* eds. Andrew Ross and Tricia Rose, 176–92. New York: Routledge, 1994.

Toop, David. *The Rap Attack: African Jive to New York Hip Hop.* London: South End Press, 1984.

———. *Rap Attack 2.* Boston: Consortium Press, 1992.

Torella, Chris, Dino & Terry, and 2 Hillbillies. "Explorer's Guide to House, 2nd Edition." *Streetsound* (August 1993): 20–25.

Troy, Sandy. *One More Saturday Night: Reflections with the Grateful Dead, Dead Family, and Dead Heads.* New York: St. Martin's Press, 1991.

Turner, Victor. *The Ritual Process: Structure and Anti-Structure.* Chicago: Aldine, 1969.

———. *The Anthropology of Performance.* New York: PAJ Publications, 1986.

Van der Leeuw, Gerardus. *Religion in Essence and Manifestation,* 2 vols. New York: Harper and Row, 1963.

Van der Leeuw, Gerardus. *Sacred and Profane Beauty: The Holy in Art.* New York: Holt, Rinehart, and Winston, 1963.

Van Gennep, Arnold. *The Rites of Passage.* London: University of Chicago Press, 1960.

Ventura, Michael. "Hear That Long Snake Moan." *Whole Earth Review* (Spring and Summer 1987): 28–43 and 82–93.

Vincent, Rickey. *Funk: The Music, the People, and the Rhythm of the One.* New York: St. Martin's Griffin, 1996.

Wach, Joachim. *The Sociology of Religion.* Chicago: University of Chicago Press, 1944.

———. *The Comparative Study of Religions.* New York: Columbia University Press, 1958.

———. *Types of Religious Experience: Christian and Non-Christian.* Chicago: University of Chicago Press, 1970.

Wafer, James. *The Taste of Blood: Spirit Possession in Brazilian Candomble.* Philadelphia: University of Pennsylvania Press, 1991.

Walker, Sheila S. *Ceremonial Spirit Possession in Africa and Afro-America: Forms, Meanings, and Functional Significance for Individuals and Social Groups.* Leiden: E. J. Brill, 1972.

Walser, Robert. *Running with the Devil: Power, Gender, and Madness in Heavy Metal Music.* Hanover: Wesleyan University Press, 1993.

Waterman, Richard. "African Influences on Music of the Americas." In *Acculturation in the Americas,* ed. Sol Tax, 207–18. Chicago: University of Chicago Press, 1952.

Weinstein, Deena. *Heavy Metal: A Cultural Sociology.* New York: Lexington Books, 1991.

West, Cornel. "On Afro-American Music: From Bebop to Rap." *Black Sacred Music* 6:1 (Spring 1992): 282–94.

Williams, Peter. *Popular Religion in America: Symbolic Change and the Modernization Process in Historical Perspective.* Englewood Cliffs, N.J.: Prentice-Hall, 1980.

Williams, Raymond. *The Sociology of Culture.* New York: Schocken Books, 1982.

Wilson, Olly. "The Significance of the Relationship between Afro-American Music and West African Music." *Black Perspective in Music* 2:1 (Spring 1974): 3–22.

———. "The Association of Movement and Music as a Manifestation of a Black Conceptual Approach to Music-Making." In *More than Dancing,* ed. Irene V. Jackson, 9–23. Westport, Conn.: Greenwood Press, 1985.

Zuckerkandl, Victor. *Sound and Symbol: Music and the External World.* Princeton: Princeton University Press, 1956.

Index

Abenaa, Otutuwa, 48–49
AC/CD, 157, 159
Accelerando, 22, 138
Acid house, 120–23
Acid jazz, 74, 133
Acid rock, 7, 85
Acid tests, 83–84
Adrenalin rush, 164
Aerosmith, 191, 258
Africa, 15–16, 18
African American churches (Black churches), 7, 56, 58, 63, 184, 207, 212, 214; Baptist, 56, 58; Holiness, 58; Methodist, 56, 58; Pentecostal, 58
African American culture, 17
African American music (Black music), 16–17, 45, 58–66, 71, 182–83, 185–88, 211, 232–33; musicoreligious practices, 58; religious music, 22, 241
African American religion, 6, 192, 200
African diaspora, 5, 16, 19, 53–58, 64
African music, 16–17, 50–53, 56–57, 119, 183–84; participatory nature of, 51, 57, 62, 119, 183; religious, 22; view of music and religion, 42; vocal techniques, 52, 56–57, 59, 62
Afrika Bambaata, 71, 188–91
Albanese, Catherine L., 5
Ali, Muhammad, 185
Altamont, 85, 154–55
Altar (altars), 46–47, 141
Altered states of consciousness (ASCs), 10, 26, 36, 105, 147
Alternative (culture, orientation), 12, 146, 151, 202, 234
Alternative spirituality, 10, 140–41
American Bandstand, 67
American Beauty (The Grateful Dead), 86
Amoaku, W. Komla, 41

"Anarchy in the U.K." (the Sex Pistols), 74
. . . And Justice For All (Metallica), 259
Angola, 54
Anthem of the Sun (The Grateful Dead), 85
Antistructure, 11–12, 35, 98, 103–4, 113, 176, 181, 233
Aoxomoxoa (the Grateful Dead), 85
Armored Saint, 157
Arnett, Jeffrey, 157, 158, 159–60, 163, 258
Ashanti, 45, 232
Atkins, Juan, 120
Australian aboriginal religion, 19

Backspinning, 189
"Ball of Confusion" (the Temptations), 263
Bangs, Lester, 258
B-boy, 189
B-boy Summit, 201, 210
Beastie Boys, the, 192
Beatles, the, 12, 69–70, 72, 73
Beck, Jeff, 153, 257
Bee Gees, 118, 242
Beer, 159
Benin, 45, 232
Berry, Chuck, 65, 66
Big Brother and the Holding Company, 85
Big Drum, 55
Biker (motorcycle) subculture, 153, 154
Black Sabbath, 153, 156–57
Blacking, John, 27–28
Blackmore, Ritchie, 258
Bland, Bobby Blue, 62–63
Block party, 200, 203–5, 209
Blue Oyster Cult, 258
Bluegrass, 83, 84
Blues, 7, 12, 45, 59, 61–65, 68, 153, 182, 184, 187–88, 192, 194, 212, 214, 217, 240, 262
Blues For Allah (the Grateful Dead), 87

Blues-rock, 153–54
Body, 6, 11–12, 21, 23–25, 31, 41–44, 216–18; in-body, 11; in-body in electronic dance music (raves), 129, 130–31, 142; in-body in Grateful Dead concert experience, 100, 108; in electronic dance music (raves), 119, 129–33, 142–45, 148; in Grateful Dead concert experience, 95, 100, 107–9; in heavy metal concerts, 169, 173–74; language, 4; locus of integration, 24; /mind split, 6, 12–13, 18, 43, 215; movement, 22–23, 25–26, 31, 48, 72, 217–18; movement in electronic dance music (raves), 143–5; movement in Grateful Dead concert experience, 108, 217; movement in heavy metal concerts, 159, 173, 217; movement in rap music, 196–97, 207–9; mutilation, 8; out-of-, 11; out-of-, in electronic dance music (raves), 133, 142; posture, 23, 48; in rap music, 196, 207–9; somatic experience, 11, 23, 37, 217
Bon Jovi, 162, 258
Bonham, John, 156
Boone, Pat, 67
"Born To Be Wild" (Steppenwolf), 153
Bowie, David, 242
Boyz In The Hood (dir. John Singleton), 195
BPM (beats per minute), 119, 128, 138, 144–45
Bralove, Bob, 93
Brando, Marlon, 67, 153
Brass bands, 59
Brazil, 55–56, 183, 208
Breakbeats, 145, 189, 200
Breakdancing, 182–83, 189, 196–97, 200, 203–5, 208
Brown, H. Rap, 185
Brown, James, 71, 182, 185–87
Buddhism, 84, 115; mantra chanting, 20
Bull-roarer, 19
Burkina Faso, 184
Burning Man, 126

Call and response, 51–52, 56, 59, 62, 183, 206–7
Campbell, Lucie, 63
Candlemas, 172
Candomble, 7, 31, 54, 214

Capoeira, 183, 208
Caribbean, 54–55, 59
Catholicism, 6, 54–55; saints, 55
Chakras, 132, 143
Chanting, 19–20; Buddhist mantra, 20; Gregorian, 20, 29; Hindu mantra, 32; Krishna devotional, 21; Santeria, 200–201
Charles, Ray, 185
Chernoff, John Miller, 51
Chic, 186, 190
Chicago, 118, 120, 127, 144, 210
Chi-Lites, 263
Chill room, 122, 138, 141
"Chocolate City" (Parliament), 186
Christianity, 57; Bach cantatas, 20; Gregorian chant, 20, 29; liturgy, 20, 58, 63; liturgy combined with rave elements, 124, 140, 252
Chuck D, 198, 199, 212
Churinga, 19
Civil rights movement, 186, 214
Clapton, Eric, 153, 257
Clark, Dick, 67
Clash, the, 74
Classical music, 22, 27
Clinton, George, 186–87, 242
Communitas, 8, 11–12, 35, 146, 176, 233
Cone, James, 64
Congo Square, 60–61
Craddock-Willis, Andre, 187–88
Cream, 153
Crescendo, 22, 138, 170, 205
Crew (posse), 189, 205–6, 209
Cross, Brian, 193
Cross-fade mixer, 188, 197, 213
Crossroads, 12, 64
Crowley, Aleister, 178
Cultural religion, 5
Cyberspace, 33, 110

Dance, 8, 217; accompaniment to music, 22, 51, 62, 119, 183; African American churches, 57; blues, 63; breakdancing, 182–83, 189, 196–97, 200, 203–5, 208; Congo Square, 60; electronic dance music (raves), 117–51; Grateful Dead, 92, 107–9; Hopi Kachinas, 19; possession, 6, 22, 25, 43–44, 46–50, 55, 66; Sufi, 20
"Dark Star" (the Grateful Dead), 116

DAT (digital audio tape), 206
Day of the Dead, 94
Deadheads, 8, 12, 77, 83–116, 122, 152, 159, 164, 172; hallway dancers, 89–90, 106; parking lot scene, 89, 106; spinners, 90, 99, 103–4, 107–8, 111; tapers, 87–88, 89, 106; tour and tourheads, 87, 102, 106, 244–45
Dean, James, 67
Deee-Lite, 251
Deep Purple, 157, 258
Def Leppard, 161, 258
Detroit, 120, 185
Detroit Electronic Music Festival, 126
Diddley, Bo, 65
Dio, 157
Dionysian, 10, 73, 98, 157
Disco, 8, 71, 74, 117–18, 183, 186–87, 242, 250
Dixon, Willie, 155
DJ (disc jockey), 3, 118–21, 127–30, 138, 141–42, 147, 183, 184, 188–90, 197–98, 200, 203–7, 263
DJ Breakout, 190
DJ Kool Herc (Clive Campbell), 71, 188–90, 263
D-Mob, 122
DMX, 195
Dr. Dre, 195
"Do Ya Think I'm Sexy" (Rod Stewart), 250
Dokken, 161
Domino, Fats, 65, 66
Dorsey, Thomas, 63
Drum, 19; ensemble, 31, 47, 50–53, 61; water drum, 19, 31
Drum machine, 118–20, 188, 213
Drumming, 19, 43, 48, 60, 185, 200; sonic driving, 22

Earth, Wind, and Fire, 186
Easy Rider, 153
808 State, 121, 125
"Electric Funeral" (Black Sabbath), 156
Electric guitar, 62, 152, 155, 157–58, 161, 170–71, 179
Electric Kingdom, 196
Electronic dance music, 3, 77, 117
Eliade, Mircea, 38
Elliot, Joe, 258
Eminem, 195

England, 69, 73–74, 117, 121–26, 135, 141, 145, 155, 156, 161, 243
Epoche, 82
Eric B. and Rahim, 191
Erzulie, 46
Ethiopian minstrelsy, 59
Europe 72 (the Grateful Dead), 86
"Evil Woman" (Black Sabbath), 156
Ewe, 41, 45, 232
"Eyes of the World" (the Grateful Dead), 116

Fear of a Black Planet (Public Enemy), 192
Fernando, Jr., S. H., 188
Fetishism, 10, 234
"Fight The Power" (the Isley Brothers), 263
Fikentscher, Kai, 119, 120
Fine, Isabel, 208
Fisk Jubilee Singers, 63
Floyd, Samuel, 16
Fon, 31, 45–46, 54, 60, 184, 214, 232
Four Tops, the, 263
Fox, Matthew, 140, 252
Franklin, Aretha, 71, 185
Friedson, Steven M., 43–44, 217
Funk, 8, 71, 118, 182–83, 186–88, 242
"Funky President (People, It's Bad)" (James Brown), 263

Ga, 45, 48, 50, 232
Gambia, the, 184
Gangs, 264
Gangsta rap, 193, 195, 199
Gans, David, 94
Garcia, Guy, 126
Garcia, Jerry, 83, 84, 90, 93, 94, 105, 106, 110
Gay, Marvin, 263
Georgia, 56
Ghana, 15, 41, 214, 232; Kisame, 49, 238; Konkonuru, 48, 238; Nungua, 50, 238
Gibson, William, 33, 236
"Give More Power to the People" (the Chi-Lites), 263
Glam, 74, 242
Goa Trance, 141
"God Save The Queen" (the Sex Pistols), 74
"Good Times" (Chic), 190
Gordy, Berry, 185
Gospel choir, 31, 185

Gospel music, 20, 185
Graffiti, 182, 189, 200
Grandmaster Flash, 71, 189; and the Furious Five, 187, 190, 191
Grand Wizard Theodore and the Fantastic Five, 190
Grateful Dead, the, 3, 8, 77, 83–116, 214, 221, 250; stealie, 88–89
Grateful Dead (the Grateful Dead), 86
Grateful Dead concert structure, 92–93, 103, 136, 170; break, 92, 103; Drums, 93, 103–4; first set, 92, 103; jams, 84, 92, 93, 105, 114; second set, 92–93, 103; "Space," 93, 103–5
Grateful Dead Movie, The (dir. Leon Gast), 87
Great Awakenings, 58, 70, 240
Greeley, Andrew, 78
Greenberg, Gary, 111
Grenada, 55
Grim Reaper, 157
Grimes, Ronald, 37
Groove, 51, 119, 129, 142, 185–87, 207–8, 211
"Groove Is In The Heart" (Deee-Lite), 251
Grunge, 74–5
Guinea, 184
Guitar, 15, 58, 61–62, 83
Guns N' Roses, 258

Haight-Ashbury, 8, 84
Hancock, Butch, 66
Hard rock, 258
Hardy, Ron, 120
Harlem Renaissance, 184
Hart, Mickey, 83, 93, 98
Headbanger, 152, 159, 173
Headbanging, 159, 164, 173, 217
Healing, 49–50, 100, 109, 218
Heaven and Hell (Black Sabbath), 157
Heavy metal, 3, 7–8, 12, 74, 77, 152–81, 242, 258; black metal, 162, 179; death metal, 162, 179; lite metal, 162–63; metal/rap, 163; thrash/speed metal, 159, 162–63, 173; white/Christian metal, 162
Heavy metal concerts, 160, 163–66, 168–76; temporal sequencing, 169–72
Hell's Angels, 85, 153
Henderson, Jocko, 184–85

Hendrix, Jimi, 86
Hill, Lauryn, 195
Hinduism: deities (Ganesha, Kali, Krishna, Vishnu), 141; Krishna sects' devotional chanting, 31; mantra chanting, 32; Nada Brahman, 20, 42; OM, 140; view of music and religion, 42
Hip hop, 3, 8, 77, 182–213, 221; culture, 182, 200–201
Hippie counterculture, 8, 70, 154–55; psychedelic, 80, 83, 86, 117, 124; 60s counterculture, 85, 154
History of religions, 5
Holly, Buddy, 66
Holy Spirit, 57
Hopi Kachina dances, 19, 22
Hopkins, Lightnin', 62
House, 8, 74, 117, 118–21, 127, 133, 134, 137, 142, 144
Howlin Wolf, 62, 153, 155
Hughes Brothers, the, 195
Hughes, Langston, 184
Human Be-In, 84
Hunter, Robert, 83, 114–16
Hussain, Zakir, 93

"I Got You (I Feel Good)" (James Brown), 186
Ibo, 45, 232
Ice Cube, 195, 199
Ice-T, 195
In The Dark (the Grateful Dead), 93
Internet, 110, 112–13, 249
Iommi, Tony, 156
Iron Maiden, 157, 161, 172
"Iron Man" (Black Sabbath), 156
Islam: call to prayer, 31; Qur'an chanting, 20
Isley Brothers, the, 263
It Takes A Nation of Millions to Hold Us Back (Public Enemy), 192

Jackson Five, the, 263
Jackson, Mahalia, 63
Jali (griot), 184, 199, 200, 262
Jamaica, 55, 263
James, William, 81–82
Jay-Z, 195
Jazz, 7, 59, 61, 68, 184, 262
Jazzy Five, the, 190

Jefferson Airplane, 85
Jefferson, Blind Lemon, 62
Jefferson, Marshall, 120
Johnson, Frank, 59
Johnson, Robert, 62, 153
Joplin, Janis, 86
Jordan, Louis, 185
Judaism: cantor's chanting, 20; lyre used by
    prophets and King David, 20; shofar, 20;
    Yom Kippur, 20
Judas Priest, 157, 165
Juice (dir. Ernest R. Dickerson), 195
Jungle (drum and bass), 144–45

Keil, Charles, 62–63, 185
Kent State shootings, 86
Kid Rock, 163
Kilminster, Lemmy, 174
King, Albert, 62
King, B.B., 62–63, 153
King Diamond, 172
King, Freddy, 62
King, Jr., Martin Luther, 185
King, Rodney, 193
Kinks, the, 69
Kiss, 258
Knuckles, Frankie, 118–20
Kool and the Gang, 71, 186
Korn, 163
Kpledzo festival, 50
Kreutzman, Bill, 83, 93
KRS-One, 192, 198, 212
Kumina, 55
Kwasitutu, 48

LaRock, Coke, 190
Last Poets, the, 185
LaVey, Anton, 178
Led Zeppelin, 153, 155–56, 157, 171, 172,
    257
Lennon, John, 69
Lesh, Phil, 83, 106
Levine, Lawrence, 184
Lewis, Jerry Lee, 65, 66, 68
Liminal, 8, 11–12, 35, 46, 98, 103, 139, 146;
    liminality, 176, 233
Limp Bizkit, 163
Little Richard, 65, 66, 68
LL Cool J, 191
Loa, 46, 55, 57

Long, Charles H., 5, 79–80, 215–16, 234
Los Angeles, 125, 161, 162, 191, 193, 209;
    South Central, 193
Love Parade, the, 126
LSD, 84, 90, 91, 98, 117, 121
Ludwig, Arnold, 26

Macoumba, 55
Madonna, 251
Makuta, 208
Malawi, 43, 217
Malcolm X, 185
Mali, 15, 184
Malmsteen Yngwie, 258
Manding, 184
Mantra, 20, 31–32
Marcus, Steve, 94, 244
Marijuana, 84, 90, 154, 159
Martin, Sallie, 63
Mase, 195
Master Juba, 59
Master P, 195
Maultsby, Portia, 16–17, 59
May, Derrick, 120
MC, 190, 198, 200, 204–7, 212
MC Hammer, 192
McAllester, David, 20–21, 26–27
McClary, Susan, 24, 216
McKernan, Ron (Pigpen), 83, 244
McLoughlin, William, 70
McNeill, William, 217–18
MDMA (ecstasy), 117, 121, 128–29,
    131–32, 143, 144
Megadeth, 162
Melle Mel, 191
Menace II Society (dir. the Hughes Broth-
    ers), 195
Mercyful Fate, 162
"Message, The" (Grandmaster Flash and
    the Furious Five), 187, 191
Metalheads, 77, 152–81
Metallica, 162, 259
Metronome sense, 51, 238–39
Mischel, Frances and Walter, 23
"Miss You" (the Rolling Stones), 250
Moby Grape, 85
Monterey Pop Festival, 85
Moreira, Airto, 93
Morrison, Jim, 86
Mosh pit, 73, 159, 173, 258

Mothership Connection (Parliament-Funkadelic), 186
Motley Crue, 161, 172
Motorhead, 157, 174
Motown, 185–86, 263
MTV (Music Television), 94, 161, 192, 195; *Yo! MTV Raps*, 192
Mursell, James, 22
Muscular bonding, 218
Musical improvisation, 52, 59, 62, 84, 99–100, 103–4, 111
Musical motto, 11, 31–32, 105, 138–39, 170–71, 215

Nattiez, Jean-Jacques, 30
Neher, Andrew, 21–22
Nelson, Angela Spence, 192, 193
Nelson, Harriet and Ozzie, 67
Nelson, Jon Wiley, 78
New Age, 151
New Jack City (dir. Mario Van Peebles), 195
New Orleans, 59
New York City, 117, 118, 120, 200, 209, 242
Nigeria, 45, 232
Nommo, 184, 198
North America, 15, 17–18, 55
Notorious B.I.G. (Christopher Wallace), 195, 264
Nugent, Ted, 258
Number of the Beast, The (Iron Maiden), 157
Numinous, 4, 5, 39–40, 80
N.W.A., 193, 194
NWOBHM (New Wave of British Heavy Metal), 161

Oakland, 140, 191, 192
Oakland Underground, 194, 202, 209–10
Occult western magical traditions, 10, 153, 155–57, 178
Oglala Sioux Sun Dance, 19, 22
Ogun, 46
One Nation Under A Groove (George Clinton), 186
Oral tradition, 184–85, 200
Orb, the, 125
Orisha, 46, 55, 57
Osbourne, Ozzy, 156–57
Otto, Rudolf, 39–41

Page, Jimmy, 153, 155, 171, 257
"Papa's Got A Brand New Bag" (James Brown), 186
Paranoid (Black Sabbath), 156
Parkin, David, 217
Parliament-Funkadelic, 71, 186–87
Peaks: electronic dance music (raves), 119–20, 124, 127–28, 138–39; Grateful Dead concerts, 91, 92, 112, 113; heavy metal, 170–71; rap, 189, 202
Performance studies, 11, 234
Perkins, Carl, 65, 66
Peul, 184
Peyote meeting (Native American Church), 19, 31
Pharcyde, 202
Philips, Sam, 65
Physiological dimensions of music, 21–24, 42, 235
Piano, 62
Pilgrimage, 103, 106
Pink Floyd, 73
"Planet Rock" (Afrika Bambaata), 191
Plant, Robert, 155, 257
Please Hammer Don't Hurt Them (MC Hammer), 192
PLUR (peace, love, unity, respect), 124, 150–51
Police, the, 74
Polyrhythm(s), 6, 19, 34, 50–51, 56, 59, 62, 119, 145, 183, 186, 187, 189, 211
Popular culture, 9–10, 78–80, 233
Popular music, 3, 5, 7–10, 12–13, 17, 19, 45, 65–75, 79, 161, 182, 217–20
Popular religion, 80, 216
Possession, 6, 7, 10–11, 23, 25–26, 31, 34, 46–50, 55, 60, 68, 92, 105, 129, 130, 142, 167, 196, 208; dances, 6, 22, 43, 46–50, 217–19, 232; religions, 19, 29, 31, 232
Post Mortem, 162
Postmodern, 4, 212–13, 219–20, 232
Power chord, 154, 170–71, 257
Presley, Elvis, 7, 65–66, 68, 69, 72
Protestant, 7, 55–56
Psilocybin mushrooms, 98
Psychedelics, 84, 90, 98–99, 117, 121, 159; hallucinogens, 92; psychedelic experience, 93, 99
Psychological dimensions of music, 24–27, 42

Public Enemy, 192, 198–99, 212
Puff Daddy (P Diddy, Sean Combs), 195
"Pump Up The Jam" (Technotronic), 251
Punk, 8, 73–74, 162, 242, 243, 258
Pyromania (Def Leppard), 161

Quaaludes, 159
Quicksilver Messenger Service, 85
Quiet Riot, 161

Raboteau, Albert, 184
Radical empiricism, 81–82
Rainey, Ma, 62
Raising Hell (Run-DMC), 191
Rap, 3, 8, 12, 74, 77, 182–213; rhyming po-
    etry, 183, 198
"Rapper's Delight" (Sugarhill Gang), 187,
    190
Ratt, 161
Rattle, 19
Rave Mass (Rave in the Nave), 124
Rave subculture/ravers, 152, 159, 164, 172,
    176–77
Raves, 3, 8, 12, 77, 117–51, 170, 214, 221;
    origin of, 122–23; temporal sequencing,
    137–39
Rebel Without A Cause (dir. Nicholas Ray),
    67
Reed, Jimmy, 62
Reggae, 74
Religious experience, 2, 4, 5, 10–11, 39,
    80–81, 216; electronic dance music
    (raves), 124, 127–36; Grateful Dead con-
    certs, 94–103, 105; heavy metal, 160,
    163–68, 221; rap, 195–203
"Revolution Will Not Be Televised, The"
    (Gil Scott-Heron), 185
Rhoads, Randy, 258
Rhythm, 34, 119, 127, 132, 142, 144, 147,
    180, 183, 185, 194, 196, 198, 207–9
Rhythm and Blues (R & B), 3, 45, 65–67,
    71–72, 83, 84, 182, 217
Rider and horse, 10–11, 26, 73, 129
Rigor Mortis, 162
Ring shout, 56, 183
Rite of passage, 8, 10, 35, 46, 104, 207
Ritual, 4, 8, 11, 31, 54–55, 63, 78, 81, 92, 98,
    217–19; dimensions of Grateful Dead
    concerts and tours, 102–11, 113; dimen-
    sions of heavy metal, 168–76, 181; di-

mensions of music, 35–38, 43; dimen-
    sions of rap, 194, 203–10; dimensions of
    raves, 123–24, 136–48
Ritual studies, 11, 35, 233, 234
Roberts, John Storm, 62
Robinson, Smokey, and the Miracles, 263
Robinson, Sylvia, 190
Rock, 69–75, 152–81
Rock and roll, 3, 7–9, 27, 45, 65–70, 72,
    182, 214, 217. 233
Rolling Stones, the, 69, 85, 250
Rose, Tricia, 187, 189, 211
Rotten, Johnny (John Lydon), 74
Rouget, Gilbert, 22, 24, 31–32, 138, 235
Run-DMC, 191
Rush, 258
Rushing, Jimmy, 62

"Sabbath, Bloody Sabbath" (Black Sab-
    bath), 156
Sacred Heart (Dio), 157
St. Vincent, 55
Salt n' Pepa, 191
Samba, 208
Sampler (sampling), 121, 183, 187–89, 213,
    251
San Francisco Bay Area, 8, 10, 77, 83–85,
    94, 127, 134, 140, 145, 162, 202, 209–10,
    214
Santeria, 7, 54, 200–201, 214
Sardiello, Robert, 88, 92
Sarngadeva, 42
Satanism, 152, 156, 162, 178–79
Saturday Night Fever, 117–18, 242, 250
Saunderson, Kevin, 120
"Say It Loud I'm Black and I'm Proud"
    (James Brown), 185
"Scarlet Begonias" (the Grateful Dead),
    116
Schechner, Richard, 218
Scorpions, the, 157
Scott-Heron, Gil, 185
Scratching, 189, 204
Semiological aspects of ritual, 37
Semiological dimensions of music, 29–33,
    42–43, 236
Senegal, 15, 31, 54, 184, 208
Sensation-seeking, 159–60
Sequencer (sequencing), 121, 213, 251
Sex Pistols, the, 74

"Shakedown Street" (the Grateful Dead), 250
Shakers, 55
Shakur, Tupac, 195, 198, 264
Shamanism, 10, 19, 92, 98, 100, 147
Shango cult, in Trinidad, 46
Shankar, Ravi, 42
Shapiro, Anne Dhu, 38
Shenk, David, 83–84, 87, 90
Sheperd, William C., 80, 216
Shouters, 55
Silberman, Steve, 83–84, 87, 89, 90, 91, 95, 97, 99, 102, 110–11, 115
Simpson, George Eaton, 54
Sin After Sin (Judas Priest), 157
Singleton, John, 195
Slamdancing, 73, 159, 160, 162, 169, 173, 217, 258
Slave trade, 6, 16, 45, 53–55,184
Slayer, 162, 172
Slippery When Wet (BonJovi), 161
Smith, Bessie, 62
Smith, Jonathan Z., 35–36, 105
Snoop Doggy Dogg, 195
Sonic driving, 22
Soul (music), 71, 118, 182–83, 185–88
SoulSonic Force, 190
South America, 54–55
South Bronx, 182–83, 188, 194, 203, 210
South Carolina, 56–57
Spatial aspects of: Grateful Dead concerts, 89, 105–61; music, 34–35, 43; raves, 140–42; ritual, 11
Speaking in tongues, 57
Spencer, Jon Michael, 78–79
Spiritual dimensions of music, 39–44
Spirituals, 63–64
"Stairway to Heaven" (Led Zeppelin), 156
Steal Your Face (the Grateful Dead), 88–89
"Stella Blue" (the Grateful Dead), 116
Steppenwolf, 153
Stewart, Rod, 250
Stier, Oren Baruch, 110
Straight Outta Compton (N.W.A.), 193
Stryper, 162
Subculture, 4, 231; musical, 4, 8, 62; musical youth, 7, 9–12, 45, 71, 221, 234
Sufism: dervishes, 20, 22, 90, 108
Sugarhill Gang, 187, 190
Sugarhill Records, 190, 191

Sullivan, Ed, 7, 66
Summer, Donna, 71
Summer of Love 1967, 84, 117, 124
Summer of Love 1988, 117, 123–25
Sun Studios, 65
Supremes, the, 182, 263
Sutton, Shan, 91–92
Synchronization, 22

Talamantez, Ines, 38
Techno, 8, 74, 117, 120, 121, 126, 133, 143–45
Techno Cosmic Mass, 140, 252
Technotronic, 251
Temporal aspects of: music, 33–35, 43; ritual, 11
Temptations, the, 71, 263
Terrapin Station (the Grateful Dead), 87
Testament, 172
Thatcher, Margaret, 73
"This Is Madness" (Gil Scott-Heron), 185
Thompson, Robert Farris, 49
Tigare cult, 49
Time, 126, 191
Togo, 45, 232
Trance, 6–7, 19, 31–32, 34; in electronic dance music/raves, 119, 127, 129, 138, 147; trance dancing, 43–44
Travolta, John, 117–18
Treacherous Three, the, 190
Tribal, 47, 151
Trinidad, 23, 55
Troy, Sandy, 86
"Truckin'" (the Grateful Dead), 114, 214
Tumbuka healers, 43–44, 217
Turner, Joe, 62
Turner, Victor, 8, 37, 103, 104, 139, 146, 218; Turnerian categories, 11, 35, 113, 176, 180–81, 233
Turntables, 183, 188, 197, 204

"U Can't Touch This" (MC Hammer), 192
Umbanda, 55
University of Creation Spirituality, the, 140, 152
United States, 3, 7, 54, 57, 69, 74, 117, 121, 125–26, 135, 141, 153, 155, 156, 161, 210, 243

Van der Leeuw, Gerardus, 5, 33, 40–41, 82

Van Halen, 161, 258; Eddie, 161, 258
Van Peebles, Mario, 195
Vanilla Ice, 192
Vengeance, 162
Ventura, Michael, 17–18, 60–61, 65, 68, 75
Vicious, Sid (John Ritchie), 74
Vietnam War, 186
Virtual dimensions of music, 33–35, 40–41
Virtual reality, 30, 33, 36–37, 43
Virtual space, 36–37
Virtual Time, 36–38
Vision quest, 102–3
Vodun (voodoo), 7, 31, 54, 59–61, 214
"Vogue" (Madonna), 251

Wach, Joachim, 81–82
"Walk This Way" (Run-DMC), 191
Walser, Robert, 152, 153–54, 170–71, 258
"War Pigs" (Black Sabbath) 156
Warehouse, the, 118, 120
Waters, Muddy, 62, 153
"We Call It Acid" (D-Mob), 122
Weinstein, Deena, 152, 154–55, 157, 179, 181
Weir, Bob, 83, 106
West Africa, 15, 184, 232
West African: diasporic religion, 6; essence,17; music, 184; musicoreligious ceremonies, 6, 34, 60; musicoreligious complex, 9, 66, 71, 75; musicoreligious possession complex, 7, 65, 97; musico-
religious practices, 58, 60, 99, 211, 214, 217, 232–33; possession dance, 22; possession religions, 7, 25, 45–53, 57, 63; religious impulse, 58; religious (spiritual) sensibility, 5, 7, 53, 59, 61, 63, 68; spirituality, 72, 75; view of music and religion, 41
West, Cornel, 194
What's Going On (Marvin Gay), 263
"Wheel, The" (the Grateful Dead), 115
White, Bukka, 62
Wild One, The (dir. Laszlo Benedek), 67, 153
Williamson, Sonny Boy, 62
Wilson, Al, 86
Wilson, Olly, 22–23
Wolof, 184
Wonder, Stevie, 186, 263
Woodstock, 70, 85, 154–55
Workingman's Dead (the Grateful Dead, 86
Wu-Tang Clan, 195

X-Clan, 199

Yardbirds, the, 153, 155, 257
Yemaya, 46
Yes, 73, 242
Yoruba, 31, 45–46, 49, 54, 184, 214, 232

ZOSO (Led Zeppelin), 156
Zulu Nation, 190

About the Author

Robin Sylvan is assistant professor of Religion and the Arts at the College of Wooster in Ohio.